Other books by Robert E. Kowalski

The 8-Week Cholesterol Cure

Cholesterol & Children

The 8-Week Cholesterol Cure Cookbook

8 Steps to a Healthy Heart

The Type II Diabetes Diet Book

The
Type II
Diabetes Diet Book

The Insulin Control Diet:
Your Fat Can Make You Thin

Calvin Ezrin, M.D.
Robert E. Kowalski

Lowell House
Los Angeles

Contemporary Books
Chicago

Library of Congress Cataloging-in-Publication Data
Ezrin, Calvin.
    [Endocrine control diet]
    The Type II diabetes diet book: the insulin control diet: your
fat can make you thin/Calvin Ezrin, Robert E. Kowalski.
        p.   cm.
    Previously published: New York: Harper & Row, 1990 under the
title: The endocrine control diet.
    Includes bibliographical references and index.
    ISBN 1-56565-334-3
    1. Non-insulin-dependent diabetes—Diet therapy. 2. High-protein
diet. 3. Low-carbohydrate diet. 4. Insulin—Metabolism—regulation.
I. Kowalski, Robert E. II. Title.
RC662.18.E97   1995   95-24479
613.2'5—dc20   CIP

Originally published: The endocrine control diet: how to beat the metabolic trap
and lose weight permanently. New York: Harper & Row Publishers, © 1990.
ISBN: 0-06-015919-7

Requests for such permissions should be addressed to:
Lowell House
2029 Century Park East, Suite 3290
Los Angeles, CA 90067

Lowell House books can be purchased at special discounts
when ordered in bulk for premiums and special sales.
Contact Department VH at the address above.

Publisher: Jack Artenstein
General Manager, Lowell House Adult: Bud Sperry
Text Design: Robert S. Tinnon Design
Illustrations: Wesla Weller

Manufactured in the United States of America

10 9 8 7 6 5 4 3 2

CONTENTS

This book is dedicated to the memory of Larry Carter, a mutual friend without whom we would never have met and without whom this book would never have been written. The world has been diminished by his death. We miss him.

To my wife Dawn (Kowalski) for all the years of support and love, and for sticking by me through what has truly been, "for better or for worse."

To Gerry (Ezrin), my partner in life, an outstanding wife and mother of eight, who has been an inspiration in all my endeavors.

ACKNOWLEDGMENTS

To Dawn Messenger, who for many years served my practice ably as a weight counselor, I (Calvin Ezrin) owe much gratitude. She would agree that the development of this book would have been impossible without the lessons that our patients taught us and the inspiration they engendered to share the knowledge we gained.

The weight loss diet proposed in this book reflects an approach to weight loss that has been developed under medical supervision of patients. The book has been written as a guide to be used by the patient under medical supervision of his or her personal physician.

The weight loss regimen described in this book has been designed for use specifically for those individuals with large amounts of weight to lose, those who have been classified as medically obese. Obesity is defined as being at least 20 percent over ideal weight. Increased morbidity and mortality are associated with overweight of this magnitude.

The protein-sparing modified-fast diet has been well documented as being both safe and effective, especially for those who are significantly overweight. This book describes that type of diet, guides the reader through aspects of the dietary regime including food suggestions and recipes, and provides information by which the reader can come to understand the principles of this approach. As such it can, in many instances, be a useful bridge between doctor and patient.

Chapter 1

AN INTRODUCTION TO PERMANENT WEIGHT CONTROL

Welcome to an entirely new approach to permanent weight loss, one that could revolutionize the way we think about weight loss and dieting. This is the first program ever to recognize the basic underlying problem of obesity and to offer a workable, lifelong solution.

This book delivers an important message: people with a weight control problem have a real and identifiable physiological and medical condition. It's *not* a matter of lack of willpower. For far too many years many in the medical community have callously regarded overweight patients as individuals who simply eat too much, handed them diet brochures, and told them to count calories. It's no wonder that a billion-dollar weight loss industry rife with quackery has sprung up to take advantage of people who are not getting the help they need.

If you have been on the cycle of weight loss and gain for any length of time, you have probably experienced obstacles, frustrations and feelings that are dismissed by others as imaginary or irrational. This book shows that much of what you have felt *can be documented*; your observations and feelings are real and rational.

You notice that some of your friends eat twice as much as you and never gain a pound. Everyone says you're mistaken. But it's true.

You eat just one slice of pie after counting calories for weeks, and overnight you gain 3, 4, or 5 pounds. Nobody believes you; everyone thinks you *must* have had more than that. But it's true.

You feel depressed and guilty about your eating; your depression leads to more eating which leads to more depression. Others do not believe that you feel legitimate depression that is linked to the eating cycle. But it's true.

You drink certain kinds of liquids and, even after just a moment of satisfaction, you are actually more hungry than before you took that first sip. Of course, others say that's simply because you have no willpower. But it's true.

In the meantime, doctors and dietitians keep telling you to count your calories, cut back on the foods you enjoy, put up with hunger, ignore your inability to sleep at night, forget your feelings of depression, and nibble on celery for the rest of your life. They say that the only way you can lose a pound of weight is to give up a pound's worth of calories. Well, finally you've picked up the right book. We will show you that your feelings and opinions have a foundation in medical science, specifically, the science of endocrinology. Endocrinology is the study of hormones. Hormones are bodily secretions that play a vital role in controlling many body functions, including metabolic rate and weight gain. The endocrine system holds the key to weight control, and a program based on its workings, as devised in this book, is simple and easy to follow.

In the pages to come, you'll learn about a diet that assures fast and efficient weight loss. You'll lose pounds and inches in a rapid, predictable way, and you'll do it without feeling hungry. Your psychological outlook will begin to improve almost immediately, and those blue, depressed moods will become a thing of the past. You'll sleep well at night and feel rested in the morning. Any problems with water retention that you've had will disappear. And you'll learn how to control your endocrine system to maintain the weight you want for the rest of your life.

This book is designed to be your guide and companion throughout the entire learning and weight loss period. We'll give you support and answer the questions most likely to come up at different times during the process. We anticipate the frustration and disappointment of the weight loss plateau every dieter experiences. We understand the problem of the person who's been doing so well that he or she decides to have just one little treat. Wham! The next morning the scale reads 3 or 4 gained pounds and there goes the diet. We understand why you start to feel depressed and when those periods of depression are most likely to occur. And, as they say in the old Westerns, we "head 'em off at the pass." We expect such problems, and give you advice on how to shift gears, start losing weight again, and keep your endocrine system under control.

Day by day, week by week you'll lose weight on a regular, predictable basis. And we'll be there to answer your questions and guide you through the tough spots as you get closer and closer to your goal. Probably the best part of being on the program is that you'll start feeling not only good, but good about yourself. Some people find that they get to know and appreciate themselves in a new way. Join the many men and women who have learned total endocrine control.

Before we begin telling you about the Insulin Control Diet, we'd like to introduce ourselves. Here are a few words from each of us.

ROBERT E. KOWALSKI
ON CLOSING THE KNOWLEDGE GAP

The issues of weight loss and weight control have come up again and again throughout my twenty-year career as a medical journalist. During my graduate training in medical physiology, while nutritionists were preaching that weight control was simply a matter of calories taken in and energy expended, my professors were detailing research on the appetite center of the brain that indicated there was more to obesity than overeating. Later, when I held a position with a medical association, I observed that among the many physician members who ran weight loss clinics, "rainbow therapy" was the rule rather than the exception; bottles of pills and capsules containing hormones, amphetamines, and tranquilizers were prescribed to patients whose nerves and health would be damaged as a result.

During my years as director of nutrition information for the National Dairy Council, I attended meetings, visited the labs of top researchers in the country, and prepared a wide variety of materials to help people make wiser food choices. In general, the information I helped dispense during those years was sound, but recent medical and nutritional research has shown there were some rather glaring errors.

I became a consultant for an organization called Weight Loss Clinics, whose techniques, provided through nurse-administered clinics throughout the United States and Canada, were successful in keeping clients on the program to achieve weight loss. The diet made sense to me because it not only cut the number of calories consumed, but induced a state that diminished hunger, and because it provided support through daily visits to the nurses. But the program was extremely expensive, and clients tended to gain back weight afterwards.

Now that I look back at that experience I realize that most weight loss clinics and spas, while successful in the short run, fail in the long run because of a conspicuous lack of biomedical foundation to their programs and education for their clients. After all is said and done, clients are left to fend for themselves and to attempt to limit the total number of calories consumed. Most eventually give up and regain the weight.

In 1984 nutrition took on crucial significance for me personally. I have a family history of heart disease, and that year I had coronary bypass surgery to improve the blood flow around arteries in my heart that had been clogged by cholesterol. It became imperative that I find a way to keep my cholesterol level down. The program I developed for myself, when tested in a hospital research project, proved to be extremely effective in lowering cholesterol level quickly and safely. Eventually, I shared my story and the program in my book *The 8-Week Cholesterol Cure*.

While writing that book, I addressed the issue of weight control and obesity, since weight loss alone can achieve significant declines in cholesterol levels, and obesity itself is a risk factor in terms of high blood pressure, diabetes, and heart disease. But while I could provide a lot of general information about the hazards of obesity and the benefits of weight loss, I could only encourage readers to shed those pounds by whatever means possible. For people with just a few extra pounds to lose, simply following my cholesterol-reducing regimen would gradually result in weight loss by reducing consumption of fats. But for those who had many health-threatening pounds to lose, I could offer a number of suggestions, but no definite program to follow.

Just as my book was being published, I received a call from a colleague about a physician who had an idea for a book on weight loss. Sure, I thought, yet another book that helps the writer a lot more than the reader. At any given time you can expect to find tons of weight loss books on the shelves of bookstores, and practically every week there's a diet book on the best-seller list of the *New York Times*. But, primarily as a favor to my colleague, I agreed to meet with this doctor.

My misgivings were quickly dispelled. Calvin Ezrin, M.D., is a luminary. An internationally acclaimed physician and endocrinologist, and one of our greatest authorities on the functional structure of the pituitary gland, he had the answers to weight loss questions that many have long asked. He had discovered a way to control the underlying metabolic problems that result in and maintain obesity. He had created a safe and effective way to lose weight and to keep it off. I was impressed, too, by the confidence Dr. Ezrin had instilled in his patients. As we discussed his research, theories, and clinical practice, I was convinced that this could be the book that could end the stream of diet books. I realized that here was a chance to combine his knowledge of the endocrine system with what I knew about health and nutrition to help countless people with a major personal and medical concern through the Insulin Control Diet.

CALVIN EZRIN, M.D., ON TREATING ALL THE PATIENTS

I do not consider myself to be first and foremost a weight loss doctor. Throughout my career in endocrinology, however, the links between the body's system of hormones and weight have become more and more clear. In my clinical practice I deal with a variety of metabolic disorders such as diabetes, thyroid imbalance, and abnormal production of adrenal, sex, parathyroid, and pituitary hormones. Frequently, weight problems brought patients to my office. Over the years I learned that many, if not most, of my patients who were overweight and unable to lose weight did not suffer from conventional hormonal malfunctions. Rather they were being victimized by insulin resistance and its consequences. As my theories about weight loss began to prove correct, I became successful in helping hundreds of patients lose weight.

When patients first come to my office, they often express feelings of guilt, low self-esteem, and depression. Many of them weep openly as they tell me their stories of failure in past efforts to lose weight. They begin to agree with those who brand all overweight men and women as moral deficients who simply lack the willpower to stop eating excessive amounts of food. "No one will believe me, Doctor, when I tell them that I do *not* overeat. I can't understand why I can't lose weight. The slightest slip from a diet causes pounds of weight to come right back." I do believe them. I know that their weight problems aren't their fault. As patients begin my plan and experience a rapid, encouraging initial weight loss, their attitudes and feelings of well-being improve with each week and with each lost pound of weight. The program really works.

Yet I simply cannot see every overweight person in my office, so I began to think about putting my medical advice into a book in order to share my discoveries and my program with anyone who has had trouble controlling weight. Robert Kowalski has a unique ability to make complicated concepts comprehensible, and I felt his ideas about food preparation, exercise, motivation, relaxation, and stress reduction could add a great deal to my ideas. I knew I wanted him to work with me in developing what is now our revolutionary program of weight control.

But first let me tell you how I became involved with the field of endocrinology. As a young physician, just graduated from the University of Toronto, I was particularly interested in diabetes in children. It was at the university's medical school that Frederick Banting and Charles Best had discovered and isolated the hormone insulin in 1921, marking the beginning of modern endocrinology and helping to save the lives of millions who would otherwise have died from diabetes.

In 1957 I worked with Dr. Best on a project researching the metabolic effects of the hormone glucagon on human metabolism. It was this research that showed me firsthand that the glucagon-insulin balance was important in the transformation of fat to ketones, which curb the appetite and could be helpful in the treatment of obesity. Later studies in insulin resistance showed the way in which heroic insulin, so necessary for life itself, can have a demonic side, leading to practically irreversible weight gain. This discovery, as you will see, is a cornerstone of the Insulin Control Diet.

Over the years, as a practicing physician, my heart has gone out particularly to those patients in whom weight gain seems to be almost predestined and against which they appear helpless. Until the middle of the 1960s I worked with the balanced, reduced-calorie diet, which limits the total number of calories consumed while providing nutrients from each food group. It is still the approach used by dietitians and physicians along with the exhortation to their patients that they try harder. In most cases of moderate overweight this is initially effective, but results in my resistant obese patients were poor.

I wanted to find another way to help people lose weight. Research demonstrated that *virtually everyone who has a strong tendency toward weight gain and who has a difficult time losing weight and keeping it of has an identifiable hormonal disorder*. That disorder is known as hyperinsulinism, and it is responsible for the metabolic trap that keeps weight on, causes a craving for sweets, contributes to sodium and fluid retention, and causes depression, irritability, and hunger. Fortunately, there is a way out of this trap—the Insulin Control Diet.

■ ■ ■

The Insulin Control Diet represents a revolutionary approach to weight control. Your physician may not be familiar with the principles underlying the program, so you may wish to show this book to him or her so he or she can work with you in using these concepts.

We have done our best to make this program a pleasant experience for you as you leave behind, once and for all, unwanted pounds. Every time you pick up this book, remember that we're with you every step of the way!

Chapter 2

The Critical Role of Diet in Diabetes

The first recorded diagnosis of diabetes was made by physicians in ancient Egypt. Finding that the urine of patients with the disease tasted sweet, they termed the problem *mellitus* meaning honey.

Diabetes remains defined as a disease characterized by elevated levels of blood sugar, glucose, caused by a relative deficiency of the hormone insulin. There are two major types of the disease.

The less common insulin-dependent diabetes mellitus (IDDM) termed Type I diabetes, occurs mainly in the young. For that reason it was previously called juvenile diabetes. Accounting for about 10 percent of all cases, IDD results from a near total destruction of the beta cells of the pancreas that make insulin. IDD is initiated by a virus attack and a malfunctioning of the body's own immune system. Type I diabetes patients are rarely overweight at the onset of their illness, but they can gain weight easily owing to the insulin treatment required for survival.

The more common second form of this endocrine disturbance is noninsulin-dependent diabetes mellitus (NIDDM), also termed Type II. It is not associated with insulin deficiency but rather with a substantial resistance to the hormone's blood-sugar-lowering effect. Most typically, NIDDM develops in adulthood and was previously called maturity-onset diabetes. Often NIDDM patients have normal or even increased levels of insulin in their blood, but not in sufficient amounts to keep the blood sugar within normal limits. About 90 percent of these patients are obese in medical terms.

Diet has been linked with diabetes from the beginning and it remains a critical component of treatment today. In fact, an understanding of how dietary management influences the disease is the first step in controlling it.

INSULIN RESISTANCE AND HYPERINSULINISM

While the overweight condition of diabetes patients is at least partially the result of poor eating habits, the phenomena of insulin resistance and hyperinsulinism both promote weight gain and make weight loss particularly difficult. Thus most efforts at weight control for Type II diabetics are frustrating and ultimately end in failure. Only when the factors of insulin resistance and hyperinsulinism are taken into consideration can one expect to succeed.

What causes insulin resistance? In Type II diabetes it is a strongly inherited *selective* defect in blood sugar regulation. This affects muscle predominantly but also involves the liver and fat tissue.

The action of insulin is necessary to metabolize glucose for the body to use it as fuel in the cells. But in diabetic patients, glucose resists this action of insulin. Viewed another way, the insulin is less capable of metabolizing glucose in the diabetic patient than in nondiabetics. In response, the body produces additional insulin in an effort to metabolize the rising levels of sugar in the blood. Ultimately an excessive level of insulin results, and this condition is termed hyperinsulinism.

For a time, the additional insulin may be sufficient to maintain relatively normal blood sugar levels. But we have a "catch 22" situation. Increased insulin levels favor a gain in fat weight, which, in turn, is another important cause of insulin resistance. Fat tissue produces a substance that inhibits the muscles' ability to utilize glucose as fuel or for storage as glycogen.

There comes a time when sufficient weight is gained so that the combined forms of insulin resistance exceed the ability of the pancreas to respond with adequate insulin secretion. At that point, the person is diagnosed with diabetes. Research indicates that Type II diabetes patients also have a defect in the pancreas' ability to make as much insulin as can a normal individual, whose pancreas has considerable potential reserve capacity.

These are difficult concepts to grasp, but they are very important to understand. In fact, understanding the link between hyperinsulinism/insulin resistance and weight control is the first step to success. We believe that it is the lack of this understanding which dooms most weight loss efforts to failure. Insulin itself must be controlled.

Interestingly, while we typically think of insulin in positive terms, there is a dark side to this hormone. Even in the normal person, insulin is involved with production of triglycerides and the "bad" cholesterol carrier known as LDL.

At the same time, insulin lowers levels of the "good" cholesterol carrier HDL. And it strongly stimulates growth of certain cells which play pivotal roles in arterial disease. Imagine, then, what can happen when there are excessive amounts of insulin circulating through the blood. All those negative functions are increased tremendously. It may well be that this connection explains at least part of the reason why diabetes patients are at significantly greater risk of heart disease and other cardiovascular complications that are so common in diabetics.

The recently completed Diabetes Control and Complications Trial showed conclusively that good blood sugar control led to significantly better outcomes. That is to say, Type I patients who had "tight control" over their glucose levels suffered fewer complications involving the eyes, nerves, kidneys, and blood vessels. Since Type II diabetics develop similar complications, it is reasonable to conclude that good control of blood sugar would be equally desirable for them as well .

High blood sugars and high blood insulin levels are both likely contributors to Type II diabetes complications. Ideally, levels of both sugar and insulin should be normalized. This, happily enough, can be done by following the program of weight control detailed in this book.

WEIGHT CONTROL AND DIABETES

Weight control and a reasonable program of physical exercise are the two most critical components of effective diabetes management. Since most Type II diabetics are overweight, the diet prescribed should be low in calories so that stored fat must be withdrawn to provide the calories missing from food.

Let's run that by one more time, since it is such an important concept. The excess weight you have takes the form of stored fat. That fat can be viewed as a potential source of food: your body's pantry, in effect. Your body needs a certain amount of fuel on a daily basis, energy measured in calories. Reduce the number of calories and the body can turn to that "pantry" to provide the deficit. Unfortunately, that ideal scenario doesn't always occur in the typical weight loss diet. Fortunately, that's exactly what happens in the program you're now reading about.

What are some of the particulars about an ideal diet for the diabetic patient? There is no argument among the world's authorities that sufficient protein must be included to provide the essential amino acids that the body cannot synthesize. A low-protein diet would be prescribed only if the patient were to have kidney disease.

Now what about carbohydrates and fat, the remaining two potential sources of energy? Commonly prescribed high carbohydrate diets produce higher plasma glucose and insulin levels. Obviously from what we've already discussed, that's defeating the purpose. Moreover, such diets generate significantly higher triglycerides and lower HDL levels, especially when compared to this book's program. A diet low in carbohydrates prevents those adverse responses. On this program, blood sugar and insulin levels fall dramatically, as does the level of triglycerides. A beneficial state of ketosis (see *Ketosis*) appears within two to three days, indicating that insulin levels have been sufficiently reduced to allow fat to be rapidly mobilized from stores to provide the major source of energy. As the book's title promises, your fat can make you thin!

In following this program, you'll keep dietary fat to a minimum in order to maximize the withdrawal of internal fat. You might be asked how many calories you're consuming on your diet. The correct answer would be 3,000 calories. Imagine the response you'd get to that reply. "What! How can you lose weight on 3,000 calories?" The answer is that only 1,000 of those calories come from the food you eat, while 2,000 calories are supplied by your stored fat, from your body's pantry.

KETOSIS AS PART OF WEIGHT LOSS

For many years now, health professionals have known how to feed seriously ill patients intravenously. A specially developed formula which includes emulsified fat is fed directly into the vein, and this emulsified fat can be used immediately as energy for the body.

Needless to say, if one were to inject any other kind of fat—including the fat stored in your own body—directly into the vein, the results would be disastrous. But imagine how efficient it would be if your body's fat were to be rendered in a way that it could be used directly as energy. That's exactly what happens when following this program, as your body enters a state of mild, beneficial ketosis.

Obviously, the first benefit would be the loss of the weight of that stored fat. But there are additional advantages to ketosis. You'll experience appetite control without over-stimulation of the nervous system which so often occurs when taking diet pills. Those pills also produce tolerance, despondency, and depression never seen with ketosis. Next, ketosis induces a gentle diuresis characterized by a selected excretion of sodium and water while at the same time sparing potassium, and without the significant rebound resistance that occurs with diuretic pills. Finally, ketosis spares protein by substituting for glucose as brain fuel and thereby limiting the amount of new glucose that must be made from amino acids, the building blocks of protein.

There are two types of ketosis, one good and the other bad. *It is crucial that both you and your doctor distinguish the difference.* The good ketosis just described results from the reduction of insulin, sufficient to permit rapid liberation of fatty acids from stored fat and their subsequent conversion in the liver. This results in moderate amounts of ketones that are never sufficient enough to disturb the chemical acid-base balance of the body. Point blank, the ketosis advocated in this program never produces acidosis.

The bad ketosis is an acute complication of diabetes usually occurring in Type I patients who are not receiving sufficient insulin. Physicians may rarely see the condition in Type II diabetic individuals whose insulin needs have been greatly increased owing to infection or other severe stress. In such cases, blood sugar is usually quite high, often over 400 mg percent. In severe cases the patient is dehydrated, acidotic, drowsy, and even comatose.

It is generally easy to distinguish between the good and bad ketosis early on in a Type II diabetes patient. Beneficial ketosis will be accompanied by a near-normal blood sugar. Adverse ketosis, on the other hand, would result in a high blood sugar from an obvious associated reason for loss of diabetic control. It is unusual for this to happen in Type II patients. In fact, Type II diabetes has been called nonketotic diabetes because patients, even with very high blood sugars, show little or no signs of the condition.

This is because fat cells remain very sensitive to insulin's inhibitory effect on the breakdown and liberation of stored fat. The production of ketones by the liver requires rapid mobilization of free fatty acids from fat sources, which even a small amount of insulin can still prevent.

STABILIZING AND MAINTAINING WEIGHT LOSS

You'll be learning the details of the actual dietary program throughout the book, and they are the same for both diabetic and nondiabetic individuals alike. But there are special considerations in stabilization and maintenance recommendations for Type II diabetics.

As a diabetic, you retain resistance to insulin even after weight loss has reduced the additional insulin resistance derived from obesity itself. As such, you may not have the same tolerance for carbohydrates that favors nondiabetics. Your ultimate maintenance diet, required for optimal blood sugar control, should contain somewhat less carbohydrate. Remaining calories may come from "good" fats such as canola oil and olive oil, those that do not adversely affect cholesterol levels as do the saturated fats.

EXERCISE FOR TYPE II DIABETICS

Exercise belongs in the lifestyle of every man and woman alive to promote good health and well-being. But it is even more important for the Type II diabetes patient as a crucial, indispensible factor in the treatment equation.

Exercise lowers blood sugar without involving insulin. It is, therefore, a wonderful means of reducing the amount of insulin to which the body is exposed. Exercise also increases the mass of lean muscle tissue in your body and it is that muscle which burns energy most efficiently.

What is the best fuel for exercise? Muscle contraction is fueled by a physiologic reaction involving the chemical adenosine triphosphate (ATP) as it is broken down into the metabolite adenosine diphosphate (ADP) with a resultant release of energy. ATP can be derived equally well from the breakdown of glucose and fatty acids. In fact, the preferred muscle fuel for aerobic exercise is fatty acids. So much for the common misconception that the body requires carbohydrate for energy. The only times your body would need to be fueled by carbohydrate would be during a marathon race or when running a 100-yard dash. You might ask yourself how likely it will be that you'll be involved in either event in the near future!

Indeed, recent studies have shown—to virtually everyone's delight—that a brisk walk is superior to jogging or running for burning fat. The reason, as we've just seen, is that the body prefers fats for fuel during such activity, as compared to burning glucose while engaged in more strenuous exercise.

For the Type II diabetic patient, as for the nondiabetic individual, the best exercise is a regular program of walking. Do as the English have done for years: Make walking your "daily constitutional."

Of course, any form of mild exercise you prefer is just fine. The important thing is that you will do it regularly. Bike riding, swimming, and aerobics classes are all terrific as integral components of the program. To quote the advertisement from Nike, "Just do it!"

Chapter 3

IN SEARCH OF IDEAL WEIGHT

Taste in physical beauty, particularly female beauty, varies widely from culture to culture and over time. In our fickle society one has to consult popular magazines to determine what this season's "ideal" figure is. The 1960s high-fashion passion for thinness has given way to a trend toward the "healthy" look, although the definition of what looks healthy comes down, once again, to personal opinion. Is the ideal body lean, flat, and smooth? Is it muscular with bulging biceps and triceps? Or does it have softer, fuller curves? At each swing of the fashion pendulum, some of us are luckier than others in terms of having the "right" appearance.

But should a person follow any standard other than his or her own in determining ideal weight? Clearly, the social pressure to be thin, especially on women, has led many down the unhealthy path of eating disorders such as anorexia and bulimia and to skewed perceptions of body image. But there are important reasons, quite apart from the dictates of fashion and appearance, to avoid being overweight. Medical authorities agree that excess weight is counter to good health.

THE MEDICAL CONSEQUENCES OF OBESITY

In 1985 the National Institutes of Health (NIH) held a conference to address what is now considered to be a matter of urgent concern in our society: obesity and its medical consequences. A panel of some of the nation's leading authorities in medicine, physiology, public health, nutrition, psychology, endocrinology, and other fields reached the unequivocal consensus that obesity was at epidemic proportions in the United States and that it is a killer, as much as smoking cigarettes is a killer. Presently about 30 percent of all adults in the United States, about 50 million people aged 20 to 75, are at least 20 percent over their ideal weight. Obesity is related to a wide variety of ills and contributes directly to total mortality. Dr. Jules Hirsch, the chairman of the NIH panel, emphasized that we can no longer view obesity as simply a matter of cosmetics or vanity, but must see it as a matter of life or death. In 1995, Dr. Everett Koop, former U.S. Surgeon General, reemphasized that message, noting that Americans were getting even fatter. But how does obesity kill?

The effects of overweight are greatest during the younger years, and the longer a person is overweight, the greater the influence of the condition on ultimate longevity. It takes about 10 years to develop problems associated with obesity. In later years we don't see as much influence, probably because vulnerable obese individuals have died off, leaving the hardy survivors to be considered in the statistics.

Medically speaking, anyone who is 20 percent or more over his or her ideal body weight is obese. This can be the small-framed female who should weigh 100 pounds but weighs 130 or the average-framed man whose ideal weight is 150 pounds but who weighs 195.

But problems begin even before a person is clinically obese. A man who is just 10 percent overweight (for example, 165 pounds rather than the ideal 150) is at risk of increased mortality and morbidity. For a woman risk begins to become significant at 20 percent overweight. As the weight increases, so does the risk. Mortality climbs to 12 times normal in the 25- to 35-year-old man at twice his ideal body weight. Thus one sees few elderly men at that degree of obesity.

Certainly the risk of heart disease, our nation's number one killer, increases as weight increases. And, being overweight increases all other risk factors by two. Thus, whatever a person's increased risk due to elevated cholesterol, that risk is doubled if the person is also overweight.

Interestingly, where those extra pounds are stored on the body can also make a difference. The typical male pattern of overweight—pot belly and spare tire—associates clearly with increased risk of heart disease. The same holds true for women who put weight on in this pattern. A more evenly distributed fat layer over the entire body does not have this statistical correlation with heart disease. But, regardless of pattern of distribution, as one increases the percentage of overweight from 10 to 20 to 30 and up, the risk of disease increases.

High blood pressure, or hypertension, is a contributing risk factor in heart disease and is the principal cause of stroke. The relative risk of hypertension for overweight American adults aged 20 to 75 years is 5.6 times that of nonoverweight persons in the same age and sex groups. Compared to obese black men and women, overweight white men and women are at greater risk of being hypertensive. (Ironically, though, black individuals in general have a higher rate of high blood pressure.)

A return to normal weight in hypertensives frequently means a return to normal blood pressure. At the very least, any weight loss results in a drop in blood pressure, and every millimeter of difference in blood pressure means a difference in the risk of heart disease and stroke. In addition, weight loss frequently means that patients can decrease the amount of hypertension medications they take, thus diminishing any unpleasant side effects the drugs may entail.

By now almost everyone in the nation has heard of the importance of maintaining a low level of cholesterol in the blood. It is no longer a matter of controversy: Every 1 percent drop in cholesterol means a 2 percent decrease in the risk of heart disease.

The relationship between weight and blood cholesterol level is an interesting one. Some individuals can be lean and still have a dangerously high cholesterol level; others can be stout and still have an acceptable level. (The only way to know what the level is is to do a simple blood test.) But the majority of overweight people experience a rise in the amount of cholesterol in their blood. Statistically speaking, overweight Americans aged 20 to 75 have a 1.5 times greater risk of having high cholesterol. Those aged 20 to 45 have a 2.1 times greater risk. But one thing is for certain: *Overweight individuals who do have elevated cholesterol levels are guaranteed to see those levels fall if they return to normal weight.*

The same applies to the fatty substances in the blood known as triglycerides. Triglycerides, a form of fat that is abundant in the diet and is also synthesized during digestion, circulate in the blood until they can be used by the body. They may also contribute to atherosclerosis.

More than 80 percent of diabetics are obese. For overweight adults aged 20 to 75 the risk of having diabetes is nearly 3 times that for nonoverweight persons of comparable age and sex. For those aged 20 to 45 the risk of having diabetes is nearly 4 times that for nonoverweight people. Type II or non-insulin-dependent diabetes (previously known as maturity-onset diabetes) is closely related to obesity. While it's true that some men and women are genetically predisposed to develop type II diabetes in their mature years, the disease usually will not be manifested without the development of obesity. It's as simple as that. Conversely, if an individual has type II diabetes and is overweight, *simply returning to normal weight usually means the disappearance of all manifestations of the disorder*. Even for severe cases of type II diabetes, following this program can well mean complete reversal of the disease.

Heart disease is 4 times more common in those with diabetes than in the general population. For diabetic patients, weight and cholesterol control are crucial. But beyond heart disease, stroke, and diabetes, the obese person faces other risks. For example, the man weighing twice his ideal weight has a 12 times greater risk of dying from accidents than the man at his ideal weight. Due to the strain on weight-bearing joints, the incidence of arthritis skyrockets in the overweight. Obesity is an important risk factor for osteoarthritis of the knee, particularly in women. Obese women seem to be at greater risk of developing cancer of the uterus.

Until something happens to change their attitude, most people have a feeling of immortality. They read about the incidence of heart disease, cancer, hypertension, diabetes, and other diseases, but think of them as illnesses that happen to someone else. Even when illness strikes members of the family, they tend to feel somehow protected. This natural tendency is unfortunate. Without being excessively morbid, taking a look further down the road of your life is to your benefit.

If you believed a fortune teller who told you that you would be killed in a plane crash if you flew within the next two weeks, you probably would not fly during that time. We can tell you, based on scientific and statistical evidence, that if you continue a pattern of significant overweight, your risk for illness and death will multiply. This is the time to do something about reducing that risk.

The medical data clearly point to the importance of maintaining ideal weight, but the next question to be considered is what is ideal weight or how do we define overweight? Even in medical circles the standards used have varied over time.

The height-weight tables issued by insurance companies are the most frequently cited standards. Insurance companies determined as early as the turn of the century that excessive weight is linked with shortened life expectancies.* Not surprisingly, they began to charge more for insuring obese individuals.

The Metropolitan Life Insurance Company developed the first tables listing desirable weight in the early 1940s. The tables were revised in 1959, when for the first time weight standards were varied according to height. While a number of tables have appeared since then, most are modeled after that 1959 chart. In a 1983 revision of the chart, weights were adjusted upward, which created a flurry of comments, letters, and articles in medical journals. After the dust cleared, the general consensus was that the weights proposed in the 1959 edition were more likely to be associated with better health and greater longevity. We've reprinted that chart here (Table 2.1).

One rule of thumb that has been used for determining ideal body weight for men is 106 pounds for the first 5 feet of height and 6 pounds for each inch after 5 feet, plus or minus 10 percent according to frame size. The rule for women is 100 pounds for the first five feet, and 5 pounds per inch thereafter, with the same adjustment for frame size.

---

*In 1913 the Medico-Actuarial Mortality Investigation revealed that in the years from 1885 to 1909 the lowest mortality rates among insured persons were those for people whose weight was slightly above average in the younger years of adulthood and slightly below average in the older years. Bear in mind that in those years, tuberculosis and pneumonia were leading causes of death, and those diseases are associated with underweight. But a few years later, after 1913, additional studies conducted by insurance companies showed that maximum longevity was associated with weights somewhat below average.

Table 3.1 Desirable Weights for Men and Women

Height (with shoes)	Weight, in indoor clothing (lbs)		
	Small Frame	Medium Frame	Large Frame
Men			
5′ 2″	112–120	118–129	126–141
5′ 3″	115–123	121–133	129–144
5′ 4″	118–126	124–136	132–148
5′ 5″	121–129	127–139	135–152
5′ 6″	124–133	130–143	138–156
5′ 7″	128–137	134–147	142–161
5′ 8″	132–141	138–152	147–166
5′ 9″	136–145	142–156	151–170
5′10″	140–150	146–160	155–174
5′11″	144–154	150–165	159–179
6′ 0″	148–158	154–170	164–184
6′ 1″	152–162	158–175	168–189
6′ 2″	156–167	162–180	173–194
6′ 3″	160–171	167–185	178–199
6′ 4″	164–175	172–190	182–204
Women			
4′10″	92– 98	96–107	104–119
4′11″	94–101	98–110	106–122
5′ 0″	96–104	101–113	109–125
5′ 1″	99–107	104–116	112–128
5′ 2″	102–110	107–119	115–131
5′ 3″	105–113	110–122	118–134
5′ 4″	108–116	113–126	121–138
5′ 5″	111–119	116–130	125–142
5′ 6″	114–123	120–135	129–146
5′ 7″	118–127	124–139	133–150
5′ 8″	122–131	128–143	137–154
5′ 9″	126–135	132–147	141–158
5′10″	130–140	136–151	145–163
5′11″	134–144	140–155	149–168
6′ 0″	138–148	144–159	153–173

Source: Prepared by the Metropolitan Life Insurance Company. Derived primarily from data of the *Build and Blood Pressure Study*, 1959, Society of Actuaries.

But weight alone doesn't give a completely accurate picture. More important than whether one is overweight is whether one is overfat. Think about a football player who is 6 feet tall and weighs 220 pounds. According to the standard tables he would be overweight. But is he overfat? Closer analysis would probably reveal that he is heavily muscled and has minimal body fat. On the other hand, a young girl who is underweight according to the height-weight tables might actually be overfat. The athletically conditioned person is likely to have a lower percentage of body fat than a sedentary person of identical age, sex, and genetic predisposition. And men tend to be lower in fat than women. That's just a biological fact of life.

The body is made up primarily of bone, muscle, and fat. We can't do anything about the weight or size of our bones, but the amount of muscle and fat and the ratio between the two can change appreciably. That ratio can and does change for practically everyone over the years. The man who participated in college sports and whose body fat was on the low side can gradually lose muscle tissue and replace it with fat cells. For a long time there may be no perceptible difference. The size of his body, the girth of his waist, and even his total weight may remain the same. But his muscle mass tends to atrophy. He continues to consume the same number of calories as always, noting that his weight hasn't changed a bit. He might even brag about his ability to pack away the food while still fitting in the jeans he wore at school. But one day the equation swings in favor of the fat over the lean. And, faster than he could dream possible, he begins to put weight on. He ascribes this to the inexorable passage of years. But that's not at all the reality.

To grasp the significance of body composition, we have to understand the dynamics of fat and muscle. Simply put, lean muscle tissue is the body's "engine." Only the activity of muscle can burn appreciable calories. Fat tissue cannot contribute to the burning of calories. The more lean muscle tissue one has, the more calories can be burned. As one loses that muscle tissue, the capacity to burn calories diminishes. Since fewer calories are being burned while the caloric intake remains the same, there are excess calories, and those excess calories get turned into fat. And fat, as just stated, can burn no significant calories, so more fat just keeps piling up, until the spare tire and "love handles" appear.

In this regard we're not much different from beef cattle. To get the desired well-marbled prime beef, farmers feed their livestock plenty of grain while restricting their movement. Take a look at a prime steak in the supermarket, with its white streaks of fat running through the red muscle. That's what the flesh of an overfat human looks like.

Two principal ways to determine body fat are being used today. The more accurate method is underwater weighing. The person to be weighed gets on a specially designed scale and is lowered into a pool of water. The buoyant fat does not register on the scale; only the bone and muscle get weighed. A simple calculation determines the percentage of body fat weight in relation to total body weight.

Not nearly as accurate, but a lot more convenient and adequate for many purposes, are skinfold measurements, which can be made by a trained professional. Calipers are used to measure the folds of fat at different sites on the body, principally the skinfold hanging from the underside of the arm at the triceps muscle.

Experiments are being conducted with methods to measure body fat indirectly. One, called total body impedance, uses harmless, painless electric current to measure electrical resistance, which is related to the amount of body water, body density, and body fat. The other, called near infrared interactance, uses noninvasive light to measure the actual composition of tissue at various sites on the body. The apparatus to make this measurement will soon be available in a portable system for use in hospitals, clinics, and health clubs.

We've listed the ideal percentage of body fat for men and women in Table 2.2. If you have an opportunity to be tested, we recommend that you do so. But for most people concerned about their weight, a look in the mirror will tell if the percentage of body fat—and body weight—is too high.

We strongly believe that it is important to establish a definite goal weight early in your weight loss efforts. As we've discovered, it's difficult to determine exactly what that goal weight should be, but the goal must be realistic. There are the factors of frame size

Table 3.2 Suggested Standards of Fat Percentage for Adult Men and Women*

	Men (%)	Women (%)
Essential fat	0–5	0–8
Optimal health	10–25	18–30
Optimal fitness	12–18	16–25
Athletes	5–13	12–22
Obesity	Above 25	Above 30

*A certain amount of fat in the body is essential for health, and optimal health can be achieved within quite a large range of percentages of body fat. Within that range one will find individuals in good physical condition, though not necessarily athletes. At both ends of the spectrum—either minimum body fat or a high proportion of fat—individuals are at health risk.

Source: *The Physician and Sportsmedicine*, April 1986.

and body fat percentage, and it may not be reasonable to expect an ultra-thin appearance.

For many people there is a distinct time when weight began to pile on. If you have not always been as overweight as you are now, try to remember the time when you were most content with your size. Perhaps you were at what you consider an ideal weight in college or in the military or before your first child was born. After that time, for whatever reason, you began to gain weight, you fell into the metabolic trap of insulin resistance, and the weight seemed to come faster. Go through some early photographs to see the person you once were and could and will be again. That's your goal weight.

It's tremendously important that you actually reach your goal weight in order to ensure permanent weight loss. A major weight loss center has found that those men and women who achieve goal weight are more likely to keep the weight off permanently.

To see why, let's take the example of Laura, who came to the office at 250 pounds. At 5 feet 7 inches tall, she felt she should weigh 140, the weight she enjoyed in college. Laura responded beautifully to the diet program, and the pounds started coming off on schedule. Needless to say, Laura was pleased with her progress. Then at 160 pounds she decided that she had lost enough weight. Her friends and relatives were all telling her how skinny she looked. Some even urged her to gain some of her weight back. Soon the goal weight was forgotten. Surely a weight loss of 90 pounds was enough. But, since she wasn't exactly at goal weight, Laura didn't mind too much when she gained a few pounds. There was a party here, a nibble there, and before long she had gained much of her weight back.

Kathy, on the other hand, attained her goal of 130 pounds, a full 100-pound weight loss. Just as Laura had done, Kathy responded well to the program, but Kathy remained determined to meet her goal and did so in a reasonable amount of time. She then went through a stabilization period and ultimately into a maintenance program. She learned to add calories to her diet slowly until she neither gained nor lost weight. To our knowledge, Kathy remains at her desired 130 pounds.

Why is this matter of goal weight so important? There is both a medical and a psychological explanation. In medical terms Laura was still in the metabolic trap of insulin resistance. She never got out of it. By retaining some of her excessive body fat, along with salt and fluid, Laura didn't have a chance. She teetered on the brink of weight gain from the very beginning. Moreover, she never learned the skills to maintain weight.

On a psychological basis Laura was similarly in a danger zone. Compare her with the person who attempts to stop the cigarette habit by cutting back from two packs a day to three or four cigarettes. The habit is never broken. Such a person is constantly in a state of withdrawal, an uncomfortable feeling as anyone who has quit will testify. It is a rare person who can go from being an addicted smoker to having a few cigarettes daily. It's best to quit completely.

Similarly, Laura was not completely committed to the weight loss program. Since she already had some extra pounds over ideal, a few more didn't seem to make much difference. The goal weight was a future concept. She could always achieve her goal a few days or a few weeks later; she could always lose a few pounds tomorrow. But then there was another pound and then another few pounds—just like the person who smokes just one more cigarette. No wonder, then, that Laura failed in her ultimate effort. Kathy, having made the goal weight a reality, had a feeling of pride and achievement; she had something at stake.

Let's take our comparison with cigarette smoking a step further. Most former smokers will tell you, "Once a smoker, always a smoker." Those who are committed to staying away from tobacco will never take even one cigarette, realizing that if they smoke one cigarette, they will be hooked again. But on the brighter side, the longer one stays away from the cigarettes, the easier it gets. The moments of desperately wanting a smoke grow shorter and fewer. The smoker learns to not smoke. The overweight person learns to not eat what he or she knows he or she shouldn't eat. It's all part of the process of reaching your ideal weight.

Chapter 4

WHY THIS DIET WORKS

We have no record of the first case of obesity, but we can guess that it occurred when food was plentiful for the first time and people were able to rest more than they exercised. We also have no record of the first attempt to lose weight, but we certainly have a lot of material in more recent times.

The weight loss industry is a multimillion-dollar business. Weight loss centers, clinics, spas, and support groups flourish. Issue after issue the covers of magazines announce the newest weight loss "breakthrough." Supermarket and pharmacy shelves are lined with pills, tablets, and other nostrums claiming to be magic potions. Late night television offers mail-order miracles. People go from one fad to another, convinced that the new gimmick or the new book will finally work, even though all the ones before have failed. So perpetually hopeful are they that the sale of weight loss mailing lists in and of itself is big business.

Yet with all this preoccupation with weight loss, and with all the highly touted solutions to this perplexing problem, over-weight continues to plague the population. In fact, the number of men and women who are significantly overweight grows annually. Never before has the U.S. population been so obese. Why don't these diets work? Why can't someone come up with the way out of this continuing predicament? There is no one, simple answer to these questions. But there are definite reasons why the pursuit of weight loss has so often been a difficult, if not futile, endeavor.

The wise consumer understands that there is no way that special devices, such as herbal body wraps and stimulating electrode equipment, can achieve weight loss. But people tend to be taken in more easily by diets that promise much, especially those that give fast, initial results. However, weight maintenance rather than weight loss is the more important consideration, since although many diets can produce at least some weight loss, the lost pounds tend to be regained. In fact, quite often more pounds are regained than were lost in the first place. So, when looking at the reasons for diet failure, we'll examine both weight loss and maintenance.

The difficulty with plans that virtually exclude food for a period of time, such as liquid protein diets and temporary fasting, is that the dieters never learn to handle foods in a normal way. At some point currently overweight men and women began to lose control over their eating patterns. Simply keeping them away from food doesn't teach them what they were doing wrong or how to change their habits. Many studies have shown, and our own work bears out, that in order to maintain weight loss, one must make some changes in lifestyle. This calls for both nutrition education and behavior modification.

Knowing the fundamentals of nutrition as they apply to eating habits is crucial to lasting weight loss, yet many dieters are inadequately informed about them. Ironically, many people who are overweight are nonetheless poorly nourished. When one begins to learn about how to choose foods wisely for their nutrient contributions, one is able to enjoy a wide variety of foods while still maintaining weight.

Behavior modification is integral to any weight loss plan. It can be simply adopting helpful strategies such as not eating while engaged in other activities such as watching television. But behavior modification is far more meaningful when it comes from examining not only habits but attitudes. Self-image is a significant factor that can make or break the commitment to weight loss. Any weight loss program that doesn't implement some aspect of behavior modification is unlikely to succeed. Throughout this book we offer advice and support from years of patient contact, to help implement the lifestyle changes that can really make a difference.

Many of the most popular diets involve unnatural eating patterns. Diets that have not been properly designed can pose some physical and mental problems. If a diet stresses a single food, it's unlikely one will be able to stay with it for the rest of one's life. How long can you stand to eat quantities of grapefruit every day? No matter how delectable any food is the first day, by the end of a month you might turn green just looking at it. Such a diet, if it does achieve weight loss, is doomed to fail in keeping weight off.

The same holds true for diets that stress any one category of foods. Some of these diets make some absurd claims that combinations of foods are more or less "fattening" than the foods eaten alone or eaten in a given order. They claim that the body can't digest more than one food at a time. This is nonsense. The body's various digestive chemicals are quite capable of digesting different foods at once.

When any one type of food is stressed and others are eliminated on a permanent basis, there is the danger of malnutrition and other health threats. A number of books prescribe eating huge volumes of fruit, often to the exclusion of other foods. Such a diet may lead to severe diarrhea, occasionally to the extent that hospitalization is required to combat dehydration. Irritation of the digestive tract can prevent absorption of needed nutrients. Diets that eliminate bulk forming foods on a permanent basis can cause constipation, not a trivial matter that can be eased by simply taking a laxative. We know today that inactivity of the colon is a risk factor for the development of future cancer.

Ultimately, even if some weight loss does occur temporarily from poorly planned diet programs, weight regain will occur when it becomes either physically or mentally impossible to continue to follow such limited regimens.

Dieting through the use of drugs came into vogue in the 1950s and 1960s as doctors frequently wrote prescriptions for amphetamines to depress the appetite and thus reduce calorie intake. While the drugs did often work, they fostered dependency and adverse reactions including jitteriness, irritability, and sleeplessness. All too often other drugs were prescribed to counteract those reactions. This practice, referred to in the medical community as "rainbow therapy" for the many colors of the pills and tablets, is much less prevalent today.

Manufacture of amphetamines has been greatly curtailed, but there are a number of over-the-counter nostrums that have the same, though milder, effects. Such diet pills, widely available in supermarkets and drugstores, most typically contain the drug phenylpropanolamine. The U.S. Food and Drug Administration would like to see them removed from the market not only because of their ineffectiveness, but also because of potential adverse reactions.

Given the drawbacks, danger, and ineffectiveness of the methods of dieting described thus far, most nutritionists and physicians have relied for years on the oldest weight loss advice we know of: Cut back on total calories.

As a general rule, weight gain is the result of consuming too many and expending too few calories—eating too much and exercising too little. Genetics also plays an important role. Some people are more predisposed to be overweight than others. Some people gain weight more easily than others, needing fewer calories to put on extra pounds. But everyone, regardless of family history, will gain weight if they eat too much and exercise too little.

Dietitians, then, commonly recommend diets that provide needed nutrients without unnecessary calories—usually a 1,200- to 1,500-calorie diet based on the four food groups. For many people, especially for those with only 5 to 15 pounds to lose, this is all it takes. But it doesn't work for everyone; there are distinct limitations to this program.

For one thing, not all foods work in the same way in terms of weight gain. It has been found that carbohydrates and protein provide 4 calories per gram, fat supplies 9 and alcohol 7. Now it appears that fat is an even more efficient source of calories, packing 10, 11, or perhaps even 12 calories per gram. Moreover, the body doesn't self limit fat intake in the same way it limits the intake of other foods. You never hear about someone gorging on fruit, for example, even after having eaten a quantity sufficient to suppress hunger. We have an apparently unlimited ability or tendency to consume fat. The body has a shut-off mechanism for both protein and carbohydrate, but not for fat.

Even supposing that the concept of merely reducing total calories could be effective regardless of circumstances and the type of food eaten, for the person with 50, 70, or 100 pounds to lose, it would take an inordinately long period of time for such a regimen to be completely effective. Furthermore, during that entire period of time, the dieter is bound to experience pangs of hunger regularly, and few people are willing to be hungry every day for months or even more than a year.

Another reason the simple "eat less" approach doesn't always work is that an important part of any successful weight loss program is exercise. It used to be thought that exercise was beneficial simply because it burns calories. We now know there's more to exercise than that. In addition to burning calories at the time of exertion, it increases the metabolic rate at which calories are utilized for some time after exertion. Exercise also increases one's sense of well-being and helps one to relax. It builds muscle tissue which, in turn, burns calories; that helps to explain why people with more lean muscle tend to have less of a weight problem. Exercise during weight loss inhibits the loss of muscle tissue, allowing the body to keep the lean and lose the fat. And finally it plays the crucial role of regulating insulin levels. (Exercise is discussed fully in Chapter 9.)

Even the combination of calorie reduction and exercise is often ineffective, particularly with significantly overweight men and women, and as the degree of obesity increases, so does the failure rate of dieting.

Physicians have recognized the need for weight loss in obese men and women for over three decades, and some have tried a variety of approaches in their attempts to deal with this difficult aspect of medical care. One approach was to hospitalize greatly obese patients and allow them no food at all, providing only unlimited fluids along with vitamin and mineral supplementation. The complication to this approach was a tremendous loss of muscle tissue as well as fat. Since lean tissue burns calories, the loss of muscle made the individual less calorie-efficient and thus more likely than before dieting to put on weight. In fact, they tended to regain more weight afterwards than they had lost. But, even more importantly, the body does not discriminate among muscles, and it is just as likely to break down heart muscle as any other muscle in order to provide fuel for the brain. A potential complication of starvation diets, then, became heart failure and even death. Because of such problems, starvation diets were abandoned.

But we learned something important from those early starvation diets. After three days or so patients were not hungry, even though they ate absolutely no food. Why? Hunger is the body's signal that levels of blood sugar are too low. With no food coming in, the body adapts by converting its own muscle tissue into glucose. (We'll look into this phenomenon in Chapter 5.) Researchers wondered how the supply of glucose could be maintained without destroying muscle tissue.

The answer was the development of the protein-sparing modified-fast diet. The pioneers in this approach were Drs. George Blackburn and Bruce Bistrian at Boston Deaconess Hospital. They designed a diet that provided a small amount of fat, a large amount of high-quality protein, and a limited amount of carbohydrate. The logic behind this approach was simple. Fat is a concentrated source of calories, so it should be greatly restricted. Protein is essential to sparing muscle tissue, so it should be available. But why limit carbohydrate?

With carbohydrate intake down to no more than 40 grams daily, the body would utilize its own deposits of fat to form chemicals called ketones, which the body could use just like glucose. (The high level of production of ketones by the body is called ketosis.) Doing so achieved two goals at once. Ketones took the place of glucose in the blood and thus kept the dieter from being hungry and kept the body from using its own protein for glucose production.

In its experimental stage the protein-sparing modified-fast was conducted only under strict medical supervision in a few major hospitals. Slowly, its safety and effectiveness were recognized, and the details of the diet were spelled out in medical symposia and literature.

Unfortunately, the first attempt to popularize the approach resulted in disaster. A physician marketed his formulation of a protein powder intended to imitate the diet used by Blackburn and Bistrian. But the protein was of poor quality, derived from collagen, the protein found in hair, horns, and nails. Moreover, the product provided inadequate vitamin and mineral supplementation. Overweight customers using the product, with no medical supervision and with no time limit for staying on the diet specified, lost muscle tissue. A significant number lost muscle in the heart, and more than 50 women died of heart failure.

At about the same time, Dr. Atkins published his *Diet Revolution*. In it he advocated strict avoidance of carbohydrates, but allowed all the meat and fat one wanted to eat. Because the diet worked, and readers lost weight as promised, this approach became popular. But the diet had a number of flaws. Dieters' cholesterol levels rose significantly, increasing the risk of heart disease. The state of ketosis produced by the diet was uncontrolled. When readers returned to their former eating habits, they quickly regained the lost weight because no provision was made for exercise, inadequate advice was provided about future behavioral changes, and no information was given about the causes of the initial obesity, how the diet worked, and why a return to old eating habits would cause the weight to come back.

Despite such setbacks the fundamental validity of the protein-sparing modified-fast diet could not be denied. Commercial weight loss companies developed programs that are based on natural foods, limit fat and carbohydrate, provide sufficient protein, include vitamin and mineral supplements, and recommend getting physician permission to follow the diet. Some clinics and spas use nurses and nutritionists to supervise progress.

Many of the commercial operations have the right idea. They call for mild exercise on a daily basis. Clients follow a diet of from 500 to 650 calories, which allows for a satisfying rate of weight loss. Limiting carbohydrates leads to a mild state of ketosis, which diminishes hunger. Guidance in behavior modification improves future eating habits. And tips provided by supervising nurses and nutritionists supply the support dieters need.

These programs work, but clients never learn that obesity has an underlying physiological, endocrinological cause. That's because when these programs were designed that cause had not yet been identified. And without knowledge of the causal factors, dieters frequently return to the foods that trigger weight regain. Moreover, these programs come with a high price tag that not everyone can afford.

As expensive as these well-advertised clinics and spas are, they pale in comparison with the hospital-based programs featuring liquid diets such as Optifast and Medifast. The price is in the thousands of dollars and far beyond the reach of most patients. These programs do have many positive qualities. The improved diet formulations contain high-quality protein, little fat, and restricted carbohydrates. A mild state of ketosis diminishes hunger. A weight loss of about 2 pounds a week for women and up to 4 pounds a week for men keeps dieters on the program without frustration. Counselors provide nutrition education and guide behavior modification. Exercise is encouraged. But the programs' major failing, in addition to expense, is that the underlying endocrine basis for weight gain and failure to maintain weight loss is never explained, and certain foods are left to trigger the insulin response that quickly results in regain.

During all the years of diet experimentation, researchers, including Dr. Ezrin, looked at the relationships among obesity, diabetes, and insulin. Numerous medical publications have shown that obese and diabetic individuals are extremely unresponsive to insulin. Certain foods trigger the release of large amounts of the hormone, but the body does not utilize it properly. Obese individuals almost invariably test out as having abnormally high insulin levels in the blood. And high levels of insulin lead to storage rather than usage of fats; to sodium and fluid retention; to depression, sleeping disorders, and other mental problems; and to cravings for foods that bring on the release of yet more insulin.

Recently we've learned that hyperinsulinism may also be a culprit in coronary heart disease. Insulin stimulates the body's production of an enzyme that causes the liver to produce cholesterol. Oversupply of insulin in the blood may also stimulate changes in the arterial walls that promote formation of fatty plaques, which are involved in coronary heart disease. Insulin resistance may also explain why Type II diabetics are four times as likely as non-diabetics to develop heart disease.

We call this condition of hyperinsulinism the metabolic trap. The result is that a person who has been significantly overweight for a prolonged period of time is no longer capable of losing weight by adhering to a program of decreased caloric intake and increased exercise that would work for other people. His or her body functions to maintain its weight. It makes sense, then, that an effective dietary approach must consider the role of insulin in overweight and must provide patients with an understanding of how insulin works and how to control it.

The protein-sparing modified-fast diet does, indeed, control insulin levels in the blood, allowing for the burning of stored fats and the release of previously retained fluids. Dr. Ezrin perfected this approach in treating obese patients in his practice, often those who were originally referred for other endocrine disorders.

This diet is not essential for everyone. As stated earlier, those who have just a few pounds to lose will probably succeed by simply limiting the number of calories, especially fat calories, in the diet and by increasing the amount of exercise. However, everyone can benefit from the information on endocrine function, behavior modification, exercise, support techniques, and procedures to assure stabilization and maintenance of weight loss. The coming chapters contain all that information.

The Insulin Control Diet is designed for men and women at least 20 percent over their ideal body weight. It provides a way to reverse the process of hyperinsulinism so that your body can switch gears, start to burn excess fat as fuel, supply your brain with calming neurotransmitters so you'll sleep well at night and be relaxed during the day, eliminate stored salt and water, improve your energy level, and bring your metabolism back to normal. It has all the qualities that have proven to be characteristic of successful diets. It ensures satisfying weight loss of up to 3 pounds per week for women and 4 pounds for men, all without much hunger at all. It includes an easy, enjoyable exercise regimen. It provides information on behavior modification, nutrition, and the underlying causes of obesity.

If our promise sounds just as exaggerated as those made by countless weight loss charlatans, we ask only that you stick with it. Our approach is based on proven scientific facts, with case histories to back them up. Within a reasonable amount of time you will have shed excess pounds and inches, and you will be able to show your friends and relatives that *this* diet works.

This program offers a medical solution to a medical problem. It is not to be taken lightly. It is most safe and effective when used under the supervision of your physician. It is not meant for use by those with Type I, insulin-dependent, diabetes. There are certain contraindications to following this strenuous approach to weight loss: kidney and liver disorders, recent heart attack, and pregnancy and lactation. We intend the book to be a bridge between doctor and patient, a way to work together in order to slash the considerable health risk posed by overweight.

The first step is to schedule an appointment with your doctor. Discuss the book and your desire to follow the diet. Make photocopies of this chapter and of the chapter "Doctor to Doctor" and show them to your physician so he or she will understand the program's rationale and approach. As time goes on, he or she may wish to read the rest of the book as well.

Next, schedule regular appointments. Your doctor may want to see you every two, three, or four weeks. Most of your questions will be answered in the pages of this book, but during these appointments your physician will be able to address specific, individual problems and concerns. He or she will take your blood pressure, ask about your general well-being, perhaps evaluate blood and urine samples, and adjust medication doses when appropriate. Insurance plans generally cover such medical care, since obesity, even for those who are not yet diabetic, is rightly considered to be a major risk factor in many diseases, so that most people can afford the program.

It would be great if you could attend one of the support sessions that are a mainstay of Dr. Ezrin's practice, but we know that's impossible. So we've done the next best thing by providing you with guidance normally given during those sessions and by answering the questions typically asked. That guidance, designed to increase commitment and motivation, is contained in Chapter 12. Take a look at it right after you complete this chapter to get an overview and to get a few tips you can put into effect immediately. Then read it again as you follow the program, paying particular attention to one strategy each day.

Next, start keeping a diet diary. Use some sort of bound notebook rather than loose pages. Every time you eat or drink anything, record the type and amount of food in the diary. Most people don't realize what and how much they eat. By recording everything you eat and drink you'll become aware of your true food intake. That information will be helpful in making appropriate changes. Also record where and when you eat and any unusual feelings or reactions to your circumstances immediately before and after eating. We can't stress the value of this diary too much, and we'll refer to it from time to time in the coming pages.

■ ■ ■

We'll be discussing some of the benefits of weight loss in detail, but only you know how important it is to you to lose the weight which you've come to hate and which threatens your well-being. Anything that important is worth working for, and this program does take more than a little effort. But as the days and weeks go by, we're confident that you'll agree it's all worth it!

So, get started right away. Don't put it off a day more. Here's your agenda:

- Make an appointment to see your physician.
- Read Chapter 12 on support to help your motivation.
- Make photocopies of this chapter and the "Doctor to Doctor" chapter to take to your physician.
- Start a diet diary today, recording everything you eat and drink.
- Read the balance of this book.

Chapter 5

YOUR PERSONAL ENDOCRINE SYSTEM

The body has a number of regulatory systems that function to keep it in a state of physiological balance. We can ski on snowy slopes or lie on a sunny beach, yet our internal temperature remains at 98.6°F. We can drink copious amounts of liquids one day and almost none the next, yet the amount of fluids within our tissues stays at a fairly constant level. The tendency of the body to keep everything in a steady state is referred to as homeostasis, which, literally translated from the Greek, is "same standing."

Our bodies attempt to regulate our weight from the time of maturity, but we challenge our control systems by eating too much and exercising too little. Even with such challenges, most of us maintain or can maintain approximately the same weight from our late teens or early twenties on through middle and old age. Even if we gain weight after a period of overeating, most of us can, with a degree of desire and commitment, shed the extra pounds and keep them off. However, some of us appear unable to control and maintain weight despite the best of intentions and efforts.

In order to understand such system failure and to grasp the methods by which the Insulin Control Diet works so well, we need to examine our bodies' regulatory systems, focusing on the two major control centers—the nervous system and two categories of glands.

The nervous system can be compared with a network of electrical wires interconnected with a main power source. The nerves travel throughout the body from their origin in the brain and spinal cord. They communicate information to the brain which, in turn, sends signals to various parts of the body to perform a given action. The action may be voluntary or involuntary. Unlike connected wires, however, the nerves are not directly attached. There are spaces, called synapses, between one nerve sending a signal and another one receiving it. The spaces are filled by chemical substances, called neurotransmitters, which function in a variety of ways both to facilitate nervous impulses and to affect our state of mind.

One such neurotransmitter is serotonin. This chemical regulator, produced from the amino acid tryptophan, helps to keep us calm and relaxed. Without enough of it we feel irritable and depressed and perhaps are unable to sleep well. You may know those feelings well, as they are often associated with the metabolic trap of hyperinsulinism.

Glands are groups of cells that produce and secrete substances for a variety of uses. Two types of glands are *exocrine* and *endocrine*. Exocrine glands secrete their chemical products into ducts which conduct them to where they are needed. For example, salivary glands produce saliva, which is transported through ducts to the mouth. Similarly, the pancreas produces digestive enzymes that enter the intestine by way of ducts.

Endocrine glands have no such ducts and secrete their chemical products into the bloodstream. To facilitate the transfer of product into the bloodstream, each endocrine gland has an abundant network of tiny blood vessels or capillaries. The substances secreted by the endocrine glands are called hormones. The way exocrine secretions such as digestive enzymes affect nutrition are rather obvious. The effects of the endocrine glands are not always so clear, and some work in ways that previously were misunderstood.

Not all of the endocrine glands influence digestion, nutrition, and regulation of weight. The principal ductless glands that do are the pituitary at the base of the brain, the thyroid in the neck, the islets of Langerhans in the pancreas in the abdomen, the adrenals next to the kidneys, and the gonads in the pelvic cavity (female ovaries) or the scrotum (male testes). We will consider only briefly the parathyroid glands, which have little direct influence on metabolism and nutrition.

PITUITARY

The pituitary gland sits in a well-protected cavity at the base of the skull behind the eyes and between the ears. Although it is only as large as the tip of your little finger, the pituitary gland produces at least eight hormones that we know of that have direct effects on the body and that control the function of other glands. Because other endocrine glands are to one degree or another governed by the pituitary, it is often called the master gland.

The thyroid, adrenals, and gonads are all regulated by hormones secreted by the anterior lobe of the pituitary. These are called trophic, supporting, or stimulating hormones because they trigger the production and release of other hormones in the target glands. In addition to these supporting hormones, the anterior pituitary produces growth hormone, which is responsible for skeletal growth; prolactin, which stimulates breast milk production and favors the storage of body fat; and melanocyte-stimulating hormone, which increases the production of melanin, a skin pigment. Melanocyte-stimulating hormone is derived from the larger precursor of ACTH (adrenocorticotrophic hormone). The precursor is called proopiomelanocorticotrophin, because it also provides opioids, that is, endorphins and encephalins.

The posterior portion of the pituitary stores two hormones produced in the hypothalamus, a nearby portion of the brain. Oxytocin stimulates contractions of the womb during labor and helps in milk letdown. Antidiuretic hormone causes kidneys to remove water from urine as it is formed, thus decreasing urine volume.

ADRENALS

There are two adrenal glands, one of which is located above each kidney. Each gland is divided into two segments, the outer cortex and the inner medulla. The cortex secretes three groups of hormones. Glucocorticoids maintain energy and well-being and tend to raise levels of blood sugar by blocking the action of insulin. Mineralocorticoids regulate sodium and potassium concentration and fluid homeostasis, thus affecting water retention and blood pressure. The gonadocorticoids, or sex hormones (estrogens and androgens), have little influence on nutrition and digestion, but they do affect the percentage and location of fat in the body.

The adrenal medulla synthesizes adrenaline and noradrenaline, also known as epinephrine and norepinephrine. These are the hormones involved in the "fight or flight" response to external stimulation. We've all experienced the feelings these hormones engender, when we are frightened, threatened, or excited. These hormones depress appetite, stimulate metabolism, and increase blood pressure.

GONADS

The gonads or sex glands are under complicated control, largely by way of the pituitary gland and its trophic hormones. In the female the gonadotropic hormones and the hormones produced in the ovaries and placenta regulate the menstrual cycle, maintain pregnancy, and stimulate lactation. Follicle-stimulating hormone stimulates the ovary to ripen an egg-carrying cavity called the follicle. When the follicle is ripe and the egg is ready to be released, luteinizing hormone acts to stimulate ovulation, or the release of the egg into the fallopian tube. The corpus luteum (yellow body), which produces progesterone, is then formed from the collapsed follicle. Progesterone makes the uterus more receptive to the fertilized egg.

The estrogens, a group of closely related female sex hormones, are produced in the follicle as well as in the adrenal cortex. They are responsible for the development and maintenance of secondary sex characteristics, including breast development and deposition of adipose tissue or fat in strategic areas of the body. Because of the action of the estrogens there is a higher percentage of fat in the bodies of females. While an athletically slender male's total weight will be from 12 to 15 percent fat, that of a similarly athletic and slender female will be about 20 percent.

Hormonal control is not as complicated in the male. Testes make testosterone, the most important male hormone, in cells outside the sperm factory. Luteinizing hormone, sometimes called interstitial cell-stimulating hormone, stimulates the testosterone-producing cells. Follicle-stimulating hormone and testosterone interact to promote sperm production.

THYROID

The thyroid is the most misrepresented of all the glands. It does in fact help to control the body's metabolic rate, but the often-heard claim that obesity can be traced to an underactive thyroid gland is seldom if ever true.

Located in front of the windpipe or trachea in the throat, the thyroid gland weighs less than an ounce in normal individuals. Within its tissues it combines iodine obtained from the diet with the amino acid tyrosine to form the hormone thyroxine (T4). But before the thyroid can exert its influence, thyroxine must be converted to the more active form of triiodothyronine (T3). T4 and T3 probably regulate the various enzymes that control energy metabolism and thus influence all metabolic processes, including growth. The effects of an overactive or underactive thyroid gland can be dramatic.

Both T4 and T3 are under the influence of the pituitary gland by way of thyroid-stimulating hormone (TSH). When levels of thyroid hormone in the blood fall, TSH rises, causing the production and release into the blood of both T4 and T3. An increase in the level of T4 and T3 signals the pituitary to stop releasing TSH. This is known as "negative feedback." The most accurate way to determine if the thyroid is functioning normally is to measure the level of TSH in the blood. Even the slightest drop in thyroid hormone will increase the TSH levels.

When the thyroid gland produces inadequate amounts of hormone, the person may become tired easily, have dry skin, and feel cold, even in rooms where others are comfortable. But in documented cases of such hypothyroidism (underactive thyroid), there rarely is weight gain of more than 15 or 20 pounds. That gain is mainly due to the accumulation of mucinous tissue, a gelatinous material that absorbs water. Patients with hypothy- roidism seldom if ever gain substantial amounts of adipose tissue. On the other hand, hyperthyroidism (overactive thyroid) will usually result in some weight loss. Dr. Ezrin was the man who discovered the "thyrotroph," that is, the cell of origin of the TSH in the human pituitary gland. He has subsequently worked with patients referred from hospitals and clinics around the world and has found no evidence to substantiate the idea that an underac- tive thyroid has anything to do with obesity.

Thyroid function is sensitive to dietary influences. During star- vation a significant reduction in circulating T3 is always observed. The same occurs in subjects on a carbohydrate-restricted diet, as a result of decreased conversion of T4 to T3. Normal serum levels of TSH and T4 indicate that these subjects are not hypothyroid in the usually accepted sense of the term. Treatment with T3 during diet- ing raises the metabolism somewhat, but also increases the loss of precious protein and for this reason is unacceptable. The best re- sponse to the lowered metabolism resulting from low circulating T3 in dieters is obtained from exercise, which increases the loss of fat calories, but spares and in time increases the protein stored.

Certainly, there are some people for whom thyroid hormone administration is indicated. But for most men and women, thy- roid hormone administration will not in any way improve or in- crease metabolic rates. One may be hypometabolic without being hypothyroid. The metabolism of most Americans is lower than it should be owing to an inadequate amount of regular physical ex- ercise. If you want to increase your energy expenditure, the best way is to increase your exercise.

PARATHYROIDS

There are usually four rice-grain-sized parathyroid glands found in the neck just outside the thyroid gland. They produce parathyroid hormone, the chief regulator of calcium balance in the body. Their major nutritional connection is with vitamin D, which is used to treat the low calcium state caused by parathyroid deficiency.

PANCREAS

While the role of the thyroid gland in weight gain and loss has been exaggerated, the influence of insulin has only recently been recognized. Insulin is one of the hormones produced by the pancreas, one of the most important glands in the body in terms of nutrition.

The pancreas produces two types of secretion. Digestive enzymes (exocrine secretions), which are delivered to the gut through the pancreatic duct, are produced by masses of cells called acini. Hormones (endocrine secretions) are manufactured in the portion of the gland called the islets of Langerhans. The islets contain two major types of cells. The beta cells produce insulin, and the alpha cells make glucagon. The two hormones have opposing effects and work in a system of checks and balances.

THE FUNCTIONS OF INSULIN

Most people have heard of insulin owing to its role in diabetes. For centuries physicians recognized the disease as characterized by sugar in the urine, but little was known of what caused it and how to treat it. The diagnosis of diabetes in children was a death warrant until 1921, when Frederick Banting and Charles Best isolated insulin from the pancreas and demonstrated that it could reduce blood sugar levels when given by injection.

We now more fully understand insulin's role in metabolism. The hormone acts as a kind of spark plug to the mechanism that allows glucose (blood sugar) in the blood to enter the cell where it can be used for energy. Without insulin sugar builds up in the blood to dangerous and even life-threatening levels. There are two main types of diabetes. In Type I, or insulin-dependent diabetes, the pancreas does not produce insulin or does so at inadequate levels. Thus insulin must be supplied by injection. Type I diabetes most typically occurs in the early years and so was previously called juvenile or juvenile-onset diabetes. In Type II, or noninsulin-dependent, diabetes the pancreas produces sufficient insulin, but the body does not use it efficiently, allowing blood sugar levels to rise. Type II diabetes is usually manifested in middle age and so used to be called maturity-onset diabetes.

Because of the essential role of insulin in the body's metabolism and its life-saving aspects for diabetics, most people view insulin in only the most positive light. But insulin has a number of functions other than allowing the cell to use glucose from the blood, some of which can have a negative impact in terms of weight control and general health.

After you eat a meal, the pancreas secretes mainly insulin into the bloodstream to maintain an optimal blood sugar level. However, other hormones, chiefly glucagon, but also adrenaline, cortisol, and growth hormone, act against insulin to prevent the blood sugar from dropping too low. The supply of glucose is essential not only for the body's physical energy, but also for functioning of the brain and for the survival of sensitive nervous tissue.

When there isn't sufficient food-derived glucose in the blood for the brain's fuel, the body produces its own, at first through the breakdown of stored glycogen, or animal starch, in the liver and then through a process called gluconeogenesis, literally, the production of new glucose. In gluconeogenesis amino acids are converted to glucose. If amino acids are available as part of the food supply, the body will use them for this purpose. If not, protein from muscle tissue will be broken down to provide amino acids.

Gluconeogenesis, which is inhibited by insulin and promoted by glucagon, is a natural bodily process and may be implemented at times between meals. It is the body's way to attempt to stave off starvation by quite literally feeding the brain from the body's own muscle tissue.

An alternative source of brain fuel the body can use is ketones, which can be formed from liberated fatty acids stored in adipose tissue. The ketones can supply energy almost as efficiently as glucose can, and the body will contentedly utilize them for long periods with no adverse reactions. After an extended period of starvation or carbohydrate restriction, ketones are formed by the body to supplement glucose derived from gluconeogenesis when there is not enough insulin in the blood to prevent their formation. Ketogenesis requires the influence of glucagon to proceed. The delicate balance between insulin and glucagon is critical in this regard. In a normally functioning body new glucose will be formed during the night when the person sleeps, when insulin levels are down and glucagon levels rise. Also, at such times fatty acids are readily liberated from adipose tissue and converted into fuel, just as nature intended. During states of obesity this process can be frustrated by the abnormally high levels of insulin that persist in the blood.

Gluconeogenesis and ketogenesis are then two processes affected by insulin in addition to glucose metabolism. Insulin has still other complicated actions that affect many parts of the body. Insulin is involved with the disposal of amino acids, fatty acids, and electrolytes. It causes a buildup of triglycerides, the storage form of fatty acids, and it inhibits their release from fat cells. Insulin also increases the formation of cholesterol in the liver and similar steroid hormones in the adrenals and sex glands. It favors protein buildup and storage, and it increases the formation of the liver and muscle glycogen, the only form of stored carbohydrate available for supplementary energy production. Insulin favors salt and water retention and thus can aggravate hypertension. It also increases the activity of the sympathetic nervous system which can raise blood pressure.

In total, when insulin levels are high in the blood, a number of negative things can and do occur. In people who have become obese, sometimes even those who are only 25 or 30 pounds overweight, insulin levels remain high, the efficiency of the hormone in facilitating the passage of glucose into the cells is lessened and more is required to maintain normal blood glucose levels. Insulin also is less able to minimize new glucose formation, another potential source of hypoglycemia unless more insulin is provided. This is the state of insulin resistance that leads to hyperinsulinism.

INSULIN RESISTANCE

How do cells become insulin resistant? There may be a decrease in the number of the insulin receptors on the cell membrane that bind insulin and allow it to act. The insulin receptors may no longer respond to insulin as they should to let glucose enter the cell. There may be defects within the cell that interfere with glucose utilization. Research has found that in obesity insulin resistance in muscle is not due to an abnormality of receptors that bind insulin but rather to the failure to activate enzymes which mobilize the glucose transport system within the cell.

There are four major causes for the development of insulin resistance. First is obesity itself, which develops over time, and in which adipose (fat) tissue produces a substance that moves to muscle tissue to selectively block the blood sugar-lowering effect of insulin. The second cause is Type II diabetes in which insulin resistance may precede diabetes and may or may not be associated with obesity. Third, when blood sugar levels exceed 300, or perhaps even less, the hyperglycemia can trigger insulin resistance. The fourth cause is stress, whether physical, emotional, or traumatic, it increases insulin-neutralizing stress hormones such as cortisol, adrenalin, and glucagon.

Because the blood sugar control by insulin is inefficient in some persons, the body tries to compensate by making *more* insulin and levels begin to soar. The same phenomenon occurs in obese patients with Type II diabetes. There is usually more than enough insulin in the blood, but the body simply is not using it properly. In fact, administering more insulin by injection in order to lower blood sugar levels in such patients perpetuates the problem. The answer is diet and exercise to lower insulin requirements, not to give patients more of it.

Even though sugar levels are elevated in the blood owing to the high amounts of ineffective insulin, the insulin continues to function normally in other respects. Thus the person who already has high blood sugar levels, which should normally signal satisfaction, experiences carbohydrate—especially sugary food—cravings. As more carbohydrates are consumed, the body produces more insulin to attempt to deal with them. That additional insulin enhances the body's resistance to its blood sugar-lowering action by decreasing the number of insulin receptors on cell surfaces.

Without adequate glucose entering the cell for energy and with a reduced ability to utilize fatty acids stored for alternative energy, it is little wonder that overweight men and women are tired and listless.

Obesity appears to be characterized by insulin resistance, which predisposes to the development of impaired glucose tolerance. In addition to its role in carbohydrate metabolism, insulin mediates feeding-related increases in thermogenesis, that is, the production of heat by the body. Thus insulin resistance results in less ability of the body to expend energy by producing heat. The result is weight gain and maintenance of overweight.

Now we have an overweight person, who cannot properly use glucose in the blood for cellular energy, who continues to store fatty acids in the tissues as increasing pounds of fat, who is tired, irritable, and depressed. And, they must now face yet another of insulin's adverse reactions. Part of this hormone's function is to store salt and thereby facilitate water retention. When insulin levels soar salt and water storage increase to formidable proportions, and the person gains more weight. Also, the salt retention causes blood pressure to rise. Increased responsiveness to adrenaline aggravates the tendency to high blood pressure.

In this situation typical efforts at weight loss are useless. Temporary weight loss may be achieved through water loss, but such weight quickly returns and the overweight person becomes even more depressed. As energy levels drop and sleepless nights continue, it's not surprising that such individuals engage in little or no physical activity and frequently become lethargic and close to immobile. In the worst cases the inactivity is accompanied by feeding the cravings for carbohydrates, which can never be fully satisfied.

Many an overweight person in this situation attempts to explain his or her feelings of powerlessness, but physicians, friends, and family respond by suggesting the problem is simply a lack of willpower. But this seemingly hopeless condition does have scientific foundation, as you have just read. The overweight person is caught in an insidious metabolic trap.

KETOSIS

The key to unlocking the metabolic trap is the physiological process ketosis in which the body's liver produces substances called ketones from fatty acids that have been stored as adipose tissue. Free fatty acids are normally liberated from stored triglycerides through exercise. However, free fatty acid mobilization is markedly impaired in obese subjects, most likely because of hyperinsulinism. On our low-calorie, low-carbohydrate weight loss diet, which reduces levels of circulating insulin, free fatty acid mobilization is improved. Fat thus becomes the major source of energy. The body begins to use its stored fat as fuel for the brain and energy for the body as a replacement for glucose.

To allow this process to occur, insulin production must be decreased and glucagon production must be increased. A substantial restriction of carbohydrate intake facilitates both. With less carbohydrate the body gradually slows down the excessive production of insulin and secretes more glucagon.

To reiterate and clarify the importance of this phenomenon, here's what we've seen when insulin production decreases:

1. The body can mobilize its stores of fatty acids to be used as fuel, rather than to be kept as adipose tissue.
2. Hunger and carbohydrate craving virtually disappear.
3. Salt and water retention decreases, allowing excess fluid to be excreted naturally, with concomitant weight loss.
4. Insulin in the blood returns to normal efficiency, thus ending the state of insulin resistance.
5. More amino acids are available for the normal production of calming neurotransmitters such as serotonin derived from tryptophan, thus relieving irritability and depression and allowing restful sleep.
6. Blood pressure falls due to loss of sodium and fluid, and decreased effectiveness of adrenaline in constricting arterial walls.

Most patients report entering the state of mild ketosis needed to achieve weight loss within three days after beginning the program. Some achieve ketosis in only two days. And there are rare individuals who enter ketosis within 24 hours.

Testing for ketosis is easily done with KetoStix (manufactured by the Ames Company). One collects urine in a container, dips a plastic stick into the sample, and 15 seconds later reads the color of the stick against a chart on the container. Beige indicates negative ketosis, pink mild ketosis, purple moderate ketosis, and deeper purple significant ketosis.

With this program you can expect to see pink to light purple changes in color in the stick. The deepness of color will vary with the amount of fluid that is being excreted in the urine. If one has consumed the recommended eight 8-ounce glasses of water daily, the urine will be quite diluted, and the color will not be into the deep purple range. Even mild ketosis signals lowered insulin production. When you see the stick change color to pink or light purple, you know your body is freeing itself from the metabolic trap.

THE DANGERS OF KETOSIS

Ketosis has been misunderstood by both the lay public and the medical profession. There is such a thing as good ketosis, a state that can be tolerated by the body for long periods of time, but we have to distinguish this mild, beneficial ketosis from the dangerous condition that can be produced by unbalanced and uncontrolled diets. Diets in which fat consumption is unlimited, such as those advocated by Dr. Stillman and Dr. Atkins, induce more severe ketosis, with side effects including nausea, vomiting, and dehydration. In the Insulin Control Diet the only significant fat source is the stored adipose tissue of the dieter. As a result, at no time does the degree of ketosis produced exceed the tolerance of the body. If you follow the advice of this program, you will not be striving for a deep purple KetoStix reading, and you will never enter severe ketosis. Instead, you'll experience the rich, rewarding benefits of mild ketosis.

You should also not confuse this mild ketosis with keto-acidosis, a condition associated with uncontrolled diabetes. The balance between acidity and alkalinity of blood and body fluids is called acid base balance. Normally it is maintained slightly on the alkaline side by adjustments made in the kidneys and lungs. Ketones are acidic and need to be balanced by appropriate adjustments to prevent an increase in the acidity of the body. In the severely uncontrolled diabetic ketones are massively overproduced and overwhelm the body's adaptive mechanisms. In this state of acidosis patients may proceed to coma and death. It is this association that makes physicians fear ketosis of any sort, even if it may be beneficial. In our program the body can easily eliminate the ketones, the acid-base balance is maintained, and it is not possible to proceed to a state of acidosis.

Another criticism that has been leveled against ketosis is that it can aggravate gout, a painful condition resulting from the buildup of uric acid in the blood. Critics point out that ketones and uric acid are excreted through the same pathway; thus heavy ketone production causes the uric acid to build up. If the recommended amounts of fluid are consumed, in most cases uric acid can be properly eliminated in the urine. It is true that in male patients with a tendency to high uric acid, ketosis could result in gout. However, your physician can prevent this by administering appropriate medication to lower uric acid levels, such as allopurinol.

The final criticism made against ketosis is that it may compromise nitrogen balance, resulting in a slight but important loss of protein from muscle. There is simply no evidence that this ever occurs. Moreover, the program described in this book is actually devised to preserve precious protein.

The only side effect noted by patients is an occasional feeling of tiredness during the two or three days between starting the diet and actually entering ketosis. We've found that such patients perk up considerably when they have a sugar-free gelatin as a quick pick-up.

Ketosis is an essential part of this weight loss program. As used in this program it is perfectly safe, and it is effective in unlocking the metabolic trap. Ketosis is the bridge by which one can return to a normal metabolic state.

Authorities who have utilized a protein-sparing modified fast have seen the benefits of ketosis as we have described it in this chapter. They have seen that on such a program one loses weight as fast as possible without compromising safety. There is an unavoidable minimal loss of precious protein, but ideally, only excess fat and retained salt and water are shed.

When such programs were first developed, patients remained under the supervision of physicians who closely monitored their progress. Today we know that a broad range of overweight people can embark on the modified program as described in this book with safety and the promise of success, with regular but less frequent visits to the doctor.

The concept behind the Insulin Control Diet is well founded in scientific and medical fact. It has been tested and proven safe and effective in hundreds of patients. No serious problems have been noted, and none are expected to occur in individuals who follow the program.

On the other hand, we believe that anyone embarking on any program to improve health should first consult a physician. This is true for an exercise program, a cholesterol control program, or any weight loss program. If your physician has some questions or misgivings, simply have him or her read the appropriate sections of this book as well as the medical literature we have cited as evidence of this programs validity.

You can expect some skepticism. Physicians are trained to be skeptical until they see proof. That's good. Today we have the evidence to back our statements and recommendations. Not all physicians have heard about this approach. You can help their other patients by sharing your newfound knowledge.

Now you know about how your endocrine system works and how it has worked against you. With that knowledge you are ready to unlock the metabolic trap.

Chapter 6

GOOD FOODS, GOOD MOODS

There's no question that the foods we eat have much to do with the way we feel and the way we feel about ourselves. Various substances in food create bodily reactions that affect everyone's moods. And in overweight people who have fallen into the metabolic trap, their condition can increase the potential for depression and irritability brought on by such reactions. In addition, for many people being overweight engenders a sense of helplessness and hopelessness, especially regarding their desire to lose weight. They lose interest in things and activities around them. Many feel guilty about their weight, a feeling that our society aggravates at every turn by praising and rewarding the slender and condemning the overweight. Many overweight people become socially withdrawn. And the more overweight they become, the less welcoming our society seems.

Taken together, these aspects of the overweight person's mental state—helplessness, hopelessness, guilt, loss of interests, and social withdrawal—can collectively be termed depression. Many patients who have come to my office for help simply characterize themselves as depressed.

That depression is not solely a psychological condition that can be altered by a shift in attitude or circumstance. Depression associated with being overweight has its origins in physical phenomena. Trying to treat the psychological symptoms alone, whether by seeing a therapist or taking medications, will usually not meet with success.

Many overweight patients come into the office either currently taking antidepressant drugs and tranquilizers or seeking them. Many expect that a prescription for this pill or that tablet will cure their problems—both of depression and overweight. Some pa-tients are disappointed, at first, when the prescription pad doesn't come out as expected. But almost all leave the office with an up-beat feeling. They've learned during the first office visit that there's a physical reason for their mood and a scientific basis for their persistent problems with weight—in short, that it isn't all their fault.

But we should clarify one thing at the start. When talking about depression, we must draw a line between the normal reactions of overweight men and women to their condition and an abnormal response that would be defined as pathological. Almost everyone coming into the office suffers some degree of depression, although the symptoms may vary from person to person. *But*—and it's an important *but*—only a few patients are depressed to the point where life no longer seems worth living. I have encountered some patients who, when questioned even tentatively, volunteer that they are indeed desperate or are considering suicide.

If you feel that way, then by all means seek qualified medical or psychological assistance. Your depression may be partly a result of your weight problem, but likely it's a more deep-seated condition requiring professional help. Do you have frequent feelings that life is not worth living? Do you feel that there is never any joy in life and that waking up in the morning is the beginning of another day of misery? Have you increasingly shunned social contact? Have others commented more and more frequently about your mental state? If so, seek medical help right away. Take care of those prob-lems, and then come back to this book and its program.

For most of you, the solutions in these pages will help to turn around negative feelings, as part of the process of freeing yourself from the metabolic trap.

NEUROTRANSMITTERS

Let's start with one of the most essential ingredients to living an active, enjoyable life: a good night's sleep. Many people who are seriously overweight have difficulty falling asleep, staying asleep, and waking with a rested feeling. Such sleep disorders, along with daytime feelings of irritability and anxiety, are an integral part of your total overweight problem, a part of the metabolic trap.

To understand this and to learn how to implement the solution, one must understand a bit about how your nervous system works. The brain is composed of billions of nerve cells called neurons. As we saw earlier, neurons are separated by gaps called synapses. To transmit a nerve impulse from one neuron to another and to communicate information throughout the nervous system, somehow those gaps must be bridged. This is done by way of chemicals known as neurotransmitters.

Today we know there are at least 40 known neurotransmitters, and it is likely that more remain to be discovered. All are derived from amino acids, the building blocks of protein. There are 22 amino acids. Of those, 8 cannot be produced by the body and must be consumed as part of our diet. They are called essential amino acids, meaning it is essential that we ingest them. (All the amino acids are necessary for life. Since the body can produce the other 14, they are called nonessential, meaning they are not essential parts of the diet.) Fortunately, unless one is on a particularly stringent diet, such as strict vegetarianism with absolutely no animal protein, getting enough of the essential amino acids isn't a problem.

Amino acids are sent to all parts of the body by way of the bloodstream. Those we are concerned with in reference to mood problems are the ones going to the brain. They must cross what is called the blood-brain barrier, a membrane that extends across almost all of the brain and the spinal cord. It is an extremely effective barrier, and many substances are denied permission to cross. We cannot directly measure the amount of the amino acids crossing the blood-brain barrier to get to the brain where neurotransmitters are produced, so we must look at the actions of those neurotransmitters. If we don't see the actions we can assume that the neurotransmitters are not being made or insufficient quantities are being made.

One of the important neurotransmitters in terms of feelings of well-being is serotonin. Adequate levels of this substance help us to get to sleep at night and keep us calm during the day. Conversely, insufficient amounts of serotonin in the brain produce sleeplessness, anxiety, and depression. Tests have shown that overweight men and women have lower than normal levels of serotonin. One might expect quite the opposite, since the amino acid tryptophan, which produces it, must be available in profusion in the diet of a person who eats a large number of calories. But that's not the case at all. Instead, the lack of serotonin is yet another part of the metabolic trap. And simple sugars or carbohydrates are the culprits. We call them the Number One Poison.

As we have seen, insulin resistance favors new glucose formation, particularly in obese diabetics, and to get this glucose the liver transforms amino acids (gluconeogenesis). Thus the obese person depletes his or her supply of the amino acids that should be used to make serotonin and other neurotransmitters.

Years ago the diagnosis of reactive hypoglycemia became popular. It was based on the concept that when people consumed sugar, they elevated their insulin levels, driving their blood sugar level below the level they could tolerate. Symptoms such as confusion and irritability were said to be due to lack of the major fuel, glucose, to the brain. While this was an attractive notion, when researchers attempted to prove it by measuring the blood sugar at the time patients were symptomatic, more often than not the blood sugar was normal. Insulin causes all of the amino acids, except tryptophan, to leave the bloodstream to enter liver and muscle, chiefly. It is likely that such patients suffer from a carbohydrate-induced neurotransmitter imbalance, which can be expressed in various ways, e.g., fatigue and drowsiness or anxiety and agitation. Whatever the mechanism, avoidance of simple carbohydrates and provision of sufficient protein to supply adequate amino acids seem to be effective in most cases.

Of all the amino acids, only tryptophan remains unaffected by insulin. Tryptophan, in turn, influences production of the neurotransmitter serotonin, which produces a calming effect. Unfortunately, for the insulin-resistant person, the beneficial effects of tryptophan are far outweighed by the ill effects of the insulin itself. In balance, then, there isn't enough serotonin to ensure tranquility.

Here's a possible solution for you to discuss with your physician. The very mild sedative trazadone can be very helpful for the insulin-resistant individual. Taking a small dosage of 25 to 50 milligrams of this very safe medication has two distinct benefits. First, trazadone increases serotonin which allows for better sleep at night. Second, the improved quality of sleep you'll enjoy elevates the body's own production of serotonin.

If your doctor agrees to provide you with a prescription for trazadone, take one-half to one 50 mg tablet about 30 minutes before bedtime. You can regulate the dosage to that which suits you best.

RELAXATION THROUGH DIURESIS

Beyond causing amino acid and neurotransmitter depletion, insulin resistance affects mood in other ways. As we have explained, high levels of insulin can lead to retention of salt and water. This can result in water intoxication, during which mental states deteriorate. In some cases patients can actually accumulate fluid in the brain, leading to a swelling of the brain and subsequent mental abnormalities, including irritability, headaches, and inability to think clearly.

Our program of diet and exercise can do much to relieve the buildup of salt and water in the tissues. As insulin levels return to normal, the tendency to retain salt and water is diminished. To further enhance the removal of retained water, we recommend a technique known as diuresis of recumbency.

That might sound like a mouthful, but the concept is simple. Diuresis is the excretion of water from the tissues through the urine; recumbency means a reclined position. The technique is a relaxing method of getting rid of built-up water by simply taking a rest. Here's how to do it.

Lie down on a bed or couch in an inclined rather than a completely prone position. Prop the upper part of your body up at a 45-degree angle with a few pillows. Relax in that position for about 20 minutes. You'll find that you arise refreshed and feeling the need to urinate. That's because the fluid has drained from the tissues of your body and filled your bladder. The technique works by increasing the circulation to the kidneys, making them function more efficiently.

This is a useful technique that will help you to get through those frustrating "plateau" periods when it seems that even though you are following the diet faithfully, the weight isn't coming off as fast as you'd like. Diuresis of recumbency helps to get the next few ounces of fluid out, and weight loss proceeds. And you'll enjoy the additional benefits of a brief period of relaxation while you are ridding the body of the excess fluid that can generate irritability and even depression.

RELAXATION THROUGH KETOSIS

Throughout the period of following this program, you'll find that ketosis produces a mild state of relaxation. No one understands exactly how this happens, but there's no question that almost every patient who enters and stays in ketosis experiences a calming effect. It's the desire to experience that kind of calm that leads people to take sedatives and tranquilizers. Unlike tranquilizers, though, ketosis calms without causing drowsiness or sluggishness.

It may well be that part of the "religious experience" of fasting may be due to the tranquilizing effects of the ketosis that would be generated by fasting.

FOOD SENSITIVITIES

Some people find they can further elevate their moods by drinking coffee. The caffeine is, of course, a mild stimulant. In reasonable amounts caffeine can help to lose weight, working in the same way as amphetamines or other prescription drugs to depress appetite. By drinking coffee in small amounts, one can obtain the benefits of caffeine without the nerve-jangling adverse reactions of the notorious "diet pills." But the operative phrase here is "small amounts." Don't have more than two cups daily. And if even that amount starts to get you edgy, cut back to one cup. (If you enjoy the pleasure of a hot cup of coffee, but can't take the caffeine, switch to one of the new water process decaffeinated brands. But then, of course, you will not be drinking coffee for its stimulant or appetite-depressing effects.)

Just as there are some people who react adversely to even the slightest bit of caffeine, certain individuals experience ill effects from other foods. Those physical reactions can definitely affect one's mood, especially if you don't know what's causing the problem.

One of the major offenders is milk. Many people cannot digest lactose, the sugar found in milk. Lactose-intolerant individuals do not produce enough of the enzyme lactase to break down the milk sugar into its two component simple sugars, glucose and galactose. The lactose remains in the digestive tract, begins to ferment, and leads to a variety of gastric symptoms. The symptoms may include flatulence, bloating, and diarrhea. The less lactase one produces, the more severe the symptoms can be. Since we hear so much about the "goodness" of milk, many of us never think to question the wisdom of its use for all people. The fact is that many people experience ill effects from drinking as little as one glass. This is especially true for blacks, Asians, and those of Mediterranean and Middle Eastern origin, but others develop the problem as well, particularly in adulthood.

During the weight loss phase of this program milk is restricted. If you have regularly suffered gastric upset in the past, you may find that, for the first time in years, your symptoms go away. During the maintenance phase you may wish to start drinking milk again (skimmed milk, of course, because you certainly wouldn't want any extra fat and calories). If you find that gastric symptoms begin to recur, there are three solutions.

First, consider eliminating milk and perhaps other dairy foods from your diet. Calcium can be supplied by calcium carbonate tablets to reduce the potential development of osteoporosis. Second, try LactAid, a brand of milk in which the lactose has been predigested by the addition of the enzyme lactase. Third, take lactase tablets, available in health food stores, after consuming dairy foods.

A similar kind of intolerance syndrome exists for some people who eat foods sweetened with sorbitol, a sugar substitute especially popular with diabetic patients who cannot tolerate sugar candy. Sorbitol-sweetened products include candies, gums, and other treats.

Intolerant individuals cannot break sorbitol down properly. As with lactose, it may remain in the digestive tract and begin to ferment. The result is a variety of symptoms including flatulence, bloating, and diarrhea. Symptoms may be mild to severe, and both children and adults may be afflicted. It's difficult to be in a good mood when one has such symptoms.

Some people must avoid sorbitol-sweetened products completely, but others may have a piece or two of such foods without an adverse reaction. During the first phase of this program, your carbohydrate intake will be greatly reduced, and such sweets will be eliminated. Later on you may choose to go back to sorbitol products. If so, let moderation be your rule.

While artificially sweetened treats may be a problem for some people, chocolate can create difficulties for others. Researchers at Bowman Gray Medical School have linked that favorite indulgence of chocoholics to heartburn. The culprit may be a caffeine-related chemical, theobromine, found in chocolate. During weight loss you won't be eating chocolate, and perhaps symptoms of heartburn will subside, giving you one more good reason to stay on the diet.

Eliminating the symptoms of food sensitivities can certainly improve anyone's mood.

RELIEF FROM PREMENSTRUAL SYNDROME

Patients afflicted with premenstrual syndrome (PMS) report mood swings, depression, irritability, anxiety, and a variety of other disturbed mental states. Authorities agree that diet plays a major role in the incidence and severity of PMS.

PMS patients often have an inordinate craving for carbohydrates. The diet you consume while following this program will be of enormous benefit if you suffer from PMS since it is low in carbohydrates and high in protein. The restriction of carbohydrates helps to curb the craving for them, since, ironically, the more one eats, the more one wants. Abundant protein helps to improve neurotransmitter status which is typically altered in those women complaining of PMS symptoms.

There is also a distinct tendency toward salt and water retention during PMS. Our diet will also help to eliminate puffiness, bloating, irritability, and the feeling that the brain is clouded reported by many PMS victims.

■ ■ ■

Food presents an interesting, if not disturbing, paradox. While we crave specific foods to satisfy some ill-defined need, the actual consumption of those foods all too often creates the opposite effect. How many times have you craved a piece of pie or cake, only to find that, after eating it, far from satisfied, you feel anxious and irritable? This is part of the metabolic trap. How often have you eaten an entire container of ice cream when you wanted only a taste, and then felt not only guilt, but also a profound depression? That's also part of the metabolic trap. Add to those feelings the physical discomfort produced by certain food sensitivities. How can you be expected to be in a good mood? But now you're learning how to escape from this metabolic trap, and nothing creates as good a mood as freedom!

Chapter 7

NUTRITION FOR A LIFETIME

In their food choices many people who are overweight focus on the calorie content to the neglect of other nutritional concepts. Even so, their ideas about what foods are "fattening" are often misguided. To bypass overall nutrition in a program targeted at weight loss is to put oneself at great disadvantage—healthwise and weightwise. Studies have shown again and again that dieters who learn about nutrition during the weight loss phase have a statistically superior chance of maintaining weight loss in the years to come. On the other hand, you certainly don't have to become an expert nutritionist; a basic knowledge of the foods available in the market and how to choose them and prepare them goes a long way in keeping one on track.

But, you might object, I'm eating so little food on this program, why do I need to know about foods and nutrition? The answer is that you'll soon be out of the weight loss phase, eating a wide variety of foods. By making the healthful choice, you'll be consuming the foods least likely to add weight.

The food choices we make should involve not only the tastes of foods but their role in health and well-being. What many dieters find is that with increased knowledge of food's nutritional makeup, tastes change; we can no longer enjoy, say, a bowl of ice cream when we know its fat and sugar content are doing us harm. And to discover some of the misconceptions we have about foods helps us to see how those misconceptions affect our weight.

NUTRITION BASICS

Going into the supermarket, we can choose from thousands of different foods. Down the street in the specialty shops we find even more choices. Does a food taste good? Will it fit into the menu for the evening? Will our friends and family like it? Is the cost within our budget? These and other considerations enter the decision-making process. Certainly these factors are important.

But consider this. Every food we put into the shopping cart goes into our bodies. Shouldn't the effect it has be an even more important factor? Every food contains nutrients that are used by our bodies in a variety of ways. Those nutrients, the components of foods, provide materials to build, repair, and maintain body tissues. They supply the chemicals we need for regulating bodily functions and the fuel we need for energy.

The combinations and permutations of how all these substances work within the body are formidable, but basically there are just six classes of nutrients: protein, carbohydrates, fat, vitamins, minerals, and water. Within the six broad categories there are about 50 specific nutrients. Each nutrient has its individual function, often working together with one or more other nutrients.

But the average person doesn't need to know about all the individual functions. Nutrients tend to occur together and work together, and 10 of them are used most frequently in the body. The 10 leading nutrients are protein, carbohydrates, fat, vitamin A, vitamin C, thiamin, riboflavin, niacin, calcium, and iron. Eat enough of the 10, and you'll have plenty of the others.

WATER

In addition to the leader nutrients, water in sufficient quantities helps to maintain good health, *and* it plays a major role in helping to control weight. In fact, water is *the* most important nutrient. Without it, we cannot live. Stranded on a desert island, we could go for days and even weeks without food, but without water we would die within a week.

Water accounts for one-half to three-fourths of the body's entire weight. For overweight individuals, that amount may be even more. Water is used in the production of tissue, acts as a solvent, and regulates body temperature. It carries nutrients to cells and carries wastes away. Water is the principal component of blood. It aids in digestion. It is required for a wide spectrum of chemical reactions in all parts of the body.

We lose water every day in a variety of ways. The biggest loss is through the manufacture of urine to flush out body wastes. The feces also contain a large amount of water. Some is lost through perspiration, both perceptible and imperceptible, as the body strives to maintain a constant temperature. All this fluid must be replaced.

The standard advice is to consume eight 8-ounce glasses of water daily. We believe that that is the minimum amount needed for good health, especially while following this program. Total fluid intake can take into account not only plain water, but also calorie-free diet sodas, carbonated mineral waters, and coffee and tea. During the weight loss phase of the diet, of course, you won't be consuming milk, vegetable juices, or fruit juices, but during the stabilization and maintenance phases those fluids will be added to your diet and will also count toward your total intake for the day.

Many people, particularly women, find that increasing fluid consumption is difficult. Our culture has something to do with that. Girls are often trained to avoid using the rest room frequently, and the less one drinks, the less need there is to urinate. And because public women's rest rooms are often notorious for having long lines, girls and women have more reason to cut back on fluids.

Women pay a price for such conditioning. The incidence of urinary tract infections is considerably higher for women than for men, due to the buildup of bacteria that results when such pathogens aren't continually flushed from the system. Those afflicted with recurring urinary tract infections will find that they can reduce, and possibly eliminate, them by simply increasing fluid consumption during the day.

Does it seem paradoxical that we're urging those who tend to store fluids to increase fluid consumption? There really is no contradiction: Fluid buildup in the tissues has nothing to do with the amount of fluid being consumed. The culprit in obesity-related fluid storage is insulin working through salt retention, and the Insulin Control Diet is designed to eliminate that aspect of the metabolic trap, by reducing insulin's salt- and water-retaining effect. Ketosis itself also acts as a diuretic, adding to the fluid loss.

Water can facilitate weight loss in other ways as well. Fluids help to suppress the appetite, and drinking a glass of water or soda can replace eating fat-producing foods.

Water can help relieve constipation. If the body does not have sufficient fluid intake, less water is passed out in the feces. As fluid consumption increases, the stools become larger and softer, thus facilitating bowel movements (and preventing colon cancer).

Make it a point to increase your fluid intake significantly every day. Note the amount you're drinking in your diet diary. Check every now and then to see how your consumption pattern has improved.

Do you work at a desk? Keep a pitcher or Thermos bottle filled with water nearby to sip at throughout the day, or set a timer to go off once an hour to signal a trip to the water fountain. At home never sit down in front of the television or to read without a big glass of water; that will also help avoid the temptations of snack foods. For trips in the car bring along water in a commuter mug (the kind with a lid to prevent spilling. Bring a canteen of water to the beach or on a hike through the woods. To fulfill part of the program, you'll need to drink some kind of fluid almost every one or two hours. Take a look at your routine and think of other ways to increase your intake.

At the beginning drinking water may be a chore, but after a while it will become a regular part of your life, a good habit you won't want to give up even after you reach your goal weight. And you'll find that maintaining your weight will be much easier when your fluid intake is high.

PROTEIN

Probably the first essential nutrient that comes to mind when thinking about nutrition is protein. We need protein to build, maintain, and repair body tissues, to make hemoglobin in the blood to carry oxygen to the body's cells, to form antibodies to protect us against foreign substances, and to produce enzymes and hormones that regulate bodily functions. Excess protein may also be used, though inefficiently, as an energy source. While some nutrients can be stored for later use, protein must be part of the daily diet.

Eating protein in our food supplies us with the amino acids—the building blocks of protein—our bodies need. We can't utilize the protein found in food until we first break it down to its component amino acids, which we can then reassemble to form our own protein. Of the 22 amino acids, only 8 need to be supplied by the diet (essential amino acids); the others can be synthesized from other substances within our bodies (nonessential amino acids).

Getting enough protein is one of the easier and more pleasant aspects of practicing good nutrition. An abundance of both animal and vegetable protein-rich foods are available and they are typically quite tasty. In fact, if anything, most of us consume far more than we need. One criticism of a high consumption of protein is that it can interfere with calcium metabolism. Scientists point to societies where protein intake is low and the amount of calcium required to build healthy bones is much lower.

How much protein is enough? To satisfy the needs of normal-weight individuals, about 45 to 60 grams daily is the Recommended Dietary Allowance (RDA). To put that into perspective, a 3½-ounce serving of meat provides at least 20 grams of protein, an egg 6 grams, a 3½-ounce serving of roast chicken without the skin about 30 grams, an 8-ounce glass of milk 9 grams, a ⅔-cup serving of dry lentils nearly 8 grams. In fact, almost all foods contain at least some amount of protein.

During the weight loss phase of this program you'll need to preserve precious protein which might be used as fuel. Protein intake should be increased to about 1½ grams per kilogram of your ideal weight (there are 2.2 pounds in one kilogram).

VITAMINS

We need 13 vitamins, each of which plays an essential function in our bodies. The National Academy of Science's Recommended Dietary Allowances are the amounts needed to prevent the onset of certain deficiency diseases. For example, without the recommended amount of vitamin C, one might develop scurvy, a condition characterized by bleeding gums and other symptoms. In the well-balanced diet there are far more vitamins than the minimum amounts given by the RDAs. Knowing a bit more about the vitamins, where they are found in the diet, and what their functions are helps to assure good health through a good diet.

There are basically two types of vitamins. Fat-soluble vitamins, including A, D, E, and K, are stored in the fatty tissues of the body. Water-soluble vitamins, including vitamin C and all the B vitamins, are not stored. When the body receives an excess amount of water soluble vitamins, unneeded amounts are excreted in the urine. Since the fat-soluble vitamins are stored, they may build up to toxic levels in the body if one consumes more than the body can use. It's unlikely that one would overconsume vitamins unless one is taking supplements.

Let's take a brief look at each of the necessary vitamins. RDAs for each are listed in Table 7.1 on page 74.

Vitamin A helps to build cells in the body, is necessary for seeing in dim light, and prevents certain eye diseases. We obtain this nutrient in vegetables, including carrots, sweet potatoes, and greens, as well as in enriched foods such as milk and cereals.

Vitamin D aids in building bone tissue and in absorbing calcium from the digestive tract. Fish, fortified milk, and other dairy foods supply all we need.

Vitamin E protects vitamin A and unsaturated fatty acids from destruction by oxidation. While deficiencies can lead to sexual dysfunction, excessive amounts cannot promote sexuality, as has been claimed. Similarly, claims for the protective role of vitamin E in heart disease have never been proved. Dietary sources of vitamin E include vegetable oils, green leafy vegetables, whole-grain cereals, wheat germ, butterfat, and egg yolks.

Vitamin K is essential in blood clotting. It is produced in large amounts by intestinal bacteria. Dietary sources include spinach, cabbage, and liver.

Vitamin C forms the substances that hold the cells and body together, hastens the healing of wounds, and increases resistance to infection. Found in a variety of fruits and vegetables, vitamin C is also added to a number of foods and beverages.

Vitamin B₁ (thiamin) contributes to the proper functioning of the nervous sytem and the immune system, promotes a normal appetite, and aids in the use of energy by the body. It is found in nuts, fortified or whole-grain cereal products, and lean pork.

Vitamin B₂ (riboflavin) promotes healthy skin and eyes and aids in the utilization of energy. Milk, yogurt, and cottage cheese are excellent sources.

Vitamin B₃ (niacin, or nicotinamide) promotes healthy skin, nerves, and digestive tract and plays a role in energy utilization. Natural sources of niacin include yeast, meats, fish, poultry, peanuts, and fortified or whole-grain cereal products.

Vitamin B₆ (pyridoxine) assists in red blood cell aggregation and helps to regulate the use of protein, fat, and carbohydrates. It is the most important of the B vitamins for maintaining immunity. It is found in various meats, soybeans, lima beans, bananas, and whole-grain cereals.

Vitamin B₁₂ (cyanocobalamin) aids in the maintenance of nervous tissue and in normal blood formation. Only animal foods supply this nutrient. Sources include fish, dairy foods, and meat.

Folic acid (folacin) assists in maintaining nervous tissue and blood cells. It is found mainly in green leafy vegetables, nuts, and legumes. There is some evidence that women taking contraceptive pills need more folic acid than the RDA minimum. Much more is needed in early pregnancy to prevent neural tube abnormalities including spinal bifida.

Biotin, another B vitamin, does not have an RDA at this time. It helps regulate carbohydrate metabolism. There is no problem with deficiencies. It is found in most fresh vegetables and in milk and meats.

Pantothenic acid is another vitamin without an RDA. This nutrient aids in general nutrient metabolism. It is found in whole-grain cereals and legumes.

Having read these brief descriptions of vitamins, you may now be questioning a dietary program that suggests that you reduce or eliminate whole sources of these nutrients. Happily, this is not a problem.

First, the period of weight loss during which you will significantly reduce your dietary intake of these nutrients is limited. In fact,

Table 7.1 Recommended Daily Dietary Allowances (RDA) for Major Nutrients

	Age (yr)	Weight (lb)	Height (in)	Energy (kcal)	Protein (g)	Vitamin A (IU)	Fat Soluble Vitamins	
							Vitamin D (IU)	Vitamin E (IU)
Infants	Birth–6 mos	14	24	kg × 117	kg × 2.2	1400	400	4
	7 mos.–1 yr	20	28	kg × 108	kg × 2.0	2000	400	5
Children	1–3	28	34	1300	23	2000	400	7
	4–6	44	44	1800	30	2500	400	9
	7–10	66	54	2400	36	3300	400	10
Males	11–14	97	63	2800	44	5000	400	12
	15–18	134	69	3000	54	5000	400	15
	19–22	147	69	3000	54	5000	400	15
	23–50	154	69	2700	56	5000		15
	51+	154	69	2400	56	5000		15
Females	11–14	97	62	2400	44	4000	400	12
	15–18	119	65	2100	48	4000	400	12
	19–22	128	65	2100	46	4000	400	12
	23–50	128	65	2000	46	4000		12
	51+	128	65	1800	46	4000		12
Pregnant				+300	+30	5000	400	15
Lactating				+500	+20	6000	400	15

(Continued)

Table 7.1 Recommended Daily Dietary Allowances (RDA) for Major Nutrients (continued)

	Water-Soluble Vitamins							Minerals					
	Ascorbic Acid (mg)	Folic Acid (mcg)	Niacin (B_3) (mg)	Riboflavin (B_2) (mg)	Thiamine (B_1) (mg)	Pyridoxine (B_6) (mg)	Cyanocobalamin (B_{12}) (mcg)	Calcium (mg)	Phosphorus (mg)	Iodine (mg)	Iron (mcg)	Magnesium (mg)	Zinc (mg)
Infants	35	50	5	0.4	0.3	0.3	0.3	360	240	35	10	60	3
	35	50	8	0.6	0.5	0.4	0.3	540	400	45	15	70	5
Children	40	100	9	0.8	0.7	0.6	1.0	800	800	60	15	150	10
	40	200	12	1.1	0.9	0.9	1.5	800	800	80	10	200	10
	40	300	16	1.2	1.2	1.2	2.0	800	800	110	10	250	10
Males	45	400	18	1.5	1.4	1.6	3.0	1200	1200	130	18	350	15
	45	400	20	1.8	1.5	2.0	3.0	1200	1200	150	18	400	15
	45	400	20	1.8	1.5	2.0	3.0	800	800	140	10	350	15
	45	400	18	1.6	1.4	2.0	3.0	800	800	130	10	350	15
	45	400	16	1.5	1.2	2.0	3.0	800	800	110	10	350	15
Females	45	400	16	1.3	1.2	1.6	3.0	1200	1200	115	18	300	15
	45	400	14	1.4	1.1	2.0	3.0	1200	1200	115	18	300	15
	45	400	14	1.4	1.1	2.0	3.0	800	800	100	18	300	15
	45	400	13	1.2	1.0	2.0		800	800	100	18	300	15
	45	400	12	1.1	1.0	2.0		800	800	80	10	300	15
Pregnant	60	800	+2	+0.3	+0.3	2.5	4.0	1200	1200	125	18+	450	20
Lactating	80	600	+4	+0.5	+0.3	2.5	4.0	1200	1200	150	18	450	25

Note: Vitamins mentioned in the text for which there is no RDA at this time include biotin and pantothenic acid. Minerals needed in only trace amounts include sodium, chlorine, potassium, sulfur, manganese, cobalt, and copper.

Source: Adapted from Food and Nutrition Board, National Academy of Sciences/National Research Council.

owing to the efficiency of this diet, you will be back to a balanced diet far faster than with many other programs. During the stabilization and maintenance phases of the program you'll be consuming a diet rich in all the nutrients necessary for optimum health.

Second, if you examine your diet past and present, you'll probably find that you haven't been eating the wide variety of foods that would assure an optimal intake of all the nutrients. Numerous surveys have shown that the intake of vitamins A and C, iron, and calcium is less than adequate for many individuals, especially women.

Third, by following this program you'll be learning about foods and how to choose them wisely for the rest of your life. As you enter the stabilization and maintenance phases, your nutritional status will be absolutely optimal. In fact, you may well be better nourished than you've ever been in adult life.

Fourth, during the weight loss phase we strongly recommend that you take daily nutritional supplements. We'll make our specific recommendations a bit later in this chapter.

Fifth, the body is capable of synthesizing most of the vitamins it needs. Several are stored by the body. They are needed only in minute amounts, and they are re-used in chemical reactions, so their absence from the diet for a brief time will have no harmful effects.

MINERALS

Recommended Dietary Allowances have been established for calcium, phosphorus, iodine, iron, magnesium, and zinc. There are nine other minerals needed in lesser amounts, which are supplied by the same foods that give us the major six minerals. In general, minerals are required for body building and regulatory functions.

Calcium requirements continue throughout life to ensure bone health and for regulatory functions in the blood serum. Dairy foods provide most of the calcium in the Western diet. Other significant sources include canned salmon with the bones, sardines, some shellfish, and green leafy vegetables.

Most adults, especially women, do not consume anywhere near the RDA for calcium of 800 milligrams, often because they think of milk and other dairy foods as "fattening." It's rather difficult to get enough calcium in the diet on a regular basis to satisfy the body's needs. Those needs have been widely publicized in terms of preventing the bone-demineralizing disease osteoporosis.

Studies have shown that women who deposit sufficient calcium in their bones prior to menopause will greatly reduce the incidence of osteoporosis later in life. You can achieve the best bone building by consuming at least 800 milligrams of calcium daily; many authorities now recommend 1,000 milligrams. In addition to the diet, one can reduce the odds of future osteoporosis by doing regular weight bearing exercise such as walking.

During the weight loss phase of this program, dairy foods are eliminated because of their carbohydrate content. During this time, we recommend a calcium supplement. We'll specify the amount a bit later.

Iron combines with protein to make hemoglobin, the red substance in red blood cells that transports oxygen to all parts of the body. There is a continuous turnover of iron in the body, resulting in a regular need for this nutrient. This is particularly true for menstruating women, who may require supplements of iron to fulfill their requirements. Dietary sources of iron include beef and cereals, especially the fortified ones.

Phosphorus combines with calcium to form bone tissue and assists in a number of regulatory functions. Sources include milk and other dairy foods, meat, fish, poultry, eggs, whole-grain cereals, and legumes. Soft drinks and other processed foods also provide a great deal of phosphorus. Some authorities have proposed that we consume too much phosphorus, causing an imbalance between calcium and phosphorus. They recommend cutting back on soft drinks and processed foods.

Iodine helps to regulate the rate at which the body uses energy and prevents the formation of goiter. Dietary sources include seafoods of all sorts, iodized salt, and vegetables grown in iodine-rich soils. There is no risk of developing an iodine deficiency, even for those who have totally eliminated the use of table salt. In addition to the normal sources of iodine such as seafood, there is a considerable amount of the nutrient in bread and in all forms of milk, owing to current baking and farming practices.

Magnesium aids in metabolism and assists in the functioning of nerve and muscle fibers. Sources include legumes, whole-grain cereals, milk, meat, seafood, nuts, eggs, and green vegetables.

Zinc is needed for growth, protein synthesis, and the production of several enzymes and insulin. It is found in organ meats, eggs, oysters and other seafoods, soybeans, peas, spinach, and whole-grain cereals.

Copper is involved with iron storage and plays a role in the formation of red blood cells. It is found in a wide variety of foods, including seafood, meat, eggs, legumes, whole-grain cereals, nuts, and raisins.

FAT

Of all components of foods in the diet, fat is the most concentrated source of energy, or calories. While carbohydrates and protein provide 4 calories for every gram, fat contains 9 calories. Some researchers are now proposing that the actual number of fat calories may be even higher, with a gram of fat supplying 11 calories.

Any prudent diet, and certainly one designed for losing weight, will restrict the total amount of fat. In the typical Western diet fat constitutes 40 to 42 percent of total calories. The American Heart Association and the U.S. Senate Select Committee on Nutrition and Human Needs have long recommended that people of all ages should consume no more than 30 percent fat. We believe that the total amount of fat in the diet should be no more than 25 percent, possibly as low as 20 percent.

Low rates of heart disease have long been observed in societies in the world that traditionally have low fat intake. There is strong evidence that a low-fat diet can play a protective role against the development of cancer. And, of course, a low-fat diet helps to ensure maintenance of desired weight.

In Dr. Atkins's *Diet Revolution* readers are advised that they can eat unlimited amounts of meat and fats of all kinds. The effectiveness of that program was achieved by the development of ketosis through limiting carbohydrate intake. But those who followed the high-fat diet often found themselves with a significantly elevated cholesterol level and thus at increased risk of coronary heart disease. As you follow the program in this book, you will enjoy remarkable success, but you will do so safely, and you will begin a low-fat regimen that will serve you well for the rest of your life.

While we typically think of fat in negative terms, some fat in the diet is essential for life and health. Fat supplies essential fatty acids, carries the fat-soluble vitamins, and is an integral aspect of the metabolism of all food. In the body it is a component of cell walls, cushions vital organs, and provides insulation. People who reduce fat intake to 10 percent of total calories or even lower may develop symptoms including lackluster hair, dull fingernails, and sallow skin. Thus too much and too little should be avoided when it comes to fat intake.

You'll find fat in both animal and vegetable foods, as well as in all varieties of cereals. Fats can be classified, based on molecular structure, as saturated, monounsaturated, or polyunsaturated. Saturated fats are hard at room temperature (for example, butter and lard), while unsaturated fats are liquid (for example, corn oil). Saturated fats are linked with atherosclerosis, in which arteries become clogged with cholesterol, and increase our risk of cancer. Foods high in saturated fat are beef, pork and lamb, butter and milkfat, coconut and palm oils, and many commercial shortenings found in processed foods.

Saturated fats tend to increase insulin resistance in diabetic patients. Thus it is especially important that you significantly limit saturated fats to no more than 10 percent of your total calories, preferably even less.

Polyunsaturated fats are found in vegetable oils such as corn, safflower, cottonseed, soybean, sunflower, and sesame seed oils as well as most margarines. Monounsaturated fats predominate in olives and olive oils, canola oil (Puritan and other brands), peanuts and peanut oil, cashews, and avocados. Research has demonstrated that replacing saturated fats with polyunsaturated and monounsaturated fats can lower cholesterol levels. Monounsaturates have the added benefit of lowering only the harmful LDL (low-density lipoprotein) cholesterol, sparing the protective HDL (high-density lipoprotein). Most authorities today recommend that no more than one-third of the total fat consumed should come from saturated fat, with the balance coming from polyunsaturated and monounsaturated, with the emphasis on the latter.

The body needs a certain amount of cholesterol to form the sheath for nerves and parts of cell membranes, to aid in the digestive process, and to manufacture hormones, but too much leads to high cholesterol levels in the blood and clogging of the arteries. Cholesterol is found exclusively in animal foods. There is no cholesterol in any vegetable food. But even if you consume absolutely no cholesterol in the diet, the body will manufacture its own. In some people the liver produces too much cholesterol, and even if they follow the most rigid diet, they can still have a dangerously high blood cholesterol level. However, for most people modified diet alone can greatly reduce cholesterol levels, and you'll find that following this weight loss program will lower your count.

CARBOHYDRATES

Sugars and starches are the two main types of carbohydrates in the diet. The molecules of these chemically related substances differ in complexity and size, hence the terms "complex carbohydrates" (starches) and "simple sugars." For those who have been unsuccessfully fighting a weight problem, we label sugar the Number One Poison. Sugars trigger the release of insulin, which leads to retention of salt and water and to inhibition of the breakdown of fats stored in the body. They promote dental caries, especially when eaten in sticky forms that cling to the teeth. They elevate levels of triglycerides in the blood, increasing risk of heart disease. They replace other, more healthful foods in the diet. And they contain no fiber.

But the simple sugars aren't the only culprits when you are trying to control weight. The body breaks down complex carbohydrates to form sugars in the blood. While the reaction to the starches may not be as dramatic in terms of weight gain, salt and water retention, and irritability and depression, all carbohydrates must be restricted at the outset of a weight loss effort.

Certainly for both weight maintenance and good health, you'll want to include in your diet complex carbohydrates in the form of whole-grain cereals, vegetables, and fruits. But there's really no good reason to include simple, refined sugars. The complex carbohydrates provide necessary energy. The foods containing those carbohydrates also supply important nutrients. Also, the complex carbohydrates contain dietary fiber, now recognized as important to good health.

There are two kinds of fiber: water soluble and insoluble. Water soluble fiber has been shown to reduce cholesterol levels by binding to the by-products of cholesterol, the bile acids, in the gut and shunting them out of the body. Insoluble fiber speeds up the passage of food through the gut, thereby improving the health of the intestines and helping to prevent the development of colon cancer and possibly other kinds of cancer as well. Soluble fiber is found in oat bran, rice bran, corn meal, and dried beans and peas. Insoluble fiber is found in wheat, fruit, and vegetables. One should include both in the diet.

For those concerned about weight maintenance, oat bran plays an especially valuable role. Because it is so rich in soluble fiber, it attracts water as it passes through the intestines. The result is a satisfied, full feeling. Having some oat bran in the morning in the form of muffins or hot cereal will keep you satisfied until lunch, with no hunger or temptation to have a doughnut or other fat-laden snack at coffee break.

During the weight loss phase of this program, you'll be restricted to no more than 40 grams of carbohydrate daily. This will allow your body to enter ketosis; higher levels of carbohydrate intake will bring your body out of ketosis. After reaching your desired weight, you will add carbohydrates gradually until you know exactly how much you can consume without gaining weight. By that time you'll have finetuned both your metabolism and your knowledge of how your own body works.

NUTRITION SUPPLEMENTS

Theoretically, one can satisfy the Recommended Dietary Allowances for all nutrients by consuming a well-balanced diet based on a wide variety of foods. We stress the word *theoretically*. That's because few men and women consume such a diet on a regular, day-to-day basis. Surveys bear this out, showing less-than-adequate intakes of several nutrients, including vitamin A, vitamin C, iron, and calcium.

Supplementation

Moreover, an increasingly large body of evidence points to the benefits of consuming certain nutrients in amounts well in excess of current RDAs. Let's take a look at some of the arguments for supplementation.

As we've noted, calcium is important for preventing the development of osteoporosis. Not only will many women be unable to consume the RDA of 800 milligrams of calcium daily, but research now indicates the daily intake should be 1,000 milligrams (1 gram) daily. Few women want to drink that much milk or eat that many sardines.

While we've heard a great deal about reducing the amount of sodium in the diet in order to prevent or reduce high blood pressure, calcium may play an important role as well. It appears that a balance between the two minerals is necessary for optimum blood pressure; in other words, too little calcium may be as important as too much sodium.

Also, calcium may aid in the prevention of colon cancer by retarding the rapid cell proliferation that precedes the cancer. Researchers feel that 1 gram of calcium is effective. For these reasons calcium supplementation appears to be a wise decision for most people. And, since this diet restricts dairy foods, it is certainly recommended for people who are following the program.

In the past some (including the dairy industry) have questioned such supplements, saying that calcium is best consumed in the form of food. However, research reported in the *New England Journal of Medicine* in August 1987 showed that the body uses the calcium from dairy foods and calcium supplements equally well. The researchers carefully compared the calcium absorption from whole milk with that from the calcium supplements on the market—calcium carbonate, acetate, lactate, gluconate, and citrate salts. In healthy women the results were the same regardless of the source of calcium.

Of the available supplements, calcium carbonate is the least expensive and also provides a favorable percentage of calcium versus the other components of the salt. For every 1,500 milligrams of calcium carbonate in a tablet, you'll get 600 milligrams of calcium. Two tablets a day of such a preparation will give you even more than you need.

Iron is typically supplied less than adequately through the diet. Diet alone cannot bring the level up to the amounts needed for women during the years between puberty and menopause. Even though you'll eat beef and other iron-rich foods during the weight loss phase of the diet, you would do well to consider iron supplementation (18 milligrams is commonly recommended).

The same applies to other nutrients. There are a number of formulations on the market that are more than adequate for your needs. Just pick one that offers a full spectrum of both vitamins and minerals and contains at least 100 percent of the RDA for each. There is no reason to pay a premium price for these supplements; you'll receive no greater benefit from "natural" products than from others.

One last nutrient requires some attention. You've probably heard and read about the need to limit the amount of sodium in the diet. Of course, there is good reason for such advice, since the typical Western diet contains far too much sodium, and excessive amounts have been linked to high blood pressure. But while following the weight loss segment of this program, your sodium intake may actually get too low, since you'll cut out many, if not most, of the sources of sodium in the ordinary diet: processed foods, junk foods, salty snacks, and dairy foods.

Actual requirements vary from person to person, and depend on activity and exposure to heat. If sodium intake drops too low, a condition termed postural hypotension may occur. Simply stated, this refers to dizziness when one changes postures, for example, when getting up out of a chair or out of bed. The solution for those following the program is to include at least 1 teaspoon of salt in their daily diet, either in cooking or added to food at the table.

We cannot stress too emphatically that in following our program for weight loss you will actually be better nourished than before. You'll be consuming some good basic food. Your calorie needs will be met by both the foods you eat and the fatty acids you'll mobilize from your body. And your nutrient needs will be ensured through the recommended supplementation.

FOOD SELECTION

Too many people select their foods for the wrong reasons, eating whatever happens to be available or what tastes good at the moment. Little attention is paid to the nutritional value in foods. It's not surprising, then, that the typical Western diet is responsible for a number of major degenerative diseases and for obesity.

On the other hand, few of us have the time or desire to learn everything that is known about nutrition in order to make wise decisions about every food we eat. To simplify the process of selecting food for optimal nutrition, dietitians and nutritionists have developed guides based on categories of foods. The concept behind all such guides is that by eating a prescribed number of servings from each food group, one will obtain the nutrients needed on a daily basis.

By and large the four-food-groups system—milk, meat, fruits and vegetables, breads and cereals—is a good one. But some improvements can be made in the original concept for those interested in weight control, as we propose in the following listing. By taking the time now to learn about our food groups and how to use them, one can be more confident of weight control and proper nutrition in the years to come.

THE MILK GROUP

The milk group consists of fluid milk and yogurt. These provide the bulk of calcium in the diet as well as a number of other nutrients. An 8-ounce glass of milk contains 12 grams of carbohydrate. As previously stated, many people do not or cannot regularly consume milk and yogurt, and these foods are eliminated during weight loss. Calcium will be provided by a daily supplement. Other nutrients found in milk and yogurt will be supplied in other foods as well as in the multiple vitamin and mineral supplement.

While the traditional food group systems typically include cheese in the milk or dairy group, we feel that for dieters cheese belongs in the protein group, since protein is its major nutrient contribution and it can be viewed as a substitute for meat. Ice cream is also included in the dairy group in some guides, but since it is so high in sugar and fat and contributes so little nutritional value for the calories consumed, we have moved it and other frozen desserts elsewhere.

Following the weight loss segment of this program you may want to restore milk and yogurt to your diet. Adults need the nutrients found in two servings (two 8-ounce portions of milk or yogurt). The milk or yogurt should be nonfat or low fat.

THE PROTEIN GROUP

The protein group was originally referred to as the meat group— a misnomer since so many other foods also provide protein as their principal contribution. One ounce of any of the foods in this group supplies about 7 grams of protein.

Foods in the protein group include meats of all kinds, eggs, poultry, fish and shellfish, cheese, and dried beans and peas. While we recommend selecting a wide variety of these foods, it's best to make your selections according to the amount of fat the foods also contain, remembering your goal of keeping fat to 20 percent of all calories consumed. For example, equal-sized servings of chicken breast and duck contain the same amount of pro-at the fat content is dramatically higher in duck. Ham is lower in fat than pastrami or corned beef. And almost all cheese is very high in fat. For ground beef, select a lean cut of meat, such as a London broil, and have your butcher cut off all visible fat before grinding. (Familiarize yourself with the composition of commonly consumed foods as listed in the table in the Appendix, page 267.)

Choose your method of cooking carefully as well. Baking, roasting, steaming, and boiling are preferable to frying with added fat. To fry, use a vegetable oil spray and a nonstick pan. Trim off as much visible fat as possible before and after cooking.

Become familiar with portion sizes. Invest now in a kitchen scale to weigh portions of meats and other foods before and after cooking. Four ounces of raw meat typically cooks down to about 3 ounces.

The consumption of eggs has been questioned owing to their cholesterol content. A large egg (one serving) contains about 260 milligrams of cholesterol—the entire day's cholesterol limit for those who want to lower blood cholesterol levels. If you have a normal level of cholesterol, you can eat that egg without any problem and stay within reasonable limits even if you do consume some other cholesterol. For those limiting cholesterol intake, egg substitutes, such as Egg Beaters, can be used. Or, since only the yolk contains cholesterol, two egg whites can replace one whole egg both in recipes and in following this weight loss program.

If you're in the habit of nibbling at cheese without really paying attention to just how much you're eating, take a few minutes to measure out an ounce of cheese on your scale. Remember that cheese is at least 50 percent fat, and that 1 ounce of cheddar cheese contains 9.4 grams of fat. Compare that to 1 ounce of lobster with less than 0.5 gram, and 1 ounce of cooked lean hamburger with about 1 gram. Obviously, cheese should be on the "once in a while" list.

Especially at the beginning of your weight loss period, choose fish and poultry. If you begin to long for alternate flavors, add some lean beef and other meats. And only much later include cheese, preferably part-skim or reduced fat varieties.

After weight loss you may wish to broaden your protein horizons to include dried legumes (beans and peas). You'll have to avoid these foods during weight loss since they do contain a considerable amount of carbohydrate. But they're also great sources of protein, and they supply an added bonus of the water-soluble fiber that tends to lower cholesterol levels in the blood.

THE VEGETABLE GROUP

We all know that vegetables are loaded with nutritious vitamins and minerals. To get the most benefit, one should choose the broadest variety of green, yellow, orange, and red vegetables. One serving is ½ cup of cooked vegetables or vegetable juice or 1 cup of raw vegetables.

Because of their high carbohydrate content, starchy vegetables such as corn, peas, and potatoes are included in the starch group. These are entirely eliminated during weight loss, but as you enter stabilization and maintenance, you'll be able to enjoy them in moderation.

Be adventurous when going into the produce section of your supermarket. Try some vegetables that you haven't tasted before or that you haven't had in a long while. Talk to the produce manager about any exotic varieties that are new to you and ask how to prepare them. There's a whole world of flavor and good nutrition waiting for you.

THE FRUIT GROUP

Fruits of all kinds are excellent sources of vitamins, especially vitamin C. But a serving of fruit—½ cup of fresh fruit or fruit juice or ¼ cup of dried fruit—contains about 15 grams of carbohydrate and 60 calories. Some processed fruit and juice also contain added sugar. These must be severely restricted during weight loss in order to maintain ketosis. Familiarize yourself with what constitutes a serving of fruit (look at the table in the appendix).

We know that it's difficult to understand and accept the idea that we should avoid foods we know are nutritious, but remember, you'll have to avoid fruit for only a limited time and soon you'll be able to enjoy it again.

THE STARCH GROUP

As with fruit, a serving of any food in this group contains about 15 grams of carbohydrate and must be strictly limited during weight loss. One serving is defined as ½ cup of uncooked cereal, grain, or pasta or 1 ounce of any type of bread (the table in the appendix provides more details). Other foods in this group are the starchy vegetables corn, lima beans, potatoes, squashes, and peas. Dried beans and peas are also included, although they are also members of the protein group as mentioned earlier.

The recommendation to avoid all these foods during weight loss may be confusing for you. On the one hand we have long heard that starches are "fattening." More recently health authorities have been advocating a diet high in complex carbohydrates, saying that such foods are not fattening at all unless fats are poured or spread over them. Now we come along and say that you should avoid these foods now, but that you can enjoy them later.

Let us clear up some of the confusion. Yes, a diet rich in complex carbohydrates is viewed by the consensus of medical authorities as being the most healthful. It's advocated for even high performance athletes. And the baked potato is a healthful food without the butter or sour cream. And the number of calories found in starchy foods certainly is not excessive.

But this diet program is not based solely on calories. Your particular metabolism currently responds poorly to any carbohydrates in the diet. Carbohydrates, both simple and complex, lead you into the metabolic trap. You need time to readjust your metabolism. And you need the benefits of the state of ketosis. That's why we're adamant about severely limiting *all* high-carbohydrate foods during weight loss.

After you've achieved your desired weight, you'll begin to stabilize, to find the amounts and kinds of foods you can eat without gaining or losing weight. Thereafter you'll be in maintenance, we hope for many years to come, enjoying a truly wide variety of foods, including those rich in complex carbohydrates.

Although carbohydrate is regarded as the best fuel for athletic high performance, fat can do as well for all other energy needs. Free fatty acids are the preferred fuel for ordinary aerobic muscular activity and ketones can substitute for glucose to nourish the brain. Therefore, unless you are running a marathon or competing in an Olympic athletic event, there is no disadvantage in fueling your muscles with fat-derived energy. For you, high carbohydrate foods trigger the insulin response that has been responsible for your weight gain and your inability to lose that weight. When you start this program, you'll begin to exercise regularly and with increasing strenuousness. You'll begin to change the way your body's metabolism works. As you increase the amount of exercise you do and as your percentage of lean body weight increases, your ability to metabolize glucose without involving insulin increases, thus decreasing your need for insulin. The resultant low insulin levels ensure adequate release of free fatty acids from fat cells for energy needs.

When you achieve your weight goal you will be *required* to eat an increasing amount of carbohydrates during the stabilization phase of the program. That increase in carbohydrate intake will continue throughout the maintenance phase also, and for the rest of your life, unless you need to re-enter the weight loss phase.

If you do not exercise, you'll continue to be a potential victim to the ill effects of carbohydrates. If you engage in moderate exercise, you'll eventually be able to eat a moderate amount of carbohydrates. But if you progressively increase your exercise level, you have the potential for needing and enjoying a diet rich in carbohydrates, and you'll reap the health benefits of carbohydrates, which provide important dietary fiber.

In the meantime, your body still requires fiber intake. That's why we urge that you choose your limited allocation of starch wisely, opting for whole-grain breads and cereals (especially oat bran, rice bran, cornmeal, and oatmeal) for their content of soluble and insoluble fiber.

THE FAT GROUP

Most of the members of the fat group are fairly obvious: butter, oil, lard, and margarine. But there are a number of hidden fats in the diet you should be aware of while you lose weight and in the coming years of maintaining that weight loss. For example, one medium California avocado supplies more than 300 calories and 30 grams of fat, as well as 12 grams of carbohydrate. Even during your years of maintenance you will want to go easy on this fat-laden fruit. Depending on type and size, olives pack about 20 calories and 2 grams of fat each.

But the biggest offender in the average snacker's diet is the seemingly innocent nut. We've been told that nuts are "health foods" and nothing but good for you. In fact, a handful of 12 to 15 almonds has 90 calories and more than 8 grams of fat. Just 1 ounce of peanuts or peanut butter has 150 to 170 calories and 12 to 14 grams of fat, with 1 tablespoon of peanut butter weighing in at 86 calories and over 7 grams of fat. If you're making a dish with pine nuts (pignolis or pinons) count on 95 calories and over 9 grams of fat for just 2 tablespoons.

Once you're aware of sources of fats and their attendant calories, you can start to avoid some and select the preferred types when you do consume fat. We've all heard about the need to cut back on saturated fats. In addition to avoiding animal fats, read nutrition labels to find the "unholy trio" of vegetable oils: palm oil, palm kernel oil, and coconut oil. These contain fat that's actually more saturated than lard.

When possible, choose reduced-fat products. For example, regular mayonnaise contains 11 grams of fat and 100 calories per tablespoon. You can cut that down to just 4 grams of fat and about 36 calories by switching to a reduced-fat brand.

Learn to read nutrition labels, which come on most packaged foods, processed foods, and foods making any sort of health or nutrition claims such as "low fat" or "reduced calorie." Start with the list of ingredients. Ingredients are supposed to be listed in descending order of volume. Next look at the nutrient table to find the number of calories and grams of fat, carbohydrate, and protein per serving. Note that what the manufacturer calls a serving may not coincide with your idea of a serving. You may typically consume two or three times the amount suggested by the manufacturer.

In the average family the items written down on the shopping list remain fairly consistent week after week. To familiarize yourself with the nutritional content of at least those foods that commonly enter your household, allow an extra 20 minutes for your next three trips to the market. Spend that time examining labels. Of course, while you're following the weight loss phase of this program, your food choices will be limited. If you are not shopping for your family, you might put off this learning process until you enter stabilization. Otherwise, you'll want to start making some changes in your family's diet now to ensure your family's good health.

Having heard that turkey is low in fat and calories, your instinct when shopping for sandwich meat might be to select a turkey-based product such as turkey bologna or turkey ham rather than sliced ham. But a look at the labels will show you that standard ham, especially a low-fat variety, is actually lower in fat and calories than the turkey products. That's because turkey thighs and byproducts that are high in fat are used rather than the low-fat breast meat.

You might assume that all breads and rolls are about the same in terms of fat and calories, but that's not at all the case. Some are made with more shortening than others. Moreover, some brands employ the saturated palm and coconut oils or lard.

Whether buying milk, cheese, or yogurt, choose nonfat varieties. If your family has been drinking whole milk, you might want to ease them to nonfat (skim) milk by switching first to 2-percent fat milk, then to 1-percent fat milk, and finally to nonfat milk. Owing to all the publicity about cholesterol and heart disease, you'll find more and more dairy foods available that contain reduced amounts of fat. Some products have had the animal fat completely removed and replaced with vegetable oils.

NUTRITION LABEL TERMS

Those who learn to read nutrition labels reduce their chances of being deceived. Just reading the claims on the front of the package can be confusing, if not outright misleading. Fortunately, the government has intervened to help consumers by mandating clear definitions for what various claims really mean. Let's look at some of those claims and their meanings.

Diet and dietetic are terms mandated by the U.S. Food and Drug Administration (FDA) to mean that a food contains no more than 40 calories per serving or that it has at least a third fewer calories than the regular version of the product.

Enriched and fortified foods have added vitamins, minerals, or protein beyond the natural content of those foods.

Good, choice, and prime refer to grades of beef based on fat content. The more fat or "marbling," the higher the grade, and, of course, the higher the calorie count.

High in polyunsaturates is a nebulous phrase that doesn't signify a specific ratio of polyunsaturated to saturated fats. Generally speaking, products so labeled will contain vegetable oils other than coconut, palm, or palm kernel oil.

Imitation means a product that looks and tastes like another, but contains different ingredients. It also implies nutritional inferiority.

Substitute means a product that looks and tastes like another, but contains different ingredients. It implies that the nutrient content is as good as that in the food it replaces.

Lean meat and poultry may contain no more than 10 percent fat by weight and *extra lean* no more than 5 percent, according to new U.S. Department of Agriculture (USDA) regulations. *Leaner* means the product has at least 25 percent less fat than the regular product. In all cases, the actual fat content will be listed.

Light (lite) has almost no consistent meaning. It can mean the product weighs less or even has a lighter color than the regular version. Don't be lulled into thinking you're buying less fat or fewer calories. Read the nutrition labels to see exactly what the content is.

Low calorie means the food contains either no more than 40 calories per serving or fewer calories than the regular product. The nutrition label will be more exact.

Low fat can mean different things on different products. On milk it means no more than 2 percent fat and no less than ½ percent fat. On meat it means no more than 10 percent fat.

Natural may or may not mean anything at all. It has no significance on baked goods and is simply an advertising word. On meats and poultry it means no artificial coloring or additive has been used. Let the buyer beware.

Naturally flavored refers *only* to the flavor. A product can be naturally flavored, but still have artificial colors, preservatives, and other additives.

Naturally sweetened has no specific meaning. Sucrose is a "natural" sweetener because it comes from a vegetable source rather than from a chemical factory. Some manufacturers use the term to refer to other naturally occurring sweeteners.

No preservatives means exactly what it says, but that's not necessarily good. Many of the preservatives used in food technology today are completely safe. In many instances the preservatives pose far less risk than the bacterial contamination resulting from potential spoilage.

Organic has no legal meaning whatever, and manufacturers can use the term to their hearts' content. Suffice it to say that all food is organic because all food is composed of carbon, hydrogen, and oxygen. The term is sheer hype.

Reduced calorie means the food must have at least a third fewer calories than the regular product. A comparison must be shown on the label.

Low salt and *low sodium* are terms that provide an insight into the minds of the advertisers. Salt is not the only source of sodium in the diet. A product could be low in salt, yet still high in sodium. Read the nutrition label for the precise sodium content of such foods.

Sugar-free and *sugarless* both mean that the product does not contain sucrose, but it may contain any number of other sugars or artificial sweeteners.

No cholesterol means just that. But the food could be loaded with fat, which is known to raise blood cholesterol levels.

Cholesterol-free means the product has less than 2 milligrams of cholesterol.

Low cholesterol means the food contains less than 20 milligrams of cholesterol.

Cholesterol-reduced implies that the food contains 75 percent less cholesterol than a comparable product.

Once you're familiar with the products that are best for you and your family in terms of calories and total health, you'll automatically know which brands to reach for, without having to read the labels.

The supermarket can be a "nutrition laboratory" for learning about foods. As with all learning experiences, it's helpful to take notes. Keep detailed records of what you learn in your diet diary. Noting which of four brands of a food you found to be the best will save you time in the future. And such notes are essential when viewing the results of the program. Those with the greatest success in losing weight and maintaining that loss keep excellent diaries.

GUIDELINES FOR GOOD NUTRITION

We can think of no field of scientific study that applies more directly to every man, woman, and child than nutrition. While it's certainly true that the metabolic trap keeps you from losing weight once the pounds have accumulated, the initial weight gain frequently was the result of poor nutritional patterns. Correcting those patterns is an essential step in assuring weight control for the rest of your life. If you have children who are improperly nourished today, they are at greater risk of future problems with weight control as well as diabetes, heart disease, and cancer. Everyone in your family will benefit from improved food habits.

For many years those who had more than a passing interest in nutrition were labeled "health nuts." Few medical authorities or practitioners showed much inclination to include nutrition counseling as part of health care. Yet today most governments have issued statements regarding the importance of good nutrition in the attainment and maintenance of optimal health, and they've provided specific recommendations.

The U.S. Department of Agriculture and the Department of Health and Human Services have published a set of recommendations titled "Nutrition and Your Health: Dietary Guidelines for Americans." Seven specific suggestions have been agreed upon to assure good health:

1. *Eat a variety of foods.* This is the best approach to assuring that the diet includes all the nutrients needed.
2. *Maintain desirable weight.* The medical world has agreed that overweight is associated with increased illness.
3. *Avoid too much fat, saturated fat, and cholesterol.* While specific recommendations vary from different organizations, all authorities agree we're eating far too much fat and cholesterol and urge reductions.
4. *Eat foods with adequate starch and fiber.* While you will restrict such foods during the weight loss phase, follow this recommendation during stabilization and maintenance.
5. *Avoid too much sugar.* This advice for the entire nation is particularly true for those in the metabolic trap. The ideal, in fact, would be no simple or refined sugar at all.
6. *Avoid too much sodium.* This holds true particularly for people with high blood pressure. Those in the weight loss phase of our program may actually have to add a bit to the diet, as stated earlier. Those in stabilization and maintenance should limit salt and other sodium-containing foods since excess amounts can lead to water retention.
7. *If you drink alcoholic beverages, do so in moderation.* While losing weight, alcohol is completely eliminated in any form. Moderation applies to stabilization and maintenance periods.

Will following these guidelines guarantee health? No, but compliance will certainly improve your odds both for health and for maintaining your weight loss for years to come.

Chapter 8

THE INSULIN CONTROL DIET

Y ou are about to learn the details of the Insulin Control Diet. It is a radical departure from the diets you've heard about, possibly tried from time to time, and routinely failed with. When you have a lot to lose, the typical, balanced diet, regardless of the number of calories provided, just will not take weight off effectively. You know that because you've tried time and time again, without any lasting success.

The weight loss program we advocate is not meant to be a permanent way of eating. It's a tested, effective method that, combined with the exercise advocated in Chapter 9, will help you to reduce both pounds and inches safely and in a minimum amount of time.

Even before you begin to follow the program, read the chapter on support. You'll learn how to motivate yourself, how to get over the rough spots, and in general to gear up for success. As you've learned in Chapter 5, most seriously overweight men and women have lost control of their body's endocrine balance. Excessive insulin produced by the pancreas has led to sodium and water retention, improper metabolism of sugars, and inability to utilize the body's stored fatty acids. Within a short period of time, the Insulin Control Diet returns the body to normal endocrine control. Insulin production is greatly reduced, and the body uses the insulin that is produced more efficiently. Water and sodium are excreted rather than stored. And the body begins to break down its fat deposits and to use that fat for energy.

The weight loss you experience during the first week or two will be dramatic owing to the amount of water you'll be losing. Quite frankly, many diets do the same thing. Don't get too excited about it. But do get excited about the weight loss that invariably follows. Women can expect to lose up to 3 pounds each week. Men will lose up to 4 pounds weekly. Your rate of weight loss will depend on the amount of excess weight you're carrying, your age, amount of exercise, and other individual differences.

The most significant aspect of your success with the Insulin Control Diet is that you will lose *fat*. That's not the case with far too many other diets, on which you also lose lean muscle tissue. That's so important that it deserves reiteration and emphasis here.

As we have explained, only muscle tissue has significant capability of burning calories, of using food for energy. Fat, on the other hand, is food—it cannot burn appreciable calories. Men typically can get away with eating more calories than women, because they have a larger metabolic "engine" by the way of their larger muscle mass. So you want to keep all the lean muscle you possibly can in order to burn calories most effectively now and in the future.

Lean muscle tissue also makes for a more attractive figure, both for men and women. Muscle gives us shape. As we replace fat tissue with lean tissue, not only do we lose pounds, but inches as well. You can measure your progress with both a scale and a tape measure.

Take your measurements today, before you start on the program. Measure your waist, hips, thighs, chest, and arms. You'll soon be seeing a dramatic difference. One of the most frequently cited thrills of those who have successfully lost weight with this program is seeing themselves in new clothes.

But there's an even more important reason for a diet that maintains lean muscle tissue. As we have said before, several well-known diets in the past have resulted in rapid loss of enormous amounts of weight. But much lean tissue was lost at the same time, and that muscle loss wasn't restricted to the arms or legs. Heart muscle was lost as well, and that led to cardiac arrhythmias (irregularities of heart beat) that were sometimes fatal. When one starves to death, the actual cause of death is either heart failure or a lethal disturbance of heart rhythm (arrhythmia), owing to the loss of heart muscle tissue or pneumonia due to weakened breathing muscles. The most notorious of such diets was the Last Chance Diet which advocated a liquid protein diet. Sixty women actually died while following that program.

Medical authorities concerned with weight loss for greatly obese patients began developing the protein-sparing diets to achieve rapid weight loss without significant loss of muscle. The Insulin Control Diet has brought these medically proven methods, employing low calorie diets, to the current state of the art. The most notable difference is that after just three days of adhering to the program, you will experience almost no hunger whatsoever. That's not idle speculation, but an observation based on years of clinical experience.

In the weeks to come you will consume as little as 650 to 1,000 calories daily. You'll lose water and fat during the first week or two, and lots and lots of fat in the weeks after that. Yet you won't be hungry. The reason is that while you're eating only approximately 650 to 1,000 calories daily, your body will be using about 2,000 calories each day. The extra 1,000 to 1,400 calories will come directly from the fatty acids stored in your body in the form of adipose tissue. Your fatty acids will be released into the blood, where they will become your body's major source of fuel. And all the while you'll be consuming the right amounts of protein and fat for optimal nutrition as well as complete satisfaction.

After just three days of following the Insulin Control Diet, the amount of insulin your body produces will drop dramatically, while the amount of glucagon will increase substantially. The body will produce ketones, which curb feelings of hunger. In the place of glucose or blood sugar, your body can also use those ketones as brain fuel, so that more precious protein can be spared.

One of the nice things about this aspect of the program is that you can observe directly how your body is adapting by measuring the degree of ketosis. (The use of KetoStix is described in Chapter 5.) Usually within three days of following the program the KetoStix will turn a shade of purple, indicating that you've entered a state of mild ketosis. On the Insulin Control Diet, the ketosis remains mild, never developing to a state severe enough to pose potential damage, as I have warned against in *The 8-Week Cholesterol Cure* and my other writings.

As stated earlier, the Number One Poison for overweight people is sugar. Even the slightest amount of simple sugars in the diet causes an increased flow of insulin. While complex carbohydrates are certainly healthful in the form of breads, cereals, fruits, and vegetables, the overweight person's body cannot always discriminate between the complex and simple sugars. Until the body's endocrine balance becomes restored, both simple sugars such as table sugar and complex carbohydrates such as pasta, cereals, and fruits will result in the same insidious cycle of insulin release, insulin resistance, sodium and fluid retention, fat storage, weight gain, and depression. For a brief time, it is necessary to restrict severely the amount of *all* carbohydrate entering the body. We have to give the body a rest so that eventually it can discriminate between nutritious carbohydrates and bloating sugars.

While the diet we're proposing may at first appear to be radical, ask yourself if you wouldn't be able to deal with some temporary deprivation if you were given the virtual guarantee that (1) you will be able to lose fat more effectively than ever before, (2) you will do so without hunger, and (3) you will be able to maintain that weight loss for the rest of your life. That is what the Insulin Control Diet has to offer.

The diet is divided into three phases: weight loss, stabilization, and maintenance. How long you will be in the first phase depends on how much weight you have to lose. If you have more than 50 pounds to lose, you'll shed between 8 and 12 pounds of combined water and fat during the first two weeks. Thereafter, as we've said, you'll lose up to 3 pounds a week if you're a woman and up to 4 pounds a week if you're a man, until you've reached your goal. You can see that the Insulin Control Diet gets you to your ideal weight within a reasonable period of time. You'll then enter the stabilization phase in which you'll learn to keep your weight constant, neither gaining nor losing, while eating a variety of food. And finally, you'll learn the techniques of weight maintenance, assuring a lifetime of optimum weight and health.

The diet itself is remarkably simple. You won't have to count calories, read complex charts, or rely on specific foods. The entire regimen has been scientifically designed to provide good nutrition, with all the nutrients your body needs and in a way that will put you on the track to wise food choices for the rest of your life.

For the duration of your weight loss period, we ask that you limit your total carbohydrate intake to 20 to 35 grams. This means that, for a limited period of time, you will have to eliminate a great number of the foods you've become accustomed to and which, under other circumstances, are excellent, nutritious foods.

On the Insulin Control Diet, what you do not eat is far more important than what you eat. In other words, more than 40 grams of carbohydrate in any form will trigger your overproduction of insulin and return you to the weight gain cycle you know so well. Isn't it worth it to do without breads and pastas and to cut down on fruits and starchy vegetables for a while, knowing that this diet plan will absolutely and positively eliminate your weight problem?

We recommend that you divide your allocated calories into three meals. This will help establish a healthful eating pattern. If you are not able, for any reason, to eat three meals, you can consume all your food in two meals, perhaps with snacks. But do try to eat breakfast, even if you haven't been doing so in the past.

We'd like you to get into the healthful habit of drinking lots of fluids throughout the day. Fluids will help satisfy your need for oral satisfaction in place of some of the snacking you've been doing in the past. At the same time they flush out wastes into your urine. Water is still the best fluid to consume but you may also wish to include diet sodas, iced tea, herbal teas, decaffeinated coffee, and club soda or mineral waters, for a total of at least eight 8-ounce glasses daily. While it's true that most diet sodas contain no carbohydrates and no calories, they may remind you of other sweets. As much as possible, start switching from artificially sweetened sodas to club soda and seltzers and mineral water, perhaps flavored with a twist of lemon or orange.

For a particularly elegant drink, try serving mineral or sparkling water over ice in a large wine goblet. And here's a special bartender's trick: Twist an orange peel over a lighted match to release a drop or two of the orange oil into the drink. The oil will flame and sizzle momentarily, releasing a lovely burnt orange flavor. Since no alcohol is permitted during your weight loss period, this makes a nice substitute for a social cocktail. Until you are well established in maintenance, with weight loss secure, avoid alcohol. It interferes with achieving endocrine balance, and its 7 calories per gram are empty calories. (See the table in the appendix for the caloric content of various alcoholic beverages.) Today there's a definite trend away from the heavy use of alcohol. Get on the bandwagon.

You will gradually come to enjoy drinking healthful amounts of water. Journalists often say that their typewriters "run" on a perpetual flow of coffee. What they're saying is that they're in the habit of sipping as they sit at their typewriters. While the caffeine in coffee can jangle the nerves and perhaps contribute to health problems, the coffee mug can be filled with other fluids to satisfy the same pleasant sipping habit.

We've included snacks in the program, but since sugar is the Number One Poison, you want to eliminate refined sugars entirely. To satisfy a sweet tooth on occasion, we suggest sugar-free gelatin. Keep a good supply on hand, and keep some prepared in your refrigerator. This is one snack you can eat to your heart's content. For variety, try preparing different flavors and colors and adding fruits or salad greens as your meal plan allows. (Some recipe suggestions are given in Chapter 13.) Many patients say that the gelatin dessert is a lifesaver in keeping them going during the first weeks of the Insulin Control Diet. Just knowing that it's there in the refrigerator gives comfort. And even after the weight loss period, patients continue to enjoy this Insulin Right snack.

Lettuce, celery, and leafy greens, such as spinach and cabbage, can also be eaten in large amounts on the program. Limit yourself to one full head of lettuce or its equivalent each day. The greens add few carbohydrates to your total dietary plan, and they provide lots of fiber and satisfaction. Leafy greens are also definitely Insulin Right foods.

Since breads are not permitted during the weight loss period of the Insulin Control Diet, lettuce comes to the rescue. When you crave a sandwich, wrap some meat, a bit of onion, and a dash of pepper sauce in two large leaves of romaine lettuce instead of using bread. Sauces and condiments that add zing to your sandwich without adding too many carbohydrates include mustard, horseradish, and some salad dressings. (The composition of some salad dressings is given in the table in the appendix.)

Carbohydrate content is the most important consideration in determining the Insulin Right and Insulin Wrong foods. To make things simpler for you, we've prepared a listing of foods in the various food groups from which you should choose. Take a look at the lists on the following pages. Then we'll talk about daily food plans.

The following lists provide just an overview for you to see the foods you'll restrict, those you'll completely forego, and those from which you can choose freely during the weight loss phase of the program. For a more complete analysis of the nutrient composition of foods, including the amount of carbohydrate, fat, and protein each provides, see the charts starting on page 268.

Foods from the Starch and Bread List are to be avoided almost entirely during weight loss as these are principal contributors of carbohydrates. You can see specific carbohydrate contents on pages 268–279. You may elect to replace a serving of fruit with a bread serving from time to time, as described in more detail on pages 114–117, to individualize your calorie intake. Be advised, however, that regardless of total calories consumed, carbohydrate intake for the day should never exceed 40 grams.

During weight loss you'll be eating more protein foods than you would normally consider part of a balanced diet. First, these foods provide nourishment without carbohydrates. Second, and most important, they supply a defense against protein loss from muscle tissue normally seen in rapid weight loss, especially during fasting. The period of time you'll be eating large quantities of these foods, including meats, fish and seafoods, and poultry, will be limited. We'll talk about specific amounts to eat daily during the phases of weight loss, stabilization, and maintenance in the coming pages.

By studying the charts on pages 268–279 you'll see specific amounts of protein provided in servings of meats, fish, and poultry. On average, three ounces of cooked beef yields 25 grams of protein. A serving of chicken breast delivers nearly 31 grams. Servings of fish and other seafood provide a bit less. As a rule of thumb, you can count on about 7 grams of protein per ounce of protein-rich foods. The RDA for protein, as shown in the chart on pages 74-75, is about 46 to 60 grams of protein for adult men and women. To achieve that goal, you'd need from six to eight ounces of protein-rich food daily. And during weight loss, your needs are even higher.

THE STARCH AND BREAD LIST

During the weight loss phase of the Insulin Control Diet, all foods on this list are prohibited or restricted. Avoiding these foods will help you remain in ketosis. As you complete weight loss and enter your stabilization phase, you will gradually reinstate many of these nutritious foods into your diet. Fiber-rich complex carbohydrates will be a major, healthful part of your maintenance diet. (See the table in the appendix for the composition of these foods and average serving sizes.)

Cereals, Grains, Pastas

Bulgur
Cereals, cooked
  (rice, wheat, oatmeal)
Cereals, ready-to-eat (bran,
  flakes, puffed, shredded)

Pasta
Rice (white, brown)
Wheat germ

Dried Legumes

Beans (kidney, pinto, white)
Lentils

Peas (yellow, green, blackeye)

Crackers, Snacks

Animal crackers
Graham crackers
Matzoh
Melba toast
Oyster crackers

Popcorn
Pretzels
Rye Crisp
Saltines
Whole wheat crackers

Starchy Vegetables

Corn
Lima beans
Peas
Plantain

Potatoes
Winter squash (acorn, butternut}
Yams, sweet potatoes

Breads

Bagels
Biscuits
Breads (white, rye,
   whole wheat, oatmeal)
Breadsticks
Croutons

English muffins
Muffins
Pita
Rolls and sandwich buns
Tortillas, tacos

Other Starchy Foods

Chow mein noodles
Cornbread
French fried potatoes
Pancakes

Stuffing, dressing
Taco shells
Waffles

THE PROTEIN LIST

These are the foods that will maintain your lean muscle tissue while you're losing weight. During the weight loss phase you'll look to foods in the protein list to provide at least 80 grams of protein. During the stabilization and maintenance periods you'll add a bit more protein, rarely exceeding 100 grams daily. (See the table in the appendix for the protein content of these foods and average serving sizes.)

Fish

Fish (all varieties, fresh and
   frozen)
Shellfish (crab, lobster, scallops,
   shrimp, clams, oysters)

Tuna (packed in water)
Herring (uncreamed)
Sardines

Poultry

Chicken
Cornish hens (without skin)

Turkey

Meat

Veal (choose the leanest cuts)	Pork tenderloin
Beef (choose the leanest cuts, good or choice rather than prime grade; remove all visible fat)	Ham (brands labeled at least 95 percent fat-free)
	Canadian bacon

Cheese

Varieties of cheese (skim milk or low-fat types)	Cottage cheese (low-fat)

Eggs

Whole eggs (unless cholesterol level contraindicates)	Egg whites
	Egg substitutes

THE VEGETABLE LIST

If you aren't already a vegetable lover, this is the time to start. The vegetables listed here are lowest in carbohydrates. Use a wide variety of them throughout the weight loss, stabilization, and maintenance periods. A serving of cooked vegetables or vegetable juice is ½ cup; a serving of raw vegetables is 1 cup.

Artichoke	Kohlrabi
Asparagus	Leeks
Beans (green, wax, Italian)	Mushrooms
Bean sprouts	Okra
Beets	Onions
Broccoli	Pea pods
Brussels sprouts	Peppers (green, red, yellow)
Cabbage (green, red, sauerkraut)	Rutabaga
	Spinach
Carrots	Summer squash (yellow, zucchini)
Cauliflower	
Eggplant	Tomato
Greens (collard, mustard, turnip, beet)	Turnips
	Water chestnuts

THE FRUIT LIST

Fruits, while they do contain carbohydrates, provide excellent nutrition. Learn to enjoy a wide variety, keeping intake within limits, during your weight loss period, and continue to include them in the stabilization and maintenance periods. Most fruits contain about 15 grams of carbohydrate per portion.

Fresh, Frozen, and Unsweetened Canned Fruit

Apple	(1)
Applesauce	(½ cup)
Apricot	(4)
Banana	(½)
Blackberries	(¾ cup)
Blueberries	(¾ cup)
Cantaloupe	(⅓ cup)
Cherries	(12 fresh; ½ cup canned)
Fig	(2)
Fruit cocktail	(½ cup)
Grapefruit	(½ medium; ¾ cup segments)
Grapes	(15)
Honeydew melon	(⅛)
Kiwi	(1 large)
Mandarin orange	(¾ cup segments)
Mango	(½ small)
Nectarine	(1 medium)
Orange	(1 medium)
Papaya	(1 cup cubed
Peach	(1 medium; ¾ cup canned)
Pear	(1 small; ½ cup, 2 halves canned)
Persimmon	(2)
Pineapple	(¾ cup cubed; ⅓ cup canned)
Plum	(2)
Pomegranate	(½)
Raspberries	(1 cup)
Strawberries	(1¼ cup)
Tangerine	(2)
Watermelon	(1¼ cup cubes)

Dried Fruit

Apples	(4 rings)
Apricots	(7 halves)
Dates	(2½ medium)
Figs	(1½)
Prunes	(3 medium)
Raisins	(2 tbsp)

Fruit Juice

Apple juice or cider	(½ cup)
Cranberry juice	(⅓ cup)
Grapefruit juice	(½ cup)
Grape juice	(⅓ cup)
Orange juice	(½ cup)
Pineapple juice	(½ cup)
Prune juice	(⅓ cup)

THE MILK LIST

Milk and yogurt are excluded during the weight loss phase, as they contain a great deal of carbohydrate. (Cheese is included in the protein group.) Milk and yogurt are permitted and encouraged during the stabilization and maintenance phases.

Nonfat milk	Nonfat yogurt
Low-fat milk	Low-fat yogurt
Whole milk	Premium yogurt

THE FAT LIST

While fats and oils contain no carbohydrate, they are a concentrated source of calories. Too much fat is a prime offender in the onset of many diseases. Consumption should be used sparingly during weight loss. During stabilization more of the "good" fats should be added to achieve a maintenance balance of calories with the help of additional complex carbohydrates.

Fats

Avocado	Bacon
Margarine	Lard
Mayonnaise	Cream
Butter	Salt pork

Nuts and Seeds

All nuts (almonds, cashews, pecans, peanuts, walnuts, and others)	All seeds (sunflower, sesame, pumpkin, and others)

Oils

Corn oil	Safflower oil
Olive oil	Canola oil
Peanut oil	Other vegetable oils

Salad Dressings

Cream dressings	Oil dressings

THE FREE FOOD LIST

Although these foods contain very low amounts of carbohydrate, if any at all, the term "free" must be considered within reason. Limits, if any, during weight loss, stabilization, and maintenance are discussed elsewhere in the chapter.

Drinks

Bouillon (chicken, beef, vegetable)	Coffee, tea (decaffeinated)
Carbonated water, club soda	Diet sodas
Cocoa powder, unsweetened (1 tbsp)	Drink mixes (artificially sweetened)
	Tonic water (sugar-free)

Nonstick Vegetable Oil Spray

Vegetables

Cabbage	Hot pepper
Celery	Mushroom
Chinese cabbage	Radish
Cucumber	Zucchini
Green onion	

Salad Greens

Endive	Romaine
Escarole	Spinach
Lettuce	

Seasonings

Spice and herbs (basil, cinnamon, chili powder, pepper, and others)	Dehydrated vegetables (garlic powder, onion powder, mixtures)
Extracts (vanilla and others)	

Sweeteners

NutraSweet (Equal)	Sugar Twin
Saccharin (heavy use to be avoided)	

Topping

D-Zerta

Dessert

Sugar-free gelatin

MEAL PLANS FOR
WEIGHT LOSS PHASE

Now that you've glanced at the food lists, let's look at how we put foods together in daily meal plans for the weight loss phase of the Insulin Control Diet. Later we will discuss applications of the food lists during the periods of stabilization and maintenance. We've made suggestions in the meal plan section, but this is your program and you should adapt your choices to meet your needs while sticking to the overall plan of food groups and amounts.

As a general overview of the program, you're permitted a total of 7 ounces for women, 10 ounces for men, of protein foods such as fish, poultry, or lean meat, in addition to 1 egg or 2 ounces of low-fat cottage cheese. Each day you'll have ½ cup of any vegetable other than those listed with starchy foods. You'll also have one serving of fruit a day, or, if you prefer, one serving of juice. On some days you may wish to substitute 1 slice of bread or ½ cup of cereal (not made or eaten with milk) for your serving of fruit. You are permitted free access to a wide variety of greens, such as lettuce and spinach. Some free vegetables, such as radishes, mushrooms, and green onions, can be used to provide color and added enjoyment to your two daily salads. The daily total of greens will add up to a small head of lettuce or its equivalent. Both milk and yogurt are completely eliminated during the weight loss phase of the Insulin Control Diet. To provide calcium needed to maintain bone health and help prevent osteoporosis, we recommend daily supplements of 1,000 mg (1 gram) of calcium. It is especially important to take calcium supplements during weight loss, when you're consuming no dairy foods, but it is advisable to continue taking them later on.

The weight loss phase program contains no added fat or oil. We strongly recommend eating only lean meats and trimming all visible fat from meat servings. Moreover, we believe that during the first few weeks of your weight loss period you will be better off without meat, relying instead on fish and poultry. We urge you to use cooking methods that call for little added oil. Enjoy your foods baked, broiled, steamed, poached, and boiled rather than fried or sauteed. When you want to use the frying pan, use a nonstick pan and a light application of vegetable oil spray or use a tablespoon or two of bouillon to keep food from sticking.

Are you a dessert addict? As we mentioned, sugar-free gelatin can be a lifesaver; it has helped keep many a dieter faithful to the program. You may also save your fruit serving for dessert. When enjoying a gelatin dessert or fruit, you might want to make it more festive with a dab of D-Zerta topping. It's little touches such as this that can make the weight loss experience so much more pleasant. If you whiten your coffee with cream or nondairy creamer, try a dab of D-Zerta there as well. You'll have all the satisfaction without the fat and carbohydrate.

Since the Insulin Control Diet greatly limits the total amount of food you consume daily, albeit without any hunger, it's more difficult to obtain all the vitamins, minerals, and trace nutrients your body requires. As we discussed in Chapter 7, we recommend that you take a daily multiple vitamin and mineral supplement. Since during the period of weight loss, your body will be eliminating great amounts of both water and sodium, you will want to add enough sodium to your diet to prevent a potential sodium shortage. Try using a total of 1 teaspoonful of salt each day in cooking or as seasoning. Since foods rich in potassium have been eliminated during the weight loss period, potassium supplements may be appropriate. This is particularly true for dieters with high blood pressure currently taking diuretic drugs. By all means consult your physician about this.

For women the total calorie content of the meal plan each day is about 650. For men the total is about 850 calories. Men require slightly more protein and a few extra calories because their muscle mass and hence their metabolic engines are larger than women's. Remember that in addition to the calories provided by the food you eat, you'll be consuming your own stored supplies of fatty acids, to meet your energy requirements. That will add about an extra 1,000–1,800 calories daily. You'll be completely satisfied and never hungry, especially after ketone production has begun. That's how your fat can help you become thin!

We have listed a full two weeks of meal plans, including three meals and a snack for each day. The items marked with an asterisk are included in the recipe section in Chapter 13. When you've gone through the 14 meal plans, you may simply repeat them through the weight loss phase, or you may prefer to interchange menu items. There are enough food suggestions to keep you satisfied for months.

Each day, measure your progress by checking the color change on your KetoStix. Each week measure your improvement in inches and in pounds on the bathroom scale. Nothing breeds success like success; your 2-, 3-, or 4-pound weekly loss will encourage you to continue. During the weight loss phase of this program, we recommend that you weigh yourself only weekly. That may come as a surprise, but we have good reason for this advice. We can confidently predict up to three pounds of weight loss weekly for women and up to four for men. Individual loss will, of course, vary. But the loss on a daily basis will vary considerably for each person. One day you might see significant loss, while another day produces no progress whatsoever. That can be frustrating. Therefore we suggest that you avoid the temptation of daily weighing and stick to the weekly schedule.

Before you begin the program, we urge you to make a contract with yourself that you will continue it all the way to the end. Don't settle for a 20-pound loss when a 35-pound loss is what you want and need. As we have said, those who quit midway through the program have no chance of reaching their ideal weight and the least chance of keeping off whatever weight they do lose. Those who stay with the program can reach their goal and maintain their ideal weight.

Start planning now. Look at the food lists and the meal plans. Decide what you'll have for breakfast tomorrow morning, for lunch, for dinner, and for the next several meals, and then make your shopping list. Pick up a supply of KetoStix and your calcium and vitamin and mineral supplements on your way to the supermarket. Review the weight loss checklist.

WEIGHT LOSS PHASE: A CHECKLIST

- Total daily calories: 650–1,000 for women; 850–1,000 for men
- Total daily carbohydrate: 20 to 35 grams (maximum 40 g) of complex carbohydrates; no simple sugars
- Total daily protein: 55 to 75 grams from 7–10 ounces of fish,

poultry {skinless), or lean meat (fat trimmed) plus 1 egg or 2 ounces of low-fat cottage cheese

- ½ cup of vegetable each day from the vegetable list (not the starchy vegetables on the starch and bread list)
- 1 serving of fruit or fruit juice each day from the fruit list, *or* 1 slice of bread or ½ cup cereal (no milk)
- No milk or yogurt
- No added fat (cook without fat or use vegetable oil spray)
- No alcohol
- 8–10 8-oz glasses of fluid, preferably water, each day
- Calcium supplement (1,000 mg)
- Multiple vitamin and mineral pill (100 percent RDA)
- 1 teaspoon of salt in cooking or as seasoning
- Follow the two-week menu plan (pages 121–134), varying items
- Monitor ketosis with KetoStix before and after bedtime
- Weigh on scale weekly

As you look over the meal plans, imagine that you're glancing at the menu of an expensive, world-famous health spa. The menus and the recipes in Chapter 13 are in fact similar to the foods served at those exclusive enclaves. You're getting the very best that money can buy. And you deserve it!

ADAPTING THE MEAL PLANS

The following meal plans were designed to provide 650 to 850 calories with under 40 grams of carbohydrate daily. For women, this will be the most effective approach to rapid yet safe weight loss. Men, having higher calorie needs, may consume 100 or 200 calories more each day. We have marked in parentheses how men can add foods to total 850 calories. Some may even prefer to go as high as 1,000 calories. For the most part, women should not go higher than 850 calories, since higher calorie intake would be counterproductive. But there may be special instances in which an individual's physician will instruct the patient to consume as much as 1,000 calories. While this may seem formidably low at first, bear in mind that within a few days of starting the program you'll feel virtually no hunger. Moreover, weight loss clinics and hospitals have employed even lower calorie diets, 400 or 500 calories, safely and effectively for years. Under the supervision and with the approval of your physician, you should have no problem following the 650- or 850-calorie plan. Your physician may decide that a higher calorie regimen is best suited to your particular needs.

Although the 650- (850-) calorie plan has the advantages of somewhat faster weight loss and greater hunger control, a dieter can remain in ketosis while consuming additional calories *as long as the limit of 40 grams of carbohydrate is not exceeded*. You can do that by adding foods that provide calories and other nutrients, but not a significant amount of carbohydrate. In selecting foods to adjust the meal plan, consult the table listing the composition of commonly consumed foods and beverages in the appendix. For more complete information we recommend your getting a copy of *Food Values of Portions Commonly Used* by Jean Pennington.

If you are a woman, and decide you want to add 200 calories daily, you can simply follow the meal plans given for men. Note that the plans for men increase the size of the portion of protein food, thereby adding calories, but not carbohydrates. Or you can add a different protein food that adds calories, is low in saturated fat, and does not add carbohydrate.

Perhaps your doctor has advised that as an active male you should follow a 1,000-calorie plan. So, take the 650-calorie meal plan, add the 200 calories as indicated on the plan, and then add another 150 calories. You might add 1 ounce of low-fat cheese (100 calories) and 1 tablespoon of margarine (100 calories). If you can do without the margarine, but would prefer to have 2 ounces of cheese, that's perfectly fine. Another day you might have a taste for a cheese omelet. Adding the following ingredients to the 650-calorie meal plan will give you 1,000 calories and your omelet: 1 egg, in addition to the 1 egg in the plan (80 calories), 2 ounces of cheese (200 calories), and 1 tablespoon of margarine in which to fry the omelet (100 calories). In the foods on the protein list and the fat list, you'll find additional calories, protein, and fat, but not carbohydrates. Can you add some carbohydrate-containing foods? Yes, but it's a bit tricky, because you must stay under the 40-gram limit for the day, or you'll slip out of ketosis. When using such foods to increase the day's total calorie content, be certain to test your urine frequently with the KetoStix to be sure you're still in a mild state of ketosis. Never add foods that will contribute more than 5 to 10 additional grams of carbohydrate. Here are some examples of foods you may wish to add to your meal plan from time to time. Never include more than one such carbohydrate-containing food in a given day:

Almonds (1 ounce), 176 calories, 5.5 grams carbohydrate
Milk (low-fat, ½ cup), 60 calories, 5.8 grams carbohydrate
Triscuits (2), 42 calories, 6.2 grams carbohydrate
Raisins (1 tablespoon), 60 calories, 7.5 grams carbohydrate
Orange (½), 60 calories, 7.5 grams carbohydrate

Or you may decide that you'd like to increase the serving size of the fruits and vegetables in your meal plan. Just remember that, on the average, 1 serving of fruit or fruit juice provides 60 calories and 15 grams of carbohydrate, and 1 serving of cooked vegetables supplies 25 calories and 5 grams of carbohydrate. A serving of a starchy vegetable, such as corn and squash, gives you 80 calories and 15 grams of carbohydrate.

It would be tedious for you to try to construct an entire day's meal plan on your own. And, you might make a mistake that could throw you out of ketosis. That's why we designed the meal plans for you. So regardless of the total calories you and your doctor decide upon, start with the 650-calorie meal plans and add calories to come up with your individual total. If you don't have time to make decisions or to consult the food composition table to see what foods you could add on a given day, we have a simple rule for you to follow to be sure you are not adding carbohydrates or too many calories. Just stick with the following foods, added to the 650-calorie meal plan, and you can't go wrong:

1 ounce low-fat protein food (such as poultry and fish),
    60 calories
1 ounce lean red meat, 75 calories

1 egg, 80 calories
1 tablespoon fat or oil, 100 calories
1 ounce hard cheese, 100 to 110 calories

As you change and add foods to reach your prescribed total calories for the day, remember three important points. First, this is a diet, and you shouldn't expect or attempt to duplicate your previous eating habits. Second, the weight loss phase of the total program is temporary and, like many who have gone before you, you will be able to stick with it. Third, this is the time to restructure your eating habits, so seek a wide variety of foods, including foods new to you. A little of this and a little of that will help you in the future a lot more than getting all your added calories from one source.

If you're confused about the diet in any way, talk to your doctor. Even if you think a question seems trivial, ask it. You might even ask your physician to recommend a registered dietitian with whom you can discuss the fine points of the diet and the foods to choose. Or you can call your local chapter of the American Dietetic Association for a referral.

There's no question that the calculations for any food selection and change in serving size will take a bit of effort at the beginning. And you'll experience hunger for the first few days before you enter the state of ketosis. But when you see those pounds and inches beginning to come off, you'll know that the program is worth all the effort you are putting into it.

REDUCING FAT AFTER YOU'VE EATEN IT

Wouldn't it be great to be able to eat a little extra fat in snacks and meals and then be able to tell your body not to absorb it? There's a way to achieve just that. A newly developed and widely distributed supplement called SeQuester actually binds onto fat in the digestive tract and prohibits absorption. Here's how it works.

Each SeQuester tablet is composed of supplemental bile (sodium choleate) that has been microencapsulated in a special combination of soluble and insoluble fiber. (The amount of carbohydrate this adds is inconsequential.) Bile normally acts to break down fat, but owing to the capsule of fiber, fat is attached to but can't get to the bile, and this forms a larger particle which cannot pass through the walls of the intestine into the bloodstream. The fat is then eliminated in the bowel movement.

Each tablet is capable of "immobilizing" about six grams of fat. Thus by taking one tablet before each meal, one can cut an additional 18 grams of fat from the diet daily. This means both the potential for weight loss and cholesterol control.

No, we don't expect to reach a "zero fat" diet. That wouldn't be healthy. Nor would it be healthy to view this product as a means to eat fatty foods indiscriminately. It is just one more tool at our disposal. On the other hand, if we know we've eliminated—quite literally—a certain amount of fat, the diet can become more pleasant and easy to follow.

Package directions call for taking one tablet prior to each meal in order to get used to it. Your body will gradually become accustomed to the additional bile. Taking too many tablets initially can result in gastrointestinal discomfort (GI). Eventually you'll take two or three prior to fatty meals.

After taking the SeQuester tablets for a while, you may start to see a change in your bowel movement. The stool may take on a yellowish tinge and may even float. That's because of the increased amount of fat in the stool.

There's really no potential for any adverse reactions beyond the GI disturbances such as nausea and bloating one might experience at the start. And even those quickly pass when the tablets are discontinued. But since the product doesn't enter the bloodstream, there's no chance of serious side effects.

We don't know whether—or perhaps how much—this type of product may impair absorption of vitamins and minerals. This is another good reason to include a vitamin/mineral supplement as part of this program.

SeQuester is backed up by literally years of both animal and human studies, and additional studies are underway. The product was developed by a cardiologist at Cedars-Sinai Medical Center in Los Angeles.

The advantage of incorporating SeQuester in the Insulin Control Diet is that it enables you to relax the limitations on fat intake without compromising the total calorie intake. An extra tablespoon of olive oil definitely enhances a dish, but carries with it 14 grams of fat and 100 calories. Three SeQuester tablets balance that out. The same would apply to other fats and oils as well. A one-ounce snack of nuts can be very satisfying, and with just over 5 grams of carbohydrate it can be included in the Insulin Control Diet. But those nuts provide a significant amount of fat: 14 grams per ounce of peanuts and 16 grams for the same size serving of almonds. Again, SeQuester can enable you to enjoy that kind of snack now and then without the additional fat and calorie load.

Let us repeat, however, that this should not be viewed as a panacea. Part of the Insulin Control Diet is to provide a lifelong approach to weight control. Prudent eating habits should be the watchword. Consider SeQuester as a means to an end, rather than an end on its own. Remember: There is no such thing as a "magic pill" that will allow you to healthfully maintain weight control while paying no attention to dietary discretion.

ANOTHER APPROACH
TO LOW-CARBOHYDRATE DIETING

We believe an important part of this weight loss and maintenance program is relearning eating habits. Nutrition education is the hallmark of weight loss success stories, and the key to making wise food choices is the use of foods in their natural state. Hospital-based programs such as Optifast and Medifast rely entirely on the drink mixes and prohibit solid foods during the period of weight loss, and so they don't teach dieters to use natural foods properly.

Another important aspect of eating solid foods is that you have the satisfaction of chewing. A number of studies have shown that dieters using liquid preparations miss chewing. Those using natural foods are more compliant with the program and will, therefore, succeed more often than those using drink mixes.

Yet there may be times when, because of your schedule or inclination, you prefer the simplicity of mixing up a packet of powder and water and drinking your meal. A drink mix can be handy when you want to carry food to work, when you are traveling, or when the time you have for preparing food or eating a meal is limited. At such times a liquid preparation can save you from being tempted off the diet by fast food convenience.

The ideal might be to mix the two approaches, and now that's possible without the disadvantages of the hospital-based programs. The Twin Laboratories Company of New York has developed an excellent product called TwinFast, which is superior to the Optifast and Medifast formulations in many ways. First and foremost, the TwinFast drinks taste much better. The mixes come in vanilla, chocolate, and strawberry flavors, and you can expand the flavor range by adding a few drops of food flavor extracts such as orange and almond. TwinFast is made with high-quality protein from milk and egg whites rather than soy. The nutrition content compares favorably with Optifast, with three servings providing 100 percent of the U.S. Recommended Dietary Allowances for all vitamins and minerals as well as for protein. TwinFast provides a full 700 milligrams of potassium per serving, more than a medium banana. That means if you're using TwinFast once or twice a day, you won't have to take a prescribed potassium supplement. Twin-Fast is available in most health food stores nationally.

One serving of TwinFast, a rounded scoop as provided in the package mixed with an 8-ounce glass of water, provides 80 calories. It can be used to replace one or two meals. For those following the 800 calorie menu plan, for example, TwinFast could be used to replace breakfast, lunch, and the afternoon snack. That would add up to 240 calories, leaving 560 calories available for dinner.

TwinFast is an excellent addition to the Insulin Control Diet during all three phases of the program. During stabilization you might want to use Twinfast less frequently than during the weight loss phase, relying more on natural foods. But it will still come in handy when eating according to the menu plan is impossible. During the maintenance phase you might wish to use Twinfast to replace lunch or to satisfy the need for a midday snack. Whenever you use it, you'll know exactly what you're getting per serving: 80

calories, 15 grams of protein, only 5 grams of carbohydrate, and less than 1 gram of fat. TwinFast is available in many health food stores. A scoop may be carried in a Ziploc bag for use away from home.

TwinFast could be used to replace all natural food during a period of weight loss, just as protein mixes are used in hospital-based programs. It is the first commercially available mix that provides for a protein-sparing modified-fast diet by way of its high-protein, low-carbohydrate formulation. However, as we explained earlier, we do not believe that it's best to use any liquid exclusively, even if it is an adequate formulation. If, for any reason, you decide that you want to do so, consult your physician and follow this approach only under strict medical supervision.

We wish to state publicly that neither author of this book has any financially vested interest and no financial stake whatsoever in TwinFast or in the company that produces it.

MEAL PLAN—DAY ONE

Thought for the day: The journey of a thousand miles begins with a single step.

Breakfast

Decaffeinated coffee *or* herbal tea
1 poached egg *or* egg substitute
1 cup beef bouillon
¼ cup fruit cocktail *or* ½ peeled orange

Lunch

Iced tea *or* mineral water with lemon twist
Chicken Breast Mexicali* (4 ounces for women;
    5 ounces for men)
Salad with Low-Cal Vinaigrette Dressing*
Checkerboard Gelatin*

*See recipe section.

Snack (afternoon or evening)

1 tangerine *or* 7 or 8 grapes

Dinner

Decaffeinated coffee *or* tea
Indian Fish Curry* (5 ounces for women; 6 ounces for men)
Asparagus Chinese Style*
Salad with Dill Vinaigrette*
1 cup vegetable bouillon
Gelatin with D-Zerta topping
Additional fluids as desired to complete minimum of eight
   8-ounce servings daily

MEAL PLAN—DAY TWO

Thought for the day: Plan a special treat—a bubble bath perhaps—for taking such good care of yourself.

Breakfast

Decaffeinated coffee *or* herbal tea
1 soft-cooked egg *or* egg substitute
1 cup chicken bouillon
1 peach *or* 2 halves canned peaches

Lunch

Iced coffee *or* diet soda
Salmon Salad Sandwich* (4 ounces for women;
   5 ounces for men)
Salad with Low-Cal Vinaigrette*
Gelatin with D-Zerta topping

Snack (afternoon or evening)

1¼ cup watermelon cubes

*See recipe section.

Dinner

Decaffeinated coffee *or* tea
Chinese Fish Steaks* (5 ounces for women; 6 ounces for men)
Beans with Basil*
Salad with Parsley Vinaigrette*
1 cup beef bouillon
Gelatin and Fruit*
Additional fluids as desired to complete minimum of eight
  8-ounce servings daily

MEAL PLAN—DAY THREE

Thought for the day: Call a friend to tell her or him how excited
you are that you found the answer to your diet problems.

Breakfast

Decaffeinated coffee *or* tea
1 basted egg *or* egg substitute
1 cup vegetable bouillon
¾ cup raw pineapple

Lunch

Mineral water with a lemon twist
Chicken Cobb Salad* 14 ounces for women; 5 ounces for men)
Gelatin on a Stick*

Snack (afternoon or evening)

1 banana

*See recipe section.

Dinner

Decaffeinated coffee *or* tea
Florentine Chicken* (5 ounces for women; 6 ounces for men)
Beets*
Salad with Curry Vinaigrette*
1 cup chicken bouillon
Gelatin and Fruit*
Additional fluids as desired to complete minimum of eight
    8-ounce servings daily

MEAL PLAN—DAY FOUR

Thought for the day: As you enter ketosis, you no longer feel hungry. Your mind is free to think about so many things other than food!

Breakfast

Decaffeinated coffee *or* herbal tea
1 hard-cooked egg *or* egg substitute
1 cup chicken bouillon
¾ cup blueberries

Lunch

Diet soda
Turkey Chili* (4 ounces for women; 5 ounces for men)
Gelatin "Cookies"*

Snack (afternoon or evening)

Dried apples (4 rings)

Dinner

Decaffeinated coffee *or* tea
Salmon in Court Bouillon* (5 ounces for women;
    6 ounces for men)
Carrots*
Salad with Mexican Vinaigrette*

*See recipe section.

1 cup chicken bouillon
Gelatin and Fruit*
Additional fluids as desired to complete minimum of eight
   8-ounce servings daily

MEAL PLAN—DAY FIVE

Thought for the day: Look in the mirror and smile at the person
you see; give yourself all the love and acceptance you can.

Breakfast

Decaffeinated coffee *or* herbal tea
1 scrambled egg *or* egg substitute
1 cup vegetable bouillon
½ cup canned fruit cocktail

Lunch

Mineral water with a squeeze of lime
Sauteed Chicken Breast*
   (4 ounces for women; 5 ounces for men)
Checkerboard Gelatin*

Snack (afternoon or evening)

½ cup apple juice

Dinner

Decaffeinated coffee or tea
Chinese Chicken Stir-Fry*
   (5 ounces for women; 6 ounces for men)
Salad with Curry Vinaigrette*
1 cup chicken bouillon
Gelatin and Fruit*
Additional fluids as desired to complete minimum of eight
   8-ounce servings daily

*See recipe section.

MEAL PLAN—DAY SIX

Thought for the day: Recall the fond memories of your life that are not about food; remember what made these times happy.

Breakfast

Decaffeinated coffee *or* herbal tea
1 sunnyside-up egg *or* egg substitute
1 cup chicken bouillon
⅓ cup cranberry juice

Lunch

Diet soda
Poultry Burger* (4 ounces for women; 5 ounces for men)
Gelatin "Cookies"*

Snack (afternoon or evening)

1 banana

Dinner

Decaffeinated coffee *or* tea
New Orleans Creole Fillet* (5 ounces for women;
   6 ounces for men)
Cabbage*
Dinner Salad with Low-Cal Vinaigrette*
1 cup chicken bouillon
Gelatin and Fruit*
Additional fluids as desired to complete minimum of eight
   8-ounce servings daily

MEAL PLAN—DAY SEVEN

Thought for the day: Weight control is worth a *fortune* in good health and happiness. You're getting *rich*!

*See recipe section.

Breakfast

Decaffeinated coffee *or* tea
1 basted egg *or* egg substitute
1 cup beef bouillon
1 cup cantaloupe cubes

Lunch

Mineral water with lemon twist
Cold Shrimp with Low-Cal Vinaigrette*
   (4 ounces for women; 5 ounces for men)
Gelatin and Fruit*

Snack (afternoon or evening)

Dried apricots (7 halves)

Dinner

Decaffeinated coffee *or* tea
Poultry Meatloaf* (5 ounces for women; 6 ounces for men)
Cauliflower and Broccoli Florets*
Salad with Parsley Vinaigrette*
1 cup vegetable bouillon
Gelatin Salad*
Additional fluids as desired to complete minimum of eight
   8-ounce servings daily

MEAL PLAN—DAY EIGHT

Thought for the day: Many, many people are on diets for one reason or another; you're in good company.

Breakfast

Decaffeinated coffee *or* tea
1 deviled egg *or* egg substitute
1 cup chicken bouillon
1 cup papaya cubes

*See recipe section.

Lunch

Diet soda
Poultry Meatloaf* (leftover from yesterday's dinner—4 ounces for
   women; 5 ounces for men)
Gelatin Salad* (leftover from yesterday's dinner)

Snack (afternoon or evening)

Grapes (15 small)

Dinner

Decaffeinated coffee *or* tea
Chicken à l'Orange* (5 ounces for women; 6 ounces for men)
Julienne Strips of Beets and Carrots*
Salad with Dill Vinaigrette*
1 cup beef bouillon
Gelatin and Fruit*
Additional fluids as desired to complete minimum of eight
   8-ounce servings daily

MEAL PLAN—DAY NINE

Thought for the day: You're well into the second week of the
program. Congratulations! It only gets easier.

Breakfast

Decaffeinated coffee *or* tea
1 poached egg *or* egg substitute
1 cup vegetable bouillon
¾ cup mandarin orange segments

Lunch

Mineral water with orange twist
Italian Poultry Burger* (4 ounces for women; 5 ounces for men)
Gelatin "Cookies"*

*See recipe section.

Snack (afternoon or evening)

1 small pear

Dinner

Decaffeinated coffee *or* tea
This 'n' That Seafood Soup* (5 ounces for women;
    6 ounces for men)
Artichoke*
Salad with Low-Cal Vinaigrette*
1 cup beef bouillon
Gelatin on a Stick*
Additional fluids as desired to complete minimum of eight
    8-ounce servings daily

MEAL PLAN—DAY TEN

Thought for the day: Make a resolution to continue to succeed, no matter what the occasion. No piece of cake or treat is worth blowing it now.

Breakfast

Decaffeinated coffee *or* tea
1 soft-cooked egg or egg substitute
1 cup beef bouillon
1¼ cup watermelon cubes

Lunch

Diet soda
Salmon Salad Sandwich* (4 ounces for women;
    5 ounces for men)
Checkerboard Gelatin*

Snack (afternoon or evening)

1 small apple

*See recipe section.

Dinner

Decaffeinated coffee *or* tea
Turkey Cutlet* (5 ounces for women; 6 ounces for men)
Brussels Sprouts and Carrot Slices*
Salad with Dill Vinaigrette*
1 cup chicken bouillon
Gelatin with D-Zerta topping
Additional fluids as desired to complete minimum of eight
   8-ounce servings daily

MEAL PLAN—DAY ELEVEN

Thought for the day: Think about the diet as a hobby—be creative about your salads and gelatin desserts.

Breakfast

Decaffeinated coffee *or* tea
1 hard-cooked egg *or* egg substitute
1 cup vegetable bouillon
½ cup apple juice

Lunch

Mineral water with squeeze of lime
Turkey Cutlet* (cold, leftover from yesterday's dinner—
   4 ounces for women; 5 ounces for men)
Gelatin Salad*

Snack (afternoon or evening)

¾ Cup blueberries

Dinner

Decaffeinated coffee *or* tea
Salmon Chowder* (5 ounces for women; 6 ounces for men)
Salad with Parsley Vinaigrette*

*See recipe section.

1 cup chicken bouillon
Gelatin and Fruit*
Additional fluids as desired to complete minimum of eight
   8-ounce servings daily

MEAL PLAN—DAY TWELVE

Thought for the day: Remember the days when you were more slender and the things you used to enjoy. Soon you'll enjoy them again.

Breakfast

Decaffeinated coffee *or* tea
1 sunnyside-up egg *or* egg substitute
1 cup chicken bouillon
½ cup fruit cocktail

Lunch

Diet soda
Tuna Salad Sandwich (4 ounces for women; 5 ounces for men)
Gelatin "Cookies"*

Snack (afternoon or evening)

½ cup cherries

Dinner

Decaffeinated coffee *or* tea
Oriental Ginger Fish* (5 ounces for women; 6 ounces for men)
Carrot Strips and French-Cut Green Beans*
Salad with Low-Cal Vinaigrette*
1 cup beef bouillon
Gelatin and Fruit*
Additional fluids as desired to complete minimum of eight
   8-ounce servings daily

*See recipe section.

MEAL PLAN—DAY THIRTEEN

Thought for the day: Sometimes your best friend can be your worst enemy by talking you into a treat "just this once." Stand by your plan.

Breakfast

Decaffeinated coffee *or* tea
1 basted egg *or* egg substitute
1 cup beef bouillon
½ cup canned peaches

Lunch

Mineral water with lemon twist
Cold crab meat (snow crab, Dungeness crab, etc.—
    4 ounces for women; 5 ounces for men)
Gelatin Salad*

Snack (afternoon or evening)

1 cup raspberries (in or out of season; you deserve a treat!)

Dinner

Decaffeinated coffee *or* tea
Oven "Fried" Scallops* (5 ounces for women; 6 ounces for men)
Beans with Basil*
Salad with Curry Vinaigrette*
1 cup chicken bouillon
Gelatin and Fruit* with D-Zerta topping
Additional fluids as desired to complete minimum of eight
    8-ounce servings daily

MEAL PLAN—DAY FOURTEEN

Thought for the day: You've made it through two whole weeks, and your weight loss shows it. Congratulations!

*See recipe section.

Breakfast

Decaffeinated coffee *or* tea
1 scrambled egg *or* egg substitute
1 cup chicken bouillon
1 cup honeydew melon cubes

Lunch

Diet soda
Oriental Poultry Burger* (4 ounces for women;
    5 ounces for men)
Lettuce
Gelatin and Fruit*

Snack (afternoon or evening)

Dried prunes (3 medium)

Dinner

Decaffeinated coffee *or* tea
Beef en Brochette* (5 ounces for women; 6 ounces for men)
Salad with Dill Vinaigrette*
1 cup beef bouillon
Checkerboard Gelatin*
Additional fluids as desired to complete minimum of eight
    8-ounce servings daily

MEAL PLAN—DAY FIFTEEN AND BEYOND

Thought for the day: Keep a positive attitude that the rest of your diet program will go smoothly. Consult the suggestions in the chapter on support regularly.

Breakfast

Decaffeinated coffee *or* tea
1 egg *or* egg substitute any style
1 cup bouillon (beef, chicken, or vegetable)

*See recipe section.

Lunch

Diet soda *or* mineral water
1 protein entree of your choice (may use leftovers for
    convenience—4 ounces for women; 5 ounces for men)
Fruit or Gelatin Salad

Snack (afternoon or evening)

1 serving of fresh, canned, *or* dried fruit of your choice

Dinner

Decaffeinated coffee *or* tea
1 protein entree of your choice (stress fish and poultry; have red
    meat once a week—5 ounces for women; 6 ounces for men)
1 serving of vegetable of your choice
Salad with vinaigrette dressing of your choice
1 cup bouillon (beef, chicken, or vegetable)
Gelatin dessert
Additional fluids as desired to complete minimum of eight
    8-ounce servings daily

Chapter 9

THE INSULIN
EXERCISE EXPERIENCE

Do NOT skip this chapter, even if you have no intention of
doing any exercise. Bear with us and read the next few pages.

For many people the thought of exercise is so dreadful that they don't even want to read about it. They haven't done anything in the way of exercise in years and don't expect to again. The last thing a typically overweight person pictures is a vision of himself or herself working out à la Jane Fonda.

Take heart! We're going to make this easy for you. In fact, the more out of shape you are, the easier it will be to benefit from the insulin exercise experience.

We're not trying to fool you. Exercise is an integral part of the Insulin Control Diet. Without it you won't achieve the kind of success we've been promising. It's just that we recognize that the kind of exercise you need isn't the kind that first comes to mind. You won't have to start jogging or buy expensive equipment or do strenuous calisthenics. We'll show you how to enhance your body's ability to burn fat, to lose weight, and to become noticeably healthier and happier—in just 15 minutes daily.

The exercise program we recommend is particularly suited for those who are overweight and who haven't exercised in years or never exercised at all. Best of all, it's truly enjoyable and doesn't have to be boring. Based on our experience over the years, we're confident that you'll come to look forward to it.

But before we get down to specifics, we'd like to explain why exercise is so important for everyone interested in weight loss. We mentioned this before. Now we'll expand on it. There's more to the benefits of exercise than burning calories.

Your body contains both fat and lean muscle, but *only lean muscle is capable of burning appreciable calories*. The basic, energy-burning engine of the body is its lean muscle tissue. The fat tissue simply sits there, a storage form of energy that the body hoards. Weight reduction by diet alone can lead to large losses of lean body mass (precious protein). A person who loses considerable lean tissue is incapable of burning as many calories as before. And, when the body regains weight, it does not replace the lost muscle tissue, but adds half fat and half lean tissue for each new pound. That's why it's so important to preserve precious protein.

In addition, large losses of muscle tissue can be dangerous, for not only do you lose the muscle on legs and arms, but also you lose critical muscle of the organs, especially the heart. As cardiac muscle is lost, the ability of the heart to function properly is compromised. That's why crash diets and extended fasting can be fatal.

The last thing you want then is to lose lean tissue. You want to lose fat. That's why simply measuring the pounds you lose isn't enough. On a crash diet or when fasting, some of the weight lost is lean muscle. *Diet combined with exercise reduces the loss of precious protein and increases the burning of fat.*

Perhaps at one time or another you were a relatively lean person, but exercised little. The muscle tissue you had began to atrophy and it was replaced by fat tissue. Since you then had less lean and more fat tissue, you were capable of burning fewer calories daily.

For a while you were in equilibrium; as your muscle tissue degenerated from lack of exercise, you added fat, but your total weight remained the same. Then slowly but surely the amount of fat increased. Even if you continued to eat only as much as before, you gained weight, and the weight brought more fat tissue. During that time, of course, there came the point when your metabolic system changed for the worse and you became insensitive to the blood-sugar-lowering effects of insulin; thus you became very efficient at storing fat, not burning it.

But, you might say, you've been active all this time, working at a job or running a home. Whether you have a sedentary desk job or do work that involves physical activity, work seldom is as efficient as exercise in terms of burning calories, increasing metabolism, and building lean tissue. Regardless of how much you protest that by the end of the day you're completely exhausted, you probably have not exerted yourself in a way that is of any value so far as burning fat is concerned. Aerobic exercise is defined as activity that brings the rate of the heartbeat up significantly and keeps it there for a period of time. (We'll explain that more thoroughly in a moment.) It's only that type of exercise that achieves the goals we've been speaking of here.

HEALTH BENEFITS OF EXERCISE

A while back, dietitians and other health professionals thought that the benefit of exercise in weight loss was a matter of burning the calories coming into the body or burning off stored fat. They calculated how much of what kind of exercise it would take to burn a certain amount of calories. And, they maintained, any way you wanted to look at it, you had to burn 3,500 calories in order to lose 1 pound of fat. How discouraging to learn that even an hour of extremely strenuous activity, such as tournament level racquetball played nonstop at top speed, would burn only 750 calories. It would take someone nearly five hours of that kind of sweating exertion to burn off just a pound of fat! And most overweight men and women are more likely to jump over the moon than to engage in that kind of physical workout.

But here's the good news. We now know that the benefits of exercise don't end when you stop exercising. Rather than merely burning the calories at the moment, your body burns many additional calories for hours afterward. After a few months of a regular exercise program, the body's metabolism undergoes a significant change, and burns extra calories throughout the entire day. And, of course, the exercise builds that lean tissue which, in turn, makes your body a more effective energy-burning machine.

As you replace fat with muscle, your body can become more shapely and slender. Clothing sizes start coming down, and shopping for new, smaller clothes will be one of the rewards for following this program faithfully. When was the last time you enjoyed buying clothes?

And there are more health benefits from exercise. Three separate studies have now provided unequivocal evidence that regular aerobic exercise does indeed improve the health of the heart. These research efforts employed laboratory animals, not humans, because the scientists wanted to examine the actual hearts.

A study at the University of California at San Diego used pigs, whose hearts and circulatory systems are similar to ours. Dr. Colin M. Bloor artificially blocked a coronary artery, which supplies blood to the heart. Nine of the 18 pigs in the study were then strenuously exercised on a treadmill for 5 months; the other 9 did no exercise. At autopsy the hearts of the exercised pigs showed twice the development of collateral vessels (vessels in addition to the main coronary artery).

This has important implications. When an artery is blocked, no blood can get through. Collateral vessels form a natural bypass around the blockage, providing the needed blood flow. A good system of collateral vessels can sometimes prevent a heart attack and can lessen the likelihood of death should a heart attack occur. Collateral development can also preclude the need for coronary bypass surgery. For many years, advocates of regular exercise have cited the development of collateral circulation as a major benefit. Now we have the proof.

Another study showed that physical exercise could give some protection against sudden cardiac death. This research was conducted by Dr. George E. Billman at the University of Oklahoma Health Sciences Center in Oklahoma City. He and his associates used dogs that had had previous heart attacks. Some were given exercise, and others were not. After just six weeks of training, all the dogs were put on a treadmill for testing. None of the exercising animals showed any cardiac irregularities or other signs of weakened or malfunctioning hearts, while seven of the eight nonexercising dogs showed such signs.

Dr. James Scheuer, Director of Cardiology at Montefiore Hospital and Medical Center in New York, addressed the issue of the potential harm of exercise for those with high blood pressure in a study with rats. Ten rats were put on a program of regular swimming, and another 10 remained sedentary. All had high blood pressure. Cardiac function returned to normal in all of the rodent swimmers.

Evidence of the benefits of exercising is accumulating in human research also. A study reported in the *Journal of the American Medical Association* predicts low coronary heart disease risk for those who habitually exercise. Dr. Ralph S. Paffenbarger and his associates studied nearly 17,000 Harvard University graduates, and found that the risk of heart disease directly correlated with whether men were currently and regularly exercising. Even those who were university athletes but who stopped exercising after graduation were at risk. But those who were engaged in strenuous activity were protected. Dr. Paffenbarger makes some strong claims based on his research. He says that for every hour of time spent exercising, one could expect another hour of life. Statistically speaking, those who exercise can estimate an additional one to four years of life. With those kinds of statistics, can you honestly say you don't have the time to exercise?

Remember, too, that while most studies dealing with health and exercise have been done with men, the same benefits apply to women, along with another major advantage. Regular weight-bearing exercise has been clinically proven to reduce the risk of osteoporosis, the bone demineralizing disease we've all heard so much about in recent years. There are two reasons why exercise protects against osteoporosis. First, less calcium is lost from bone tissue in those performing weightbearing exercise. That can be as mild as regular walking. Second, calcium is better absorbed into the bones of those who exercise.

Many overweight men and women suffer from some degree of depression. As we've seen elsewhere in this book, there's a lot of hormonal involvement with such mental states. Exercise can help eliminate this depression. There's a direct chemical association between exercise and mood. When you exercise, the body releases a substance called beta endorphin, which has a soothing, relaxing effect. The more one exercises, the more beta endorphin is released into the blood and the more relaxed and contented one becomes. When this benefit of exercise is combined with the beneficial effects on mood of the Insulin Control Diet itself, one can expect to eliminate those feelings of depression and replace them with feelings of contentment.

But, you might ask, won't I be even hungrier when I exercise? Actually, quite the reverse is true. Exercise tends to decrease the appetite. That's why we advocate exercise in the evening, rather than early in the morning, for those on a weight loss program. Exercise decreases blood sugar by a mechanism not involving insulin and thus decreases the need for insulin, thereby suppressing the appetite somewhat. (And, by getting out of the house, you take yourself away from the temptations of the refrigerator.)

THE EXERCISE PROGRAM

We recommend easy, regular activity. Intense exercise should be restricted during weight loss because it tends to burn glucose rather than fat. The contribution of fat as an important energy source occurs to the greatest degree at relatively mild to moderate work intensities. In the trained state, the energy requirement during exercise is increasingly met by the burning of fat. Thus, the muscle is able to spare its glycogen (animal starch reserve) for use during more demanding circumstances.

The exercise best suited for the Insulin Control Diet to help you lose weight now and keep it off forever is nothing more than walking, fine-tuned for optimum results.

Some of you may not have walked more than a city block in years. If you fear even that amount of exercise is beyond you, nothing could be further from the truth. In fact, if you are completely out of shape, it will be easier to get the activity you need to get your metabolism going in the right direction.

Let us explain that. Many overweight people become incredibly efficient at doing little or no activity. They arrange, consciously or unconsciously, to avoid or completely eliminate movement. While watching television for the evening, they have their remote control at hand, a soft drink close by, snacks at the ready, and the telephone within easy reach. An entire evening can pass, hour after hour, without movement. For such persons simply getting off the couch and walking across the room is enough to get the heart beating rapidly. And that's exactly what we want to have happen. As we'll see, elevating the heart rate is the goal. So if you're totally out of shape, reaching that goal will be remarkably easy.

Others of you, most likely those who are in better shape, may doubt that simply walking could possibly be enough exercise to get the job done. What about the saying "No pain, no gain"? As we'll soon show you, walking can get the heart pounding for even the most athletic person.

But won't walking get boring? How can one expect to keep it up for long? We've got some tricks up our sleeves that will keep you walking for years to come.

Any form of exercise should increase your heart rate. Only when it increases well beyond the resting rate will your metabolic rate begin to change and will you begin to reap the tremendous benefits of exercise. So it's important that you understand just what's happening.

The heart beats at a rate sufficient to supply the entire body, including the heart itself, with oxygen-rich blood. When you're sitting still, you need less blood coursing through your arteries than when you're doing various activities. The average resting heart rate for adult men is about 72 and for women about 80. Children have a much higher rate, often about 100 beats per minute. The trained athlete may have a resting rate as low as 50. To find your own resting heart rate, simply place your forefinger on the artery to the side of your Adam's apple. Now count the beats for 10 seconds, watching the time on a sweep-second watch. Multiply that number of beats by 6 and you'll have your resting heart rate in beats per minute.

If you haven't been exercising regularly, don't be surprised if your resting heart rate is higher than average. This is because the heart has become inefficient at pumping enough blood to satisfy the body's needs. A strong, healthy heart can pump enough blood with little problem, requiring just a few squirts to get the blood out through the arteries. A well-trained, in-shape heart can pump a bit more blood during exercise or other activity with just a few extra beats. But the out-of-shape heart has to beat many times more. That's why when a person who has not been exercising regularly does some activity, the heart rate increases significantly.

And that brings us to your goal heart rate—the rate we'd like to have you reach during your walking sessions. Each of us has a maximum heart rate, the absolute limit of what our heart is capable of doing. Yours can be determined by subtracting your age from the number 220. It doesn't matter whether you're a man or woman, overweight or at ideal weight, in or out of shape. If, let's say, you're 40 years old, your maximum heart rate will be 220 minus 40, or 180 beats per minute.

But your heart is incapable of beating at that rate for any length of time. What you want to reach is called the training heart rate. The training rate is 80 percent of the maximum rate. For example, a 40-year-old's training heart rate will be:

$$220 - 40 = 180 \times .80 = 144 \text{ beats per minute}$$

Your goal in exercising is to elevate your heart rate to the training rate. However, you must reach the goal in stages. To start out, exercise to reach only 60 percent, rather than 80 percent, of maximum. For our 40-year-old this would be:

$$220 - 40 = 180 \times .60 = 108 \text{ beats per minute}$$

By raising your heart rate to the training level, you will begin to change your metabolism, burn fat stores more efficiently, and improve the efficiency of your heart's ability to pump blood. With only a little conditioning your resting heart rate will begin to drop. And, you will start feeling better almost immediately. That's why you don't want to put it off any longer. You don't need any special equipment, clothing, or setting. All you have to do is decide that you're going to start your Insulin Exercise Experience today.

The improvement you're going to make will be simply astounding. That's why we want you to keep an accurate record of your walking. Use a chart like the one on page 144. Each day record your resting heart rate, your heart rate while exercising, the time you walk, and a few comments about how you feel about it.

How long should you walk? We strongly believe that daily activity for a short period of time is infinitely better than longer, more intense activity done just once in a while. We'd like you to walk for 15 minutes a day, every day. The best time to do so is in the evening.

Check your resting heart rate. Then start to walk at a brisk pace. How fast is fast enough? You shouldn't be able to gaze into store windows as you pass along a street. Your mind should be set on the act of walking. As you walk, you should notice your breathing increasing. You'll probably also notice a slight sheen of perspiration on your brow. But don't overdo it. While walking, you should be able to carry on a conversation without straining or to sing a song without gasping for breath.

After walking along for a while, put your finger to your throat to feel the pulse in your artery. Count the beats for 10 seconds as timed on your sweep-second watch. How close are you to your training heart rate? Right on target? Terrific, keep it up for the full 15 minutes. A bit under the rate? Step up your pace. A bit faster than your training rate? Slow down. How fast you have to walk depends on what condition you're in. If you are out of shape, you may have to walk at a moderate pace so that you don't exceed your training rate. If you've been active, you may have to step right along.

Even the most physically fit individual can reach the training heart rate with a program of walking. Once you start getting into better shape, walking can continue to provide all the exercise you'll ever need. Simply walk a bit faster and perhaps a bit longer.

In many ways walking is superior to other kinds of exercise. Unlike jogging or running, walking is unlikely to result in any injuries. Practically every jogger will eventually succumb to shin splints, strains and sprains, stress fractures, and other muscle and bone ailments. Unlike swimming, walking can be done at any time and any place. And there's no potential of swimmer's ear infections. Unlike aerobics, walking entails no expensive fees for classes or clubs, and no chance of injury associated with high impact workouts.

Walking can and should become a habit, done each and every day. Like any habit, this one eventually becomes hard to break. Patients report time and time again that once it becomes a part of their lives, it's difficult to have to go without walking even for a single day. And, unless you're truly ill, there's no reason why you can't get those 15 minutes of walking in daily.

Daily Exercise Record

Date	Length of Walk	Resting Pulse	Peak Pulse	Comments (place walked, feelings, etc.)

Our only concern is that you don't overdo your walking when you first begin. Especially if you haven't done much physical activity recently, ease yourself into it. Start at 60 percent of your maximum heart rate, work up to 65 percent in the first month, and don't exceed 70 percent for the first two months. Check these numbers with your doctor before you begin. If your muscles feel sore, slow down a bit. You will and should feel some muscle tension; that simply shows you've been doing your exercise, and it will decrease with each day of exercising. But you don't want to ache severely.

A few men and women, particularly those with large amounts of overweight and the elderly, will be able to do only 10 minutes rather than 15 minutes of walking daily. That's just fine. Do as much as you can, within the limits we've set, on a regular basis.

Regularity is the most important aspect of walking to help you lose weight. It's far better to do 15 minutes each day than to do 35 or 40 minutes every other day. That way one improves metabolism every day. The same applies to intensity of your exercise. It's better to maintain a steady pace than to walk so briskly that you increase the risk of tripping or pull a muscle or wear yourself out so that you have to stop. If you feel after a few weeks that you're ready for more exercise, simply increase the amount of time you spend walking each day. Go from 15 minutes to 20 to 30 and so on.

When you're in better shape and walking 15 to 30 minutes every day, you may find that you can no longer reach your target training heart rate in that 15 or 30 minutes. If you have the time and inclination, you can simply walk longer distances over a longer period of time. However, if the time you have available for exercise is limited, you can increase the difficulty of your walks in order to use your limited time more efficiently. Here are a couple of things you can do to get your heart rate up faster.

First, hand weights will increase the amount of work you do while walking and you'll find your heart rate increasing. Don't overdo it. Start with the smallest weight you can find and gradually build up. The last thing you want to do is to hurt yourself.

Second, pick up a small knapsack. Place a 5-pound bag of sugar or flour in it, and walk with that amount of weight for a week.

Gradually increase the weight as you're able to do so while staying within your training heart rate zone.

For most people this increase in workload will not be necessary. You'll get the results you want if you just continue to do your 15 minutes of walking each day. Remember that the most important part of this exercise experience is consistency. Once you've gotten into the routine of daily exercise, try increasing the amount you do. Instead of 15 minutes, walk for 20 minutes, then 25, and then 30. Next try to get out not just once, but twice daily. Or, if your schedule doesn't permit that, try walking once a day and doing some other exercise some other time during the day.

ENJOYING YOUR WALKING EXPERIENCE

After just the first two or three weeks, you'll start to realize that you won't want to give walking up. Perhaps you'll want to treat yourself to a new pair of walking shoes. There are a number of high-quality shoes on the market specifically designed for walking. They look like jogging shoes, but the sole is more flexible and has less cushioning than the sole designed to soften the impact of running. Shop around for a pair that feels particularly comfortable for you.

You can walk alone or with friends. You can walk through a park, along a crowded avenue, or in an indoor shopping mall. You couldn't be getting into this activity at a better time. Walking clubs are starting up all over the country. (To find clubs in your area you might contact the American Volks-Sports Association at 1001 Pat Booker Road, Universal City, Texas 78148.)

In order to make your walking experience as enjoyable as possible, we've developed a series of suggestions to keep you interested and looking forward to the next outing. Your personal schedule will determine when you'll be able to do the various suggested walks. If you can, plan two or three days ahead, so you'll have something to look forward to.

Remember that your main purpose is to walk for the exercise. Make sure that you do your full 15 minutes of walking without stopping to look in the shop windows or to smell the roses in the park. After you've done your vigorous walking, you may wish to stroll through the park or do your window shopping. But never forget that the two types of walking are different in their purposes.

The most convenient walk is around your block. It's probably the best way to start and there will be days when it's all you'll have time to do. As you start out, time how long it takes you to walk a block, and calculate how many blocks you'll be able to walk at your training heart rate during your 15 minutes. Then map out other routes.

Some days you may wish to get into your car and drive a mile or so away to take your walk. Pick up a street map of your area. Map out the areas you want to walk in and assign yourself different chunks of your town or city for different days. Soon you'll know the city better than any cab driver! If you live in a rural area, the same principles apply. Does your city have a Chinatown, or other ethnic areas? How many parks do you have in your community? Try to do walking tours of each of them. Relive a part of the history of your area by imagining yourself to be living during an earlier time, walking, say, the route of Paul Revere.

On rainy or extremely cold days, find an indoor shopping mall where you can really stretch your legs. Some of the new ones have two or three levels, and you can really work up a good sweat in 15 minutes. Many malls open their doors before business hours so that walkers can take an indoor hike before shoppers crowd the lanes. And after your walk, give yourself a little reward such as a nice hot cup of tea.

Make a list of the places you'd like to go walking. In many cities, your list can include museums, zoos, plant conservatories, boardwalks, and various public buildings. After your walk, put your comments into your daily exercise record. Was it a walk you want to repeat? How did it rate on a scale of 1 to 10?

STRETCHING EXERCISES

We'd like to encourage you to do some simple stretching exercises that will enhance your total program of weight loss and toning. The stretches we've selected are soothing and will gradually increase your flexibility. Do them immediately after your walk each day. Do as much as you can without straining. As time goes on, you'll find that you're able to stretch farther and farther.

By increasing your flexibility at the same time you build up your stamina and lose weight, you'll be at much less risk of the injuries that so often accompany the aging process. It's the sedentary people who are more likely to experience the difficulties we associate with aging.

Do these stretches in the order given. Hold each stretch for a 5-count at first, and then work up to a 10-count. Stretch only to the point of feeling it, not to the point of pain. Relax and *breathe*.

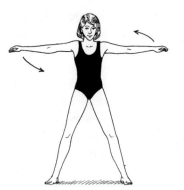

1. Stand straight and lift your arms out to the sides. Turn the upper torso to one side. Count while feeling the tension. Repeat to the other side.

2. Stand straight. Use a chair or the wall for balance. Bend one leg up to the back and grasp your ankle. Gently pull your leg toward your body and count. Repeat with the other leg.

3. In either a standing or reclining position, pull one knee to your chest. Count. Repeat with the other leg.

4. Sit on the floor with one leg outstretched toward the side and the other bent so the foot is close to the groin. Stretch to grasp the outstretched foot. Count. If you cannot reach your foot, stretch as far as possible. Repeat with other leg outstretched.

5. Kneel with arms akimbo. Slowly bend backward. Count. Push hands into sides to achieve stretch.

6. Sit on the floor and bring both feet into the groin. Gently push your knees as close to floor as possible. Sit upright. Count.

7. While comfortably seated, let your head drop slowly to your chest. Gently rotate it to the side, back, opposite side, and front. Count the repetitions. Repeat rotating in the opposite direction.

8. Stand upright and place your hands on a wall or a sturdy support. Extend one leg to the rear. Bend the other knee, pressing the heel of the extended foot downward to exert stretch on calf. Count. Repeat for other leg.

9. Stand upright. Attempt to touch the center of your back by reaching over your shoulder. Assist with your other hand by pulling gently on your elbow. Count. Repeat with the other arm.

10. Stand upright. Stretch to touch your toes (or as close as possible). Count. Stand. Repeat.

11. Stand upright. Attempt to touch the ceiling with each hand alternately, then both together for a count of 10 each.

12. Stand upright, and lift your arms out to the sides. Extend your arms as far as possible. With palms up, circle arms to the back 10 times. Circle to the front 10 times. Repeat with palms down.

13. Stand upright. Let your right hand slide down your right leg as your left hand reaches for the ceiling. Bend the torso toward the right, keeping shoulders straight forward and arm stretched. Count. Repeat on opposite side.

We've stressed moderation in your walking and your stretching. But if it's a particularly nice day and you feel like taking a walk of 15 minutes or so twice during the day rather than just once, by all means do so. Similarly, if you feel like doing some stretches in the middle of the day just to make you relax and unwind, be encouraged to do so.

OTHER EXERCISE POSSIBILITIES

While we believe that walking is the best possible form of exercise, ultimately the best is that which you will be most likely to continue indefinitely. You may prefer to do some other activity, or you may want to alternate exercise activities. And there will be times when walking is out of the question due to bad weather.

Swimming is an excellent form of exercise. As with any activity, start with a few laps and gradually build up to longer total distances. Does your YMCA/YWCA have aquatic exercise in the pool? That is a growing and enjoyable method of good exercise.

Stationary bicycles are excellent for working your heart up to the target rate. You can buy one or use one at a local YMCA/YWCA or health club. (If you do decide to buy, two brands known for high quality are Tunturi and Schwinn.)

Other apparatuses are not as efficient, and look better in principle than in action. And some may be harder on the back or other parts of the body. Investigate potential benefits and harm of any given machine before buying.

Again, the best exercise is the exercise that you *do* on a regular basis.

• • •

Thank you for bearing with us and reading this chapter. If you're still skeptical about exercising, even in the easygoing and pleasant ways we've described, we can only ask you to trust us and give it a try. Do the walking and the stretching for just a month. You certainly can do that. It's only a month, and what have you got to lose? We're absolutely positive that after a month you'll never want to quit. The Insulin Exercise Experience will become a part of your life.

Chapter 10

STABILIZATION

Congratulations! You've shed those pounds and inches and attained your desired goal weight. You have complied with our guidelines for food consumption and restriction. You have entered a program of regular exercise and you're doing some form of physical activity every day. You've kept a detailed diary of everything you ate and drank and of all the exercise you've done. It's been an effort, but it's been worth it, and now you want to make sure you never gain that weight back again.

Your success in stabilization will require a continued commitment. It's best to go along with our diet recommendations as strictly as you can. It's essential to continue your exercise program; ideally, you should exercise daily, with at least 20 to 30 minutes of walking, bicycle riding, or indoor aerobic activity. By all means continue to keep your daily diary. The odds for successful stabilization and maintenance favor those who follow these three suggestions.

But before you begin to stabilize at your current weight, be certain that this is the weight at which you really want to live the rest of your life. Too often dieters decide it's time to stop before they reach goal weight. Some look in the mirror and say this is "good enough." Others aren't really satisfied, but decide to accept a compromise. Still others are persuaded by well-meaning friends and relatives that they should stop dieting.

At the very beginning of the program you set a goal weight. If it was a realistic goal, then don't be persuaded to give up early. People who do go to goal weight are much more likely to maintain their weight loss permanently. Discuss your goal weight with your physician to determine the weight best for you as an individual.

Remember, as we said, there's no mystery in this. If you settle now for a weight that's, let's say, 10 or 15 pounds above your original goal, you'll not find it too difficult to accept just another pound or two. Then the next month it will be OK to add another pound or two. And before you know it, you've gained all that lost weight back, and perhaps even more than you started with.

So give this a great deal of thought before you leave ketosis and begin to stabilize. Be absolutely certain that you weigh what you want to weigh and that you've achieved the goal you had in mind from the start. Remember, the less fat you carry the less insulin resistance remains.

Perhaps when you began this diet you doubted the idea of limiting your carbohydrate intake so severely. You might have thought that it wouldn't really be necessary to follow the guidelines rigidly. Then you found that in order to stay in ketosis, carbohydrate intake did indeed have to be kept way down and that deviation from the guidelines took you out of ketosis.

Remember this as you enter the period of stabilization. Again, our guidelines have been proven time and again to be the most effective way to deal with this process. You might be tempted to cheat a bit or to speed the process up. Don't do it. Stay within our guidelines and you'll succeed beautifully.

PROCESS OF STABILIZATION

To understand the process of stabilization, think of your body as a beaker in which you, a chemist, are trying to create just the right solution. You will have the right solution when it turns from yellow to green. You pour one chemical into another chemical in the beaker just one drop at a time so that you can measure exactly how much of the first chemical it really takes to get the job done. Finally, one more drop in a long series is the one to complete the reaction and make the color change. If you had simply dumped a lot of the chemical in at once, the color change would have occurred, but you'd never know how much more was added than necessary. In science this process of gradual adding is called titration.

To stabilize your weight so that you neither lose nor gain, you have to determine exactly how much food and what kinds of food you can add to the diet. You know that the diet you're currently following causes you to lose weight, but now you've lost enough. Just how much more can you eat before you stop losing weight and before you begin to gain weight? No one knows. Each person is different, and there's no formula that will tell you the exact number of calories and grams of carbohydrate needed to stabilize and maintain your weight. So we titrate, that is, we add food little by little, drop by drop, to measure accurately how much and what kind causes a reaction.

During the weight loss phase, you have been feeding yourself in two ways. First, your food has provided 600 to 1,000 calories. Second, you have received about 1,000 additional calories from your stored fat which has been converted to energy.

To stop losing weight you must now begin to increase your food, and thus your caloric intake. You'll do this gradually with a combination of complex carbohydrates and monounsaturated fats.

Weight loss produces a decrease in metabolism, a phenomenon which probably evolved to ensure survival during times of famine. As you increase your calories taken as food, metabolism increases by favoring the production of the active form of the thyroid hormone. See page 45 for a review of that hormone.

Ultimately, if you are burning 2,000 calories daily, you will have to consume that number of calories to maintain a constant ideal weight. That number will vary, of course, depending upon your level of physical activity and your individual body stature. Remember that the more lean muscle tissue you have, the more calories can be burned.

How should your caloric allowance be divided into fat, protein, and carbohydrate? No more than 30 percent of the day's calories should come from fat, with the emphasis placed on monounsaturated fats from foods such as olive and canola oils, and avoiding saturated fats from animal foods and tropical oils. That means, for a person consuming 2,000 calories, 600 calories will come from fat. Since fat has 9 calories per gram, that means one's daily fat allotment would be 66 grams.

Next we calculate 50 percent of calories from carbohydrates. Again, for the person requiring 2,000 calories daily, that means

1000 of those calories will come from carbohydrates. And because carbohydrates provide 4 calories per gram, that person will consume about 250 grams of carbohydrate.

That leaves 20 percent of our daily calories, which will be derived from protein. For the person consuming 2,000 calories, this will mean 400 protein calories. Like carbohydrates, protein provides 4 calories per gram; therefore, 100 grams will yield those 400 calories.

Of course, you won't jump directly to 2,000 calories or any other pre-determined number. Rather, you will gradually add calories until you no longer lose—nor gain—weight. Perhaps you'll reach 2,000 calories. Perhaps the number will be greater or less. Regardless of the total, however, the percentage will remain the same: 30 percent as fat, 50 percent as carbohydrate, and 20 percent as protein. For diabetics the carbohydrate allowance may have to be reduced in favor of more "good" fats, to maintain normal blood sugars.

Don't be dismayed if during the stabilization period you begin to gain weight. Bear in mind the concept of titration and the need to find exactly the right caloric intake. But it's also true that those added carbohydrates may trigger salt and water retention. This may be aggravated by vigorous exercise which diverts blood away from the kidneys.

Deal with this dilemma by returning temporarily to ketosis and utilizing the concept of the diuresis of recumbency. (See page 61.) When weight has returned to goal level, you can once again add back the carbohydrate, but perhaps in smaller increments.

THYROID HORMONE AND THE STARVATION WEIGHT MODE

Thyroid hormone produced by your body's thyroid gland in the neck plays a large role in metabolism. It exerts its influence as one form, T4, is converted to T3 by way of an enzyme which is sensitive to carbohydrate. When there is less carbohydrate available, less T4 will be converted to T3, and metabolism is decreased. This is the mechanism by which the body conserves its energy in times of famine and starvation.

This has practical implications for you when following the Insulin Control Diet, because as metabolism decreases, the body produces less heat, and you may feel cold. The answer to this problem is an increase in exercise. As always, this does not mean strenuous aerobics. Rather, a slight increase in physical activity will communicate the need to step up the metabolism. Try taking an additional one-mile walk, for example. Your metabolism will increase, and you'll feel warmer.

During the stabilization phase, you'll gradually add back some carbohydrate which will directly influence the T4/T3 conversion. Again, the emphasis is on small, stepwise, incremental increases.

In the first week of stabilization, you add 5 grams of carbohydrate and 1 ounce of protein food to your daily meal plan. For example, instead of 4 ounces of chicken at lunch, make it 5. Or add another ounce of fish to your evening meal. The choice of carbohydrates is yours, but make your carbohydrate selections from the vegetable list during that first week. Perhaps it will be half a cup of green beans, broccoli, or cauliflower with your evening meal. Maybe you'd like to have a half of an artichoke to nibble on during the evening. Or you might opt for a 4-ounce glass of tomato juice before a meal or in the afternoon.

Assuming that you're continuing your program of exercise, you may lose another pound or two during that first week of stabilization. In fact, you probably will. Depending on the amount of physical activity that now marks each day, you may even lose more than that. But that's just fine, because you'll be adding foods gradually.

Add another ounce of protein and another 5 grams of carbohydrate during the second week and again during the third week. During the fourth week of stabilization, you will add a final ounce of protein to reach a full 13 to 15 ounces daily. How you divide your portions depends on your own preferences. Would you like to have a larger breakfast, with a piece of meat added to your egg? Do you prefer to have a larger portion of meat with your evening meal? The 13 to 15 ounces, however, is the maximum allotted protein throughout stabilization and as you maintain your weight for years to come.

This amount of protein, coming from your meat, fish, poultry, cheese, and eggs, will more than satisfy your body's requirements. In fact, the total amount of protein will be larger than the Recommended Dietary Allowances. No man or woman needs more, regardless of physical activity.

But, again depending on your energy output as determined by the amount of exercise you're now doing, you very well may need more calories. So, during the fourth and fifth week of stabilization you'll add one daily carbohydrate serving.

This is the time to stress the utmost importance of eating a variety of foods. Every nutrition authority concurs on the importance of such variety from the food groups. The Japanese government in its recommendations for the population urges its citizens to eat 35 different kinds of food each day. Of course, portions would be small, as in a salad or a stew containing many different ingredients.

Additional calories during stabilization may also come from fat. As always, diabetic individuals should avoid saturated fats even more stringently than the general population owing to the increased risk of heart disase. Monounsaturated fats, however, do not raise cholesterol levels and may be used interchangeably with carbohydrates in adding calories.

Remember that *all* fats add 9 calories per gram, as compared with 4 calories per gram of either protein or carbohydrate. Sources of monounsaturated fat include olive and canola oils, olives, avocados, and cashews.

The added carbohydrates will come from fruit, vegetables, breads, cereals, and pasta. You may decide to add fruit by having a larger piece instead of adding another kind; instead of a half pear, you may want a whole one.

We've neglected one food group until now—the milk group. You may now feel free to have a glass of skim milk or a serving of nonfat or low-fat yogurt. Certainly these dairy foods provide both enjoyment and nutrients, but since the calcium supplement you now take will provide all the calcium you need, there isn't a strict nutritional reason for consuming dairy foods. If you wish to, enjoy a serving of nonfat milk or yogurt during the fifth week of stabilization. This will be *in place* of both a serving of carbohydrate and a serving of protein, since milk and yogurt contain both. You must also be aware of any flavorings in the yogurt; most have added sugar and fruit which boost the carbohydrate level considerably.

By the end of the fifth week of stabilization, you will be consuming a wide variety of foods from all the food groups. The number of servings will depend entirely upon your own individual metabolism.

The stabilization process should take at least four to five weeks of gradually adding carbohydrates and protein until you reach a point of balance. Don't try to rush the process by adding two carbohydrate servings at a time. Keep that cautious chemist in mind, titrating according to your special, individual needs.

As you proceed, you'll want to keep accurate records in your diet diary. Those who add foods systematically and record those foods faithfully are far more likely to succeed.

How much carbohydrate will you be able to add to your diet? There's no way to predict the total, other than in relation to the amount of your lean muscle mass and your level of physical activity. Larger individuals, with bigger bones and more substantial muscles, will undoubtedly be able to consume more carbohydrate than smaller persons. On the other hand, smaller people who exercise a lot may be able to eat as much as larger, sedentary individuals. But there are unfortunate and unexpected exceptions to the basic rules of thumb. There are large, active men who find they can add very little carbohydrate. And there are small women who, once they lose fat tissue, are able to consume quite a bit. Some men and women will be able to go up to only 75 grams of carbohydrates daily, others up to 150 grams. Some diabetics will have difficulty with even a little more carbohydrate than they consumed on the weight loss program, and may require oral medication to control their blood sugars,

Thus far we've talked only about adding foods to the diet. There may be times when you have to subtract some. If, after two or three weeks of stabilization, you find that you're starting to gain a bit of weight, cut back on the carbohydrates. A week later try the additional carbohydrate again, and see if you gain. If you do not, continue with that amount for another week before trying the next carbohydrate increase. If you're still not gaining, go on from there.

You may go all the way through four or five weeks of stabilization without gaining a pound, only to have a sudden weight surge. This is where your food diary and exercise record will come in handy. Read them carefully. Perhaps you upped the carbohydrate intake beyond what you thought it was. Perhaps your exercise program suffered a bit owing to a slight cold. Perhaps you ate in a restaurant and did not know what all the ingredients were in the meal. Try to eliminate such variables, and see if the weight gain continues. If it does, you'll have to subtract one of the carbohydrates, perhaps going back to a half a pear rather than a whole one for a snack. Or, as we'd prefer, you can increase your exercise. Do an extra hour of walking for the week. Get in another bicycle ride. Take another aerobics class. Work that metabolism up to where you can consume that additional food without weight gain.

SIMPLE SUGARS:
STILL THE NUMBER ONE POISON

One person may be able to add carbohydrates and protein to the diet every week throughout stabilization without gaining an ounce. Another individual may find that only one or two servings of carbohydrates can be added without weight gain. Certainly there are distinct genetic differences among men and women that we have no control over. The amount of lean muscle mass will also determine the level of energy that can be burned efficiently. And, of course, the time spent in rigorous physical activity directly correlates with just how much total food, including carbohydrates, can be eaten without weight gain.

The one food that almost everyone who has had a weight problem will have difficulty with is simple sugar. Whether in the guise of a candy bar, a piece of cake, a slice of pie, or a bowl of sweetened cereal, simple sugars remain the Number One Poison for most people, even after they've lost weight and begun a regular program of exercise. Avoid them whenever possible. For some people this is easier than for others. For one patient, Margaret, for example, staying away from sugar also prevented the headaches she had suffered for years without knowing the source of her pain. Just a small serving was enough to bring on throbbing pain. So Margaret never ate enough to return her to the metabolic trap.

Concentrate on the many, many foods you can enjoy without the fear of regaining the pounds and inches you successfully shed. Whether it's a main meal or a midday snack, there are many choices available to you without dipping into food laden with sugars. Do you *really* want to risk weight gain for the small and transient pleasure of a piece of candy? Practically everyone has to come to grips with avoiding one pleasure or another for the sake of health and well-being.

For the person who quits smoking cigarettes, we know that having "just a puff" now and then or "just one" cigarette after a nice Saturday evening dinner is flirting with disaster. Certainly there is the temptation to start thinking that one no longer is addicted to tobacco and thus can enjoy that occasional smoke. But the truth is harsh and simple: The only way to stay away from the habit is to eliminate smoking completely from one's life.

On the positive side, former smokers will tell you that the times when one craves a cigarette grow more and more infrequent and the craving, when it does strike, becomes less and less intense as time goes on. Take it from a former two-pack-a-day smoker. The habit *can* be kicked for good.

And the same applies to simple sugars. As one who has been a victim of the metabolic trap, your body is far more vulnerable to the horrors of insulin resistance than others. Even though you are slender at this point, insulin levels can soar with just the smallest slice of pie or piece of cake. We wish it weren't so, but it's simply a physiological fact of life that you'll have to deal with now and forever.

To cite another analogy, many authorities now believe that alcoholism is a disease that can be genetically determined and that has little if anything to do with a person's willpower or self-control. The body of an alcoholic reacts differently to ingestion of alcohol than does the body of a social drinker, who can consume alcoholic beverages moderately for years without dependence. When the alcoholic determines to stay sober, he or she must accept the truth that even one drink is too much. It must be total abstinence for life. That's why groups refer to the sober drinker as a "recovering" rather than a "recovered" alcoholic. The disease is always there, ready to return at the first indiscretion.

It's interesting to realize, then, that there are alcoholics who have never had a drink in their lives. Alcoholism is a disease that requires a stimulus, namely, alcohol, to make itself manifest. Therefore, if one is born an alcoholic by genetic potential and a member of a nondrinking religious sect such as the Mormons or the Seventh-Day Adventists, one will never exhibit the inability to consume alcohol in moderation. And that, certainly, is a blessing.

The same can be said for those genetically determined to become non-insulin-dependent diabetics. Without the factor of overweight, the diabetes may never become manifest. Conversely, if a diabetic patient successfully loses the weight, symptoms of diabetes frequently completely disappear. Does that mean the diabetic has been "cured"? Not really, since the disease is ready to reappear with the regaining of weight.

For the alcoholic, no drink should be worth the degradation alcohol can cause. And for the formerly overweight man or woman, simple sugars, the Number One Poison, are simply not worth the return to a state of obesity. Unlike former smokers and recovering alcoholics, however, there are some now-slender dieters who can enjoy an occasional special treat. Some can take a taste of dessert and leave the rest behind. Are you one of these? Can you have just *one bite* of cake? Just one small piece of candy? Just one cookie? For some the little taste is satisfying; for others it's self-inflicted torture to be tantalized with a taste only to have the urge to gorge denied.

You may decide on occasion to say "the hell with it" and enjoy yourself with a food you shouldn't have, knowing full well that in the morning you'll have gained weight. You'll have to weigh the risks and benefits. But if you do "fall off the wagon" at a special meal or just for the pleasure of a hot fudge sundae, you have to do so with your eyes wide open. Accept the fact that you probably will gain some weight. But also anticipate that you'll go right back to your healthful diet.

The real danger in this situation is the temptation to say, well, I've gained one pound, so if I gain another pound today it won't be too bad. That kind of thinking can lead one off the straight and narrow and right back to obesity and the metabolic trap.

Another, probably safer, approach might be to anticipate an occasion where you'll want to splurge. Let's say you're invited to a party on Saturday evening, and you'll want to join the other guests in eating dessert. Knowing this in advance, you can "save up" for the party by avoiding carbohydrates all day Friday and Saturday until dinner. Perhaps you may also need to eliminate starch on Sunday as well to make up for your indulgence. But you will be able to enjoy that special treat.

As time goes on, most formerly overweight men and women come to accept their dietary limitations, rather like the smoker who, after a while, seldom thinks about having a cigarette. By avoiding the simple sugars as much as possible, you'll find it easier to achieve that state of mind. Ultimately, only you will be able to find out what works best for you and make your own decisions.

A NEW IMAGE

As you progress through your period of stabilization, concentrate on a new self-image. You are no longer an overweight person. Believe it or not, in one way or another, you've gotten used to the idea of being heavy. You may even have used it as an excuse for doing one thing or not doing another. Now it's time to make an entirely new life for yourself as a slender person.

Look in the mirror and allow yourself to enjoy what you see. Take pride in your achievement, for which you alone can take all of the credit. Say it right out loud: "I *love* myself and I *love* my new body." Now prove it by being nice to yourself. You deserve the reward for your effort.

This is the time to read our chapter on support again. Think again about the important life-style changes you must make in order to be slim for the rest of your life. You've lost the weight you wanted to lose; the period of stabilization is critical if you want to keep it off.

It's important to start thinking of yourself as a thin person.

How is a slender person different from the way you were before you lost weight? Slender people seem to have more energy and be more active. You've probably noticed those traits in yourself lately; now believe they are real changes, and capitalize on them. Slender men and women enjoy their meals without overeating. Many people who have a weight problem tend to look and act with little confidence; now try being a bit more assertive.

In the past you may have thought of yourself as a thin person in a fat body. Now perhaps you're beginning to feel like a fat person in a thin body. Think of the things you wanted to do when you were heavy but were unable to do. This is the time to take charge of your life, and enjoy it to the fullest.

It's sometimes helpful to take some snapshots of yourself today and compare them with those taken when you were overweight. Look at the difference. Convince yourself that you really are slender and that it's worth all your efforts to remain that way.

Exercise may have been quite a chore when you first started the program. As you became used to it, physical activity became easier. Now that you're slender, exercise has probably become an important positive pleasure in your life. Enjoy the way your body responds to your commands for movement. You glide across the room in comparison to the way you moved in the past; your walking stride has grace. You can feel your muscles flex and enjoy touching the firmness of your body.

Get used to the compliments you're hearing on your new slender appearance. Don't be embarrassed by them. When you receive a compliment, can't you honestly respond, "Thanks. I feel much better, too!"?

Never, never let anyone convince you that you're too thin if you feel great at your present weight, especially if that's the weight your doctor recommends. Friends and relatives may try to convince you that you looked better with "just a bit more weight" or that some people are simply meant to be on the heavy side. There are reasons why our loved ones may not be pleased with our weight loss. Change can be threatening to others. Eating and drinking love company, and our abstinence and self-control may make others uncomfortable. Competitiveness and jealousy might even be motivations. The misconception that more flesh on the bones means more robust health may still hold sway with some people.

On the other hand, if everyone seems to be telling you that you're too thin and losing too much weight, it makes sense to evaluate those concerns seriously and honestly. Are you perceiving yourself as you really are? Are you maintaining your low weight by practically starving yourself or making yourself miserable and nervous? Do you feel healthy? If you can satisfy yourself on these counts, stick to your guns. Tell them some people might be meant to be on the heavy side, but you're not one of them, and never will be again.

After five, or up to six or even eight weeks, you will have stabilized your weight. This is the beginning of the maintenance phase. That's another phase for the rest of your life.

STABILIZATION AT A GLANCE

Week One

- Weigh yourself daily.
- Maintain your dietary diary and exercise record.
- Add one vegetable carbohydrate serving to your current daily diet.
- Add 1 ounce of protein to your current daily diet for a total of 9 ounces for women, 11 ounces for men.
- Maintain daily exercise.
- Consume eight 8-ounce glasses of fluid daily.

Week Two

- Weigh yourself daily.
- Maintain your dietary diary and exercise record.
- If you have not gained or lost weight during the first week, add another vegetable carbohydrate. If you have lost weight, add one fruit carbohydrate.
- Add 1 ounce of protein for a total of 10 ounces for women, 12 ounces for men.

- Try to exercise one hour daily.
- Consume eight 8-ounce glasses of fluid daily.
- Work on your image of your new, slender self.

Week Three

- Weigh yourself daily.
- Maintain your dietary diary and exercise record.
- If you wish, you may add one more ounce of protein for a total of 11 ounces (13 ounces for men). Choose lean cuts of meat, white meat poultry, and fish.
- If you are still losing weight, add two servings of carbohydrate. These can be fruit, vegetable, or bread.
- If you are maintaining your weight, add one carbohydrate serving of your choice.
- Consume eight 8-ounce glasses of fluid daily.
- *AVOID SIMPLE SUGARS!*.

Week Four

- Weigh yourself daily.
- Maintain your dietary diary and exercise record.
- Add another ounce of protein if desired.
- You may now be approaching your maximum carbohydrate intake potential. Add one carbohydrate serving. If you gain weight, eliminate it.
- If you're not gaining weight, you may now add 1 teaspoon of oil to your daily diet.
- Continue to exercise daily.
- Consume eight 8-ounce glasses of fluid daily.

Week Five

- Weigh yourself daily.
- Maintain your dietary diary and exercise record.

- Only if you are now exercising extensively and feel that you can afford the added calories, add one more carbohydrate to your diet. Watch the scales carefully each day to be sure you don't gain any weight.

- If you wish, you may now have a glass of nonfat milk or a cup of nonfat yogurt in place of 1 ounce of protein and one carbohydrate.

- Consume eight 8-ounce glasses of fluid daily.

- At this point you are consuming a totally balanced diet and are able to consume all foods except simple sugars.

Week Six

- Weigh yourself daily.

- Maintain your dietary diary and exercise record.

- If your weight continues to fluctuate, carefully analyze your diary to determine what may be causing the weight gain or loss. Check: (1) exercise, (2) simple sugar consumption, (3) fat consumption, (4) fruit carbohydrate consumption, (5) total caloric intake. Adjust your daily diet as necessary. You may increase your exercise activity if you need to burn more calories.

- Consume eight 8-ounce glasses of fluid daily.

Week Seven and Forever

- Weigh yourself every other day.

- Add or subtract foods as needed to maintain weight.

- Maintain an energetic daily exercise regimen of brisk walking, bicycle riding, sports, or aerobics.

- Consume eight 8-ounce glasses of fluid daily.

- Practice relaxation techniques (pages 193–196) and improve your self-image.

- Enjoy your slender body and give yourself credit for success!

Chapter 11

MAINTAINING WEIGHT LOSS PERMANENTLY

Probably for the first time in your life, you have a good grasp of how your body works. You know just how much food you can eat daily without gaining or losing weight. You're feeling better because of your exercise program, and you're more in tune with your body. You're sleeping better at night, and you know how to be certain of a good night's rest. Using relaxation techniques (pages 193–196), you now feel calm and in control. You feel a strong sense of satisfaction, knowing that you've done something worthwhile in losing weight. It may well be that you've never felt better in your life. Now's the time to make a promise to yourself that this is the way you're going to feel for the rest of your life.

We'd be lying if we told you that everyone who ever lost weight with this program kept it off. But we can say that everyone who succeeded made a commitment to a lifetime of loving himself or herself enough to really care about his or her own well-being. It's up to you to make that commitment to yourself, to be absolutely certain that you won't harm yourself by regaining those pounds and inches. You now have the knowledge to make it all work, and the chapter on support will give you new skills that you can use when you need bolstering in your resolve.

Long before you fell into the metabolic trap that made you virtually helpless to lose weight, you began to gain weight slowly but surely. Regardless of the circumstances, and everyone has his or her own story to tell, that weight gain at the beginning was due to a surplus of calories and a deficit of physical activity. Only after you gained a significant amount of weight did your endocrine system join the enemy team to add to the pounds and inches. Once that happened, of course, you were out of control and almost any diet or program would have ended in failure.

But that's all changed now. You've escaped from the metabolic trap, and there's no reason to fall into it again. Massive weight gain begins with the gain of just one pound. There are two ways you can make sure you don't put on that one pound.

First, throughout the maintenance phase you can continue with the program for the last week of stabilization. Count the servings of protein and carbohydrates you eat each day, drink adequate water, exercise regularly, and weigh yourself every other day to make sure you haven't regained. This approach has worked for hundreds of men and women. You know it has worked thus far for you, and it can continue to do so forever.

Second, you can take the dietary approach that most medical and nutrition authorities agree is the ultimate way to maintain desired weight permanently and at the same time postpone the onset of degenerative disease and enhance longevity. Many people lose weight without even trying to do so when they change their diet to improve their health.

Just as simple sugar is the Number One Poison for those caught in the metabolic trap, fat is the Number One Killer when it comes to degenerative diseases including heart disease and cancer. The recommendation for a longer, healthier life is unequivocal: Eat less fat, especially less saturated fat and less cholesterol. By focusing on low fat intake, you may achieve two goals: maintaining ideal weight (without counting calories) and attaining optimal health.

Maintaining desired weight comes down to giving your body just enough food to support itself. Feed the body you want to have. If you give a 150-pound body enough food to feed a 200-pound body, predictably you'll have a 200-pound body. And, if you give a 200-pound body just enough food to feed a 150-pound body, you'll have a 150-pound body. But weight loss is not quite that simple, as you've learned through the years. When you stop feeding that 200-pound body, providing only enough for 150 pounds, the other

50 pounds start screaming: Feed me! Feed me! The challenge is to hold out long enough to make those 50 pounds disappear. And, as we now know so well, the influence of the metabolic trap makes the weight loss nearly impossible. If the weight loss you had to deal with originally was even more than 50 pounds, the odds against your success were astronomical.

But now, through this program, you've wiped the slate clean and are starting out again. You do weigh 150 pounds or 120 pounds or whatever your desired goal weight is. You can now learn to feed only those desired pounds. You may say that you've tried counting calories before and that can be a dismal and frustrating way to live your life. We couldn't agree more. There's a better way to do it.

KEEPING TRACK OF FAT INTAKE

The better way comes down to knowing how much fat you're eating daily. We've mentioned that medical authorities urge you to eat no more than 30 percent of your calories as fat. Such advice comes from nutritionists, dietitians, medical establishments, and government organizations, who point out that the percent of fat in the American diet reaches as high as 40 to 45 percent. But what does all this mean in terms of daily living? How can you go into a restaurant or supermarket and order 30 percent fat? Even when we want to follow this health recommendation, doing it is far from easy, and we soon give up.

Now we're going to tell you a simple way to determine and control your fat intake at 30 percent. As we explain this formula, you will understand even more clearly why exercise is essential for good health and desired weight. Remember that lean body mass, or muscle tissue, is your body's engine, and only such tissue burns energy in the form of calories. As you continue your exercise program, you'll develop more lean body mass to burn calories efficiently.

For a sedentary man it takes only about 12 calories to maintain a pound of body weight. If he increases his physical activity to the levels we've been recommending throughout this book, he'll boost the caloric requirement significantly. He will then need 15 calories to maintain a pound of weight. A woman's body, even at ideal weight, contains a higher percentage of fat, and females require fewer calories to maintain weight. For the sedentary woman 9 to 10 calories will maintain a pound of weight; the active woman will burn 13 or 14 calories a pound. The lower the amount of body fat and the higher the amount of lean muscle tissue, the greater the number of calories burned. And the more extensive the exercise program, the more calories burned.

That troublesome word "calorie" keeps popping up, but soon it can be completely forgotten. For the moment, however, let's use it for some calculation. We'll take two examples, a man and a woman, and we'll assume that both are moderately to extensively engaged in physical exercise, having completed the weight loss phase of this program.

Our male wants to maintain his weight at 150 pounds, and our female wants to maintain her 120 pounds. The man will require 15 calories per pound, the woman 13. Total calories for the day, then, will be 2,250 for the man and 1,560 for the woman.

$$150 \text{ pounds} \times 15 \text{ calories} = 2,250 \text{ calories per day}$$
$$120 \text{ pounds} \times 13 \text{ calories} = 1,560 \text{ calories per day}$$

Now, how much fat will our man and woman need for the day? We want them both to have 30 percent of their total calories as fat. So we multiply the total calories by .30 to give us 675 calories as fat for the man and 468 calories as fat for the woman.

$$2,250 \text{ total calories} \times .30 = 675 \text{ calories as fat}$$
$$1,560 \text{ total calories} \times .30 = 468 \text{ calories as fat}$$

But how can our examples determine what constitutes 675 or 468 calories as fat? How can they keep track of fat easily? We know that 1 gram of fat supplies 9 calories. So we can easily calculate how many grams of fat should be eaten daily by dividing the calories consumed daily as fat by 9 (the number of calories per gram). For the man this comes out to 75 grams of fat and for the woman 51.

$$\frac{675 \text{ calories}}{9 \text{ calories/gram}} = 75 \text{ grams of fat}$$

$$\frac{468 \text{ calories}}{9 \text{ calories/gram}} = 52 \text{ grams of fat}$$

If the man has 75 grams of fat daily, he'll eat 675 calories as fat. By simply keeping track of that amount of fat, it's highly unlikely that he can possibly consume more than 2,250 total calories for the day while following a balanced diet of good foods. The same holds true for the woman eating 52 grams of fat.

The next step is to be aware of the fat in your diet. How much is 75 or 52 grams of fat? The answer can be found in the super-market. Pick up a quart of milk or a loaf of bread or a can of pasta sauce and you'll see a listing of the amount of protein, carbohy-drates, and fat, as discussed in the chapter on nutrition. After just a while, you'll get to know how much fat there is in a glass of milk, a slice of bread, or a serving of sauce. And you'll know which brands to buy to get the least fat possible.

There are, of course, foods that don't come with a list of nutri-ents, such as fresh meats, fish, poultry, and fresh produce. That's why we've listed the fat content, along with other nutrient infor-mation, of many foods in the table in the appendix. Spend some time with that table and familiarize yourself with the foods you nor-mally eat. See what they actually contain in terms of fat, protein, and carbohydrate. We're not suggesting that you memorize the list; just by looking it over a few times, you will begin to have a better sense of just how much fat the foods you eat contain.

Would you gulp down a bubbling potion handed to you by a stranger without asking what's in it? Probably not. So why not question what's in the foods you eat? Just as that bubbling potion might be a deadly poison, some of the foods in the supermarkets contain dangerous amounts of the Number One Poison (simple sugars) and the Number One Killer (fats).

The gram-counting method was first developed in *The 8-Week Cholesterol Cure* as a way to reduce cholesterol levels for men and women at risk of heart disease owing to elevated counts of cholesterol in their blood. Many of the people following the program discovered to their pleasant surprise that they lost weight, if they began the program with a few pounds to shed. Those who were not overweight found to their delight that they could eat far larger amounts of food than they had been eating previously. Hundreds of letters came pouring in as testimony to the weight loss and maintenance potential of this program designed originally to deal with cholesterol levels.

Such a finding should not come as a surprise, however, if you just think about the calories coming from fat. As mentioned, each gram of fat contains at least 9 calories, whereas each gram of protein or carbohydrate contains 4. Throughout the weight loss phase of this program we've stressed the importance of choosing lean cuts of meat, fish, and poultry. Making those food selections means that you cut back on fat. So you've really been following two programs at the same time. We can guarantee that in addition to your weight loss, you've experienced a significant decline in cholesterol levels. How's that for a nice bonus?

Of course, one musn't assume that limiting the amount of fat in the diet allows one to go wild with simple carbohydrates as sugars. The simple sugars are still the Number One Poison when it comes to weight control. But, fortunately, the goals of avoiding excessive amounts of sugar and avoiding fat are not mutually exclusive.

Look at the foods listed in the table in the appendix and you'll see how many of the foods high in simple sugars are also high in fat. Cut back on or completely eliminate cookies, pies, cakes, ice cream, and chocolates, and you remove both fat and sugar from your diet. Overweight men and women didn't eat just hard candies for their treats as simple sugars. They, and many if not most other Americans, have been indulging in a deadly combination of the two worst components of the diet, fats and sugars.

ALCOHOL CONSUMPTION

Whether talking about health or weight loss, alcohol inevitably comes up. During weight loss and through stabilization we recommend the elimination of alcoholic beverages. There's no way to get around the calories they contribute to the diet, and when greatly restricting calories there's just no room for them.

But at this point you may not want to live without alcohol altogether. First, let's consider the health aspects of drinking. Certainly there's a significant risk of alcoholism, since one of every nine adults in the United States develops this disease. In alcoholics and heavy drinkers the liver pays a heavy price. Most deaths from liver disease, a leading cause of death in the United States, are attributable to alcohol abuse. There's no question that pregnant women should avoid alcohol to eliminate fetal alcohol syndrome. And, some patients must not drink owing to medical conditions such as hepatitis.

On the other hand, moderate alcohol consumption has been widely accepted in this and many other countries and cultures. There are even statistics indicating that moderate drinking is associated with greater longevity. As a specific example, levels of the protective HDL form of cholesterol are higher in drinkers than in nondrinkers, thereby affording some degree of protection from heart disease. The operational term here is "moderate" drinking.

But can one consume alcohol and maintain desired weight? Obviously, the answer is yes, since millions of people do so successfully. But alcoholic beverages are high in calories, and they are "empty" calories, offering no nutritive benefits. Alcohol tends to behave calorically more like a fat than a carbohydrate. It contains about 7 calories per gram, thus somewhere between fat and carbohydrates. (The caloric content of alcoholic beverages is listed in the table in the appendix.)

Moderate drinking is commonly defined as having no more than a drink or two daily. That might mean a cocktail before dinner or a glass or two of beer or wine with dinner. More than that can put on the pounds not only by way of the added calories, but also by lowering your guard against snack foods, which are frequently available at the times when significant drinking might occur. What begins as having just a peanut or two winds up as devouring the entire bowlful. It's no coincidence that salty peanuts and pretzels are supplied to tavern patrons; the salt produces thirst, which is quenched by more drinking, followed by more snacking, and on it goes.

We'd also like to throw cold water on the idea of the alcoholic nightcap. There's no worse thing you can do to destroy a good night's sleep. Alcohol before bed is likely to result in a restless night, interruption of deep sleep patterns, and an increased likelihood of awakening in the middle of the night unable to return to sleep. The same applies to the use of alcohol to anesthetize oneself against the adversities of life in general. Instead of that drink, take a brisk walk and a hot bath and read a good book to calm the nerves and restore the production of calming serotonin.

Determining just how much you can drink on a regular basis comes down to your personal metabolism. The woman who has a desired weight of only 100 pounds and who does little if any exercise will have a difficult time having even one drink without weight gain. The man who works out regularly in a gym, runs a few miles daily, and weighs 180 pounds of mostly lean tissue will be able to have a martini every night before dinner without gaining an ounce.

View the addition of alcohol to the diet in the same way you approached protein and carbohydrates during the period of stabilization. Have a drink or two in the evening for the next couple of days and check the results on your scale. If you gain weight by adding those alcohol calories while keeping your food calories constant, you'll have to cut down. Perhaps you'll find that one drink daily is your limit. Or maybe you'll prefer having two drinks every other day. As with other foods, you will have to titrate the amount you can ingest without weight gain. The 100-pound woman who finds that she gains weight by having just one drink may decide to make up for the additional calories by increasing her physical activity.

In no case, however, should you substitute alcohol for other foods. Alcohol provides absolutely no nutrition and cannot and should not be exchanged for food. The advice for the 100-pound woman holds true for anyone who finds that desired amounts of alcohol are not compatible with desired weight: Get more exercise to burn those excess calories.

LOSING SOME GAINED POUNDS

Remember your first attempts at riding a bicycle? As much as you persevered, you still fell off a lot. Try as you might to listen to all the good advice, you fell. But what happened after the fall? You got right back on and tried again. Finally, you got it down pat and wondered how it could ever have been difficult.

As much as we hope that you won't fall when it comes to maintaining your weight, there is a chance that it will happen. We're not referring to a pound or two that appears on the bathroom scale after a splurge weekend or a special dinner. You can handle such small deviations from your desired weight simply by cutting back on your carbohydrates and alcohol until the weight returns to normal. By diligently weighing yourself every other day you won't typically gain more than that 1 or 2 pounds, and those are rather easily shed now that you know just how your body works in relation to food and exercise.

Those episodes of 1- or 2-pound weight gains are merely slips, not falls. We're now getting down to outright falls, those times when you've completely abandoned your commitment to maintaining your weight.

Today you might shake your head and say, "Never! It won't happen to me. I worked too hard to get that weight off and I'm never going to gain it back!" We hope you're right. And there's no reason to believe that you aren't. Many people have maintained their weight loss for years.

But weight gain can occur. It may follow a major disruption such as a divorce, the loss of a job, or a significant disappointment. The reasons are not as important as the resultant weight gain. And that weight gain isn't as important as the resolve you must make as quickly as possible to get that weight off again. You've fallen, and now it's time to get right back up on your feet.

We divide weight regain into two basic categories: (1) gaining back all or a significant portion of your weight loss and (2) gaining back 5 to 10 pounds, more than can be easily handled by cutting back on a few foods or increasing your daily exercise. In both cases you've slipped back into insulin resistance and the metabolic trap, and you have to get your endocrine system back in order.

As you gain back weight, the same old syndrome returns: depression, water and sodium retention, poor sleep patterns, and an inability to lose the weight by cutting back on calories (even when the fat content of the diet is down to the grams of fat that you should have for your desired weight). The longer you remain in this state of insulin resistance, the more difficult it will be to reverse the process, to return your body to endocrine balance. So, the faster you return to your original commitment the better.

The solution, whether you fall into category 1 or 2, is to reenter the state of ketosis by severely restricting carbohydrates to less than 40 grams. Don't think that just because you've done it once before that you know all there is to know and that you can just call back the program from memory. Start at the beginning. Reread *all* the chapters and begin the program as though you had never done it before. Every chapter has a lesson in it for you. It's time to get back into a regular program of active exercise. It's necessary to relearn your lessons as to the amounts of foods you can eat daily, greatly restricting your carbohydrate intake.

If you've caught yourself when you have gained only 10 or 15 pounds, rather than after you've regained all your lost weight, you'll still have to follow the program as though you needed to lose 100 pounds. And regardless of the weight you are now committed to lose, you can count on the program to bring you back to goal weight faster and more efficiently than any other approach.

Once again, start a diet diary, carefully reporting everything you eat and drink during the day and the amount of exercise you do. Note the weight you set as your goal and the daily changes as you get closer to that desired weight.

Do not take any short-cuts. This is the fastest way possible to lose weight safely. Any short-cuts you may take, such as omitting the diary or not doing the relaxation techniques, will short-circuit the plan.

Take out your diary from the first time you lost weight and compare notes. You'll gain support from reading the progress you made last time and be reliving both the difficult times and the moments of success you recorded at the time.

But more important than anything else, you must come to grips with whatever it was that led you away from your commitment to yourself. What has happened to cause you to fall out of love with yourself to such an extent that you have allowed weight gain to occur?

Weight gain of significant proportions isn't simply a matter of having a piece of birthday cake or enjoying a party with all its temptations. You didn't gain that weight because the taste of the food was so wonderful that you just couldn't stop yourself. You know very well that no food in the world can compare to the happiness you feel when you're at desired weight and feeling terrific.

So get right back to the chapter on support. Read it and reread it. Stand in front of the mirror and say that you love yourself despite what you've done to your body. You're the same person who deserved to lose the weight in the first place, and you deserve to get rid of those extra pounds right now.

Do not—repeat—*do not* wait for the emotional or financial turmoil that caused your regain to pass before going back to weight loss and maintenance. Don't use that as an excuse. Try to view the situation from outside yourself. Would you withhold your fullest love and attention from the dearest person in your life until problems passed? Would you tell your child that you couldn't love him or her, couldn't do anything for him or her until the conditions changed? Of course not. So why deny that love from the person you should love the most in the whole world: YOU?

If this is a time of a major disturbance in life-style, you might well seek some professional assistance. It's never a sign of weakness to ask for help. And such support may mean a far easier time both in terms of weight loss and of getting over your current hurdles.

Tell yourself that you forgive yourself. Give yourself a special treat: a massage, a manicure, a pedicure, just to show yourself how much you care. You're worth it. And you're worth the effort to get right back on track with this program. You did it once, and you can do it again.

We have one word of warning, however. You must be aware that it may be more difficult the second and subsequent times to get back into ketosis. It's as though you've used this trick on the dragon that guards the metabolic trap before, and now he's wise to your craftiness. That doesn't mean that it's impossible to reenter ketosis, but only that it'll be a bit more difficult. By knowing that in advance, you should be able to cope with the frustration you may feel.

Keep at it. Pretty soon you'll look yourself in the mirror and say, "Congratulations on your weight loss!" Now's the time to commit again to a vow to maintain that weight loss permanently. As is true for the person who quits smoking or stops drinking or using drugs, it's not the times you tried and slipped or fell that count, it's the time you finally succeeded permanently. The former smoker and the recovering alcoholic do not think about anything except their current freedom from addiction. Now that you're at desired weight, enjoy your success and your good health. You've done it and you're glad. Congratulations!

• • •

As you read these pages you may feel that this is all very complicated and that you'll have a difficult time keeping track of all the elements of fat, carbohydrates, protein, alcohol, and exercise in order to maintain desired weight on a permanent basis. For you, as for anyone embarking on a new venture, we can only offer the encouraging words that it will soon become second nature to you. Think of the time when you first learned to ride a bicycle, ski down a hill, or hit a golf ball straight down the fairway. Your instructor told you to do several things at once and you thought at the time that it was impossible to do so. But you persevered and you learned and you succeeded. You will succeed at weight maintenance as well.

Chapter 12

LIFE CHANGES AND SUPPORT STRATEGIES FOR SUCCESS

Whether you have always been heavy or put on weight later in life, food played only a partial role in your overweight development. Those who believe that simply sticking to a diet will make unwanted pounds disappear permanently are due for certain failure. The only way to achieve lasting success is to restructure your life-style in a meaningful way. As effective as the Insulin Control Diet is, the program is incomplete—and harder to follow—without life-style change.

You might be convinced that it's food, not life-style or behavior, that's been your problem. If you have just 2 or 3 pounds to lose, you would probably be right. Even weight gains of 5 to 10 pounds, say after a long vacation or over the holidays, can frequently be coped with if one has sufficient motivation. But as much as we wish it weren't so, one scientific fact remains: Excessive weight is a long-term result of too many calories and too little exercise. And, if those pounds remain as fat tissue and you continue to gain weight, the problems of the endocrine system kick in. Once a person has become substantially insulin resistant, weight loss becomes difficult if not impossible, especially on a permanent basis. Often as a person gains more weight, he or she does even less physical activity. Wrong foods eaten at the wrong times for the wrong reasons make the metabolic trap close even tighter. So foods and the diet must be viewed as part of the total lifestyle.

A MATTER OF MOTIVATION

Most decisions in life seem relatively unimportant. We can decide to start playing golf, and later decide to give it up and sell the clubs. We can change hairstyles and if we don't like them, the hair will grow back. But there are some decisions which require a concerted commitment backed by heartfelt motivation.

How do you develop the motivation to make weight control a lifelong effort? Seldom is it entirely an intellectual decision. Whether it's weight control or cigarette smoking cessation or other lifestyle modification, there must be a degree of passion.

While no one can give you that passion, or teach it to you, sometimes one can be inspired by another's story. With that in mind, I (Bob Kowalski) would like to share with you the reason why I watch my own diet scrupulously.

No, I've never had a weight problem. If anything, I've always been on the slender side. My problem is heart disease. I suffered a heart attack and bypass surgery in 1978 at the age of 35. Then just six years later I was told that I'd need a second operation. But, oh, the difference between the two events.

In 1984 when my cardiologist told me my disease had deteriorated and the arteries were clogged again, I had two small children. Ross was six and Jenny was three. The surgeon was blunt: a repeat bypass was five to six times more risky than the first, and there was a significant chance that I might not get off that operating table.

I went home that day to an empty apartment. My wife was teaching school, Ross was in kindergarten, and Jenny was in preschool. All alone, I thought about my kids growing up without their Daddy. And I cried bitterly.

After the tears came the anger and then the determination to beat the disease. I knew that my elevated cholesterol level was a major cause of my disease, and I vowed that if all went well in surgery, I'd control it.

From that day forward, and now that means more than 11 years, I stuck to my diet scrupulously. No cheeseburger in the world could take the place of watching one of Ross's little league baseball games. No hot fudge sundae could replace the joy of being at Jenny's next birthday party. Those kids are my life—not food! The choice was, and remains, obvious.

That's my passion. That's my own reason for my commitment. That day in the apartment was my moment of epiphany.

Think about it. Don't you have enough passion in your life to, quite literally, save your own life?

The decision ultimately is yours. I'll never forget a time in Dr. Ezrin's office when he said—with true passion in his voice and in his eyes: "There is no better treatment for Type II diabetes, there really isn't!" You have the program at your disposal. We've provided the information, but you have to provide the passion to make it work for yourself!

LOVING YOURSELF AND EXPECTED LIFE CHANGES

Certainly one needs to modify behavior for long-term success, and many of the behavior modification tricks and techniques we read about in magazines are useful. But more fundamentally, and as a first step to revamping your life-style, you probably need to change your attitude.

Your approach to living comes down first to loving. Do you really love yourself? Enough to want the very best for yourself? Enough to do whatever it takes to get the very best?

If you answer yes to loving yourself, how can it be that you've been willing to carry the extra pounds that prevent fullest enjoyment of life and threaten life itself? If you answered no, perhaps you are not giving yourself enough credit for loving. You did, after all, start reading this book, didn't you? Probably you do love yourself, and have the potential to do so, but just as we don't always act in loving ways to those who are dear to us, we don't always know *how* to love ourselves faithfully and fully. It can be difficult to love yourself when the world seems to condemn you for being overweight. Even parents, if they're not overweight themselves, criticize children for those extra pounds. And every glance in the mirror seems to confirm the world's opinions: How can I love myself when I look like this?

It's time to make a commitment to loving yourself unconditionally. We're not so naive as to believe you can simply make that decision and have it happen like some sort of lightning flash out of the sky. It may have taken quite a few years to fall out of love with yourself, and it may take a while to fall back in love. There was a time when you did love yourself completely and unconditionally. As children, we all had innate self-love. We had to learn not to love ourselves. And now it's time to regain that child-like self-love.

Just as a marriage counselor might advise a squabbling couple to reacquaint themselves, remembering the things that first drew them together as a couple, we advise you to give yourself a chance to learn what a terrific person you really are. You're not just OK. You're wonderful!

Take a moment right now to jot down a few particularly nice things about yourself. Perhaps you are honest, trustworthy, or devoted to duty. Maybe you are especially willing to give of yourself to others. You might have career and professional achievements. Think about the physical features you've gotten compliments about over the years. Your hair. Your eyes. Your skin. Almost every person has at least one or two beautiful features. Have you forgotten about yours?

Even if you find it easier to think of your flaws, why not view your flawed self with the same compassion you give to the other people you love? Do you expect them to be perfect? Do you withhold love from them when they're not? You really are worth loving. You don't have to earn love by being perfect. To love yourself on an unconditional basis means not when you lose those pounds, but today. Not when you get your promotion, but today. Not when you find someone who tells you they love you, but today. There's no reason to be reserved or cautious; love yourself absolutely.

Next, prove it to yourself by doing some nice things for yourself. Go to the bookstore and buy that book you've been wanting to read. Go to a movie matinee. Bring home fresh flowers from the supermarket. Make it a point to do something particularly nice for yourself every week. And every day give yourself at least a gesture of your own esteem. Every person loves to hear someone say "I love you." Start saying that to yourself daily, not only in words but in deeds. Look yourself in the mirror and say "I really do love you." And as someone who is truly loved, you want the best for yourself.

Part of giving yourself the best is making an absolute commitment to this program. No turning back or finding excuses this time. You know you're in good medical hands, and this is the best possible program. After all, you don't want someone you love to be at increased risk of disease, do you? Reducing weight will reduce that risk. You want someone you love to live a long time, and this program can increase longevity. And you want your loved ones to feel good about themselves and be full of energy.

How can you ensure that commitment to the program? You need more than willpower; you need assistance in developing self-control. You could check into a hospital or clinic and have your environment and your diet controlled for you. You definitely would lose weight, but if you didn't learn techniques for making this a permanent lifestyle change, it's likely that you would gain the weight back.

You've already taken the first step in changing your life-style by making the commitment to love yourself. And you've placed your faith in the ability of this program to help you lose weight. There are also behavioral changes you can make that will enhance your success. But it's not just a matter of learning techniques; rather, you must make a commitment to doing those things that can help remove the harmful habits that have contributed to your condition of overweight. We're not just talking about tricks, such as using smaller plates to make food appear more plentiful. We're referring to new ways of dealing with your environment and the food in that environment. You can't possibly change all the negative behaviors in your life in a day, a week, or even a month. Give yourself the time it takes to make some real and profound changes. Read this chapter over and over again until it really sinks in.

Take a few minutes to review your own reasons for wanting to lose weight at this moment in life. These can be vital sources of inspiration when the program seems difficult. One good way to focus on your personal motivation for achieving and maintaining desired weight is to think about the ways your life will change when you succeed.

Make a list of how your life will change, or if you're at your goal weight, how it has changed already. Write down your feelings, and then come back to review your words from time to time. You'll find that by doing so you'll strengthen your resolve, both by reminding yourself of your reasons and by the satisfaction of seeing the predicted changes coming true.

The changes you can expect will be in a number of areas, some more important to you than others. We've provided a few guidelines, but feel free to add others, or write your own list.

- Life Changes Expected in Personal Growth
- Life Changes Expected in Self-Esteem
- Life Changes Expected in Health
- Life Changes Expected in Career
- Life Changes Expected in Social Life

CLARIFYING GOALS

The expectations of change are your motivation to realize your weight loss goals. Now let's look at what those goals are. Be realistic in your goals. You may not expect to become a fashion model (unless you were one before gaining weight), but you do have distinct goals. Nearly all successful people do set definite and achievable goals in order to turn dreams into reality. By seeing the light at the end of the tunnel you can focus your efforts more clearly, and you can start to measure your success on a step-by-step basis.

Let's turn to the analogy of a college education. That is the goal for a freshman first setting foot on campus. But to get to that goal, he or she must first achieve some significant subgoals, such as completing a course, passing an examination, writing a thesis, and so forth. Looking at the pile of books, reports, and tests a student must get through in the coming years would be enough to make any freshman turn tail and run. Instead, the freshman will pick up the books and assignments for that first semester and go on from there. Sticking with it, our freshman will become a sophomore, then a junior, a senior, and on to graduation. As the saying goes, inch by inch it's a cinch, but yard by yard it's very hard.

What are your broad goals? How many pounds do you want to lose? Focus on a realistic, achievable goal. Perhaps the weight you remember in high school. Or before your baby was born. Or before your career started gobbling all your time.

And there's more to this program than just lost pounds. You will also achieve a gradual but certain reduction in your measurements. In fact, even at times when it seems as though the pounds aren't disappearing as you hoped they would, the inches will continue to decrease.

Before starting the program, take a few minutes to measure your body. Write the measurements down, both pounds and inches, on the Body Measurement Record on the next page. Mark the date. Then return to note your improvements over time.

Now it's time to start clarifying your picture of your soon-to-be self. Close your eyes and imagine yourself with those pounds and inches reduced. Bring that picture into sharper focus by mentally arranging your clothing. Are you wearing a suit, slacks and sweater, swimsuit? Are you standing in your office or on the beach? Is the picture the way you appeared a few years ago?

If you were once the weight you now want to achieve, you can help clarify your mental image by looking at a photograph taken when you were at your desired weight. If no such photos are available, scan through a few magazines until you find a picture of someone you can model yourself after. But be realistic: Looking at pictures in *Playboy* or *Vogue* or *Gentlemen's Quarterly* won't do the trick. Concentrate on that picture of yourself. Burn it into your consciousness as one of the major accomplishments for the future and one of the most important efforts today. Each day in the coming weeks you'll want to call that image up in your mind, and each week you'll be closer to looking like that mental image.

As a sign of commitment to attaining and maintaining the goal

Body Measurement Record

Date	Pounds	Waist	Hips	Thighs	Upper Arms	Chest

weight, the formerly overweight person should simply get rid of oversized clothes. Keeping large clothes in the closet is inviting the inevitable weight gain. In doing so you're actually saying that your ideal weight is only temporary, and you'll be ready for the return of your old weight. Jackie Gleason kept three full wardrobes at all times, in large, medium, and slender sizes. He had no real expectation at any time to keep his weight down.

Some of the people who have succeeded most dramatically in losing weight have had their clothes taken in by a tailor every step of the way. Those who can afford to do so buy new outfits to keep up with their changing figures. None keep the old sizes hanging in the closet.

You've made a commitment to weight loss, and this time you really mean it. If you had just enrolled in college, you'd tell your friends and relatives. So tell them now that you've decided that with the help of this book and its program you're going to lose the weight that has been adversely affecting your life. Tell them in strong, positive tones.

You're accomplishing a great deal by making this sort of declaration to everyone around you. By telling them now that you no longer will eat certain foods, they won't be surprised later. You won't be tempted to have that special something that your mother or friend cooked or baked "just for you." If they persist in their temptations, remind them that you informed them clearly and unequivocally that you wouldn't be eating that food any longer.

You'll also be burning bridges behind you. There's no turning back on your commitment. You've told these people that you'll be losing weight on a regular and predictable basis. So now you'll have to deliver on your promise. But remember that it's *you*, not them, to whom your promise really matters.

When you make your announcements, enlist the help and support of all those around you. We all need all the help we can get, especially when it comes to particularly important projects. And when it comes to weight loss, friends and relatives can actually sabotage your efforts more effectively than all the television and magazine food advertisements you can imagine. We'll give you some specific defenses against such sabotage later in this chapter.

But people like to be asked for help, and when they feel their contribution will be of value, they are often eager to cooperate.

Would one or more of your friends like to lose weight also? Perhaps you can establish a little circle of support by doing the program together. Having a friend or two to lose weight with can help get through some of the tougher moments of temptation and frustration. Some of the greater successes with this program have been with patients who followed the program together.

But beware of the flip side to this coin. If your friend does not make a complete commitment to the program in the same way that you have, he or she could become a barrier to your success. Having abandoned the diet in favor of a box of chocolates and a cheesecake, your friend may well attempt to get you off the program as well. He or she can make it more difficult for you, and the last thing you need is sabotage.

PHYSICAL ACTIVITY

What you do need, however, is physical activity. We discussed exercise in Chapter 9, but here we are talking about physical activity as a part of one's life-style. It's a matter of movement. Some overweight people have made an art of avoiding all but the most necessary physical movement. They cruise around trying to find a parking place directly in front of a store, rather than park a block away and walk there. They take elevators and escalators, rather than climb stairs. They mail order merchandise from catalogs, rather than go to a store to shop. They use remote control for changing television channels, rather than get out of a chair. They even use prepared foods, rather than cook from scratch.

The result of such lack of movement is that the calorie-burning engine shuts down. With so little muscular activity, the body stores rather than uses incoming fuels. So not only does the person consume more calories than necessary in terms of energy used, the metabolism of the body slows down, further reducing the need for calories. Add to that metabolic slowdown the development of insulin resistance and its concomitant sodium and water retention and fat storage, and you have an inevitable and progressive state of obesity.

In addition to your daily exercise program (as described in Chapter 9), we want you to increase the amount of movement in your everyday life. But don't do it just because we're telling you to; do it because you love yourself. The next time you have a chance to climb stairs, do so. When you go shopping or out to an appointment, park the car at least a block away from the door. As time goes on, make that a block and a half, then two blocks.

Modern technology has given us a number of convenient work savers. Start turning them off. Use the old-fashioned way of getting things done. Chop vegetables by hand instead of using the food processor when making the family's meals. Use the hand mower instead of the power mower to cut the lawn. Every little bit helps to burn calories and increase the metabolic rate of your body. When secretaries were given electric typewriters to replace their manual machines in a study done many years ago, the women uniformly gained weight. You'd never imagine that such a little thing would matter. But, again, every little bit helps or hurts.

RELAXING ACTIVITIES

While we want you to do more physical activity, we also want you to relax more and to relax more often. That's not really a contradiction. A relaxed person is less likely to reach for food. A relaxed person will sleep better and will awaken refreshed to start another day of physical activity. But just as overweight people have often forgotten how to exercise, they also have lost track of beneficial relaxation.

The person who has made lack of movement an art form might think not doing anything is a kind of relaxation. But sitting and watching television with the aid of the remote control does not necessarily promote a relaxed, peaceful state; often quite the opposite is true, since activity loosens (relaxes) muscles.

At the opposite extreme is the person who works continually and "has no time" to relax. But there's always time to grab a calorie-laden snack, or to become upset over a traffic snarl, or to have three martinis before dinner to calm down.

Both extremes need to take the time to learn some techniques to make their periods of relaxation more productive in terms of weight loss and the enjoyment of life in general. Once again, the first step is to make a commitment to doing some relaxing activities every single day. We use the term "relaxing activities" to emphasize that what we recommend is more than doing nothing. You have to put some concentrated energy into being fully relaxed.

As with exercise, a type of relaxing activity that works well for one person might not be effective for another. Some relaxation techniques can be done alone, while others involve a group. And some types require some equipment. Finding something that works for you and that you can and will do regularly is the key to success.

At the beginning many people find that they appreciate assistance. For them a yoga or meditation class can be helpful. Today such classes are offered in practically every community. Check out the programs at the local YMCA/YWCA as well as those offered in health clubs, spas, and hospitals.

Yoga is a system of physical poses and postures that enables one to concentrate on relaxing both the mind and the body. It brings one more in tune with one's body, especially after perhaps years of inactivity, and helps limber up unused joints. Once the techniques are learned, yoga exercises can be done at home, at the office, or on vacation. And one can continue to attend classes for group support.

Meditation classes teach techniques for concentrating more fully on bringing the mind and body to a state of relaxed awareness. One type of meditation is called biofeedback. It uses an apparatus designed to measure galvanic skin response (in the same way lie detectors work) to determine the state of anxiety or relaxation an individual is in. Using this principle on a crude level, one could hold a fever thermometer in the grip of one's hand and read the temperature. A cold reading indicates stress, while a warm reading, in the range of the mid 80s, denotes relaxation. By then concentrating purposefully on raising the skin temperature, the state of relaxation deepens. Biofeedback devices are available to help that concentration by providing a constant tone on which to focus one's thoughts thus ridding the mind of irritating thoughts.

Most of us are unable to go for long without falling victim to negative thoughts and feelings. But as time goes on, especially with the assistance of relaxation techniques, we can improve our ability to concentrate on a pleasant concept or a neutral tone in order to relax.

If you prefer to begin your efforts in relaxation on your own, a few suggestions can help you succeed. Select a location where you can be alone for 10 to 15 minutes at a time. That may mean disconnecting the telephone for a while or telling your secretary to hold calls. It may necessitate going off to a separate room, into the garage, or sitting in a parked car.

Darken the area as much as possible. You may find that some types of music can help you stop thinking about everyday problems. The so-called New Age music is specifically designed to do just that. Such music is restful, employing soft guitar strains, harp stylings, and electronically engineered sound effects. Try listening to a recording with headphones. Then close your eyes and conjure up a pleasant idea or memory. This is called imagery.

The effectiveness of such imagery has been proven amazingly beneficial in blocking out much of the world around you. In some cases an individual—a teacher, group leader, therapist, or even a friend—will guide the imagery by telling a subject to concentrate on a given scene, describing that scene as it evolves. Perhaps it will be a guided mental tour through a path in the woods or a stroll down a beach. Details of the landscape, the scattered pine cones or the driftwoods washed to shore, are brought to mind, as the listener focuses thoughts entirely on that scene.

This guided imagery has been used by cancer specialists to help patients receiving chemotherapy. By concentrating on a soothing, peaceful scene, the patient can block out the negative images of the medication being injected. Frequently the nausea often associated with chemotherapy can be eliminated by using guided imagery.

Give imagery a try when you begin to take moments out from your day to relax. You'll find that your skills will grow with practice. In time you'll be able to transport yourself to the scenes of your choice: a beach, park, forest, or desert. Describe to yourself all the elements of your picture, as though you were describing it to a blind person. Worked into your daily routine, the art of relaxation by such forms of meditation can assist your efforts at weight loss.

In fact, you can go a step further and guide yourself in imagery relating to your weight. Draw a mental picture of yourself as you would like to appear. Daily refer to that mental image and compare it with your current weight, noting how the pounds and inches are disappearing. Many patients have found such imagery to be astoundingly effective and have succeeded at weight loss far better than others who do not use this technique.

As with exercise, your relaxation practices should not be limited to a specified period of time daily. Try to find frequent, short periods of time when you can relax. If you're caught in a traffic jam during rush hour, focus on pleasant thoughts, put on some relaxing music, and concentrate on not becoming irritated by the delays. If you are waiting for a late appointment, don't fret and keep looking at your watch. Instead, take the time to close your eyes and relax. Or take along some light reading so you can pass the time enjoyably.

MODIFYING YOUR FOOD BEHAVIOR

A key to permanent weight loss is to broaden the scope of your lifestyle horizons to avoid situations that have contributed to your present overweight condition. By that we mean replacing food-related situations with those that are incompatible with eating. Instead of continually munching on snacks while watching television, engage in an activity using your hands. It's hard to grab for a potato chip when you're knitting or building a ship in a bottle. Not only do such hobbies eliminate the temptation of snacking, but they also help you to enter a state of relaxation. Instead of centering social engagements around food, make other plans with friends, such as a walk at the botanical gardens or a drive to the beach.

The only way to zero in on all your food habits is to keep a strict food diary. Record everything you put into your mouth, both food and beverages, including times you take a drink to wash down medications or vitamins. Note the time of day, where you are when you consume, and circumstances. You might comment, for example, that you ate or drank something because of bad news just received or because you needed a reward for a tough time gotten through. Be sure to make daily entries and to keep the diary not just for a day or a week but for the months while you lose weight and learn to keep the pounds and inches off permanently.

Next, do some planning. If you have a party to go to, you know that food and drink will be served and that friends and relatives will urge you to have "just a little." Plan for that in advance. What are you going to say? How will you keep your hands busy? When offered a drink, there's no need to order a glass of water with a dour expression on your face. Instead, ask for a Perrier on ice with a twist of lemon peel. The attitude you take and the appearance of the drink itself can make all the difference in the world.

Record your victories in your diet diary. Read back through your diary now and then to see how much easier it's becoming to stick to the program. Entries at the beginning may reflect difficulties that won't be problems a few weeks later.

We'd now like to share with you some ways you can modify your behavior when it comes to food. Make an effort to implement these techniques and make them a regular part of your lifestyle.

Many good intentions for proper dieting are abandoned in the aisles of the supermarket. There are some definite do's and don'ts that can eliminate the hazards of shopping. Practice them regularly and they'll become an automatic part of your behavior.

Plan your grocery shopping on a weekly basis and do not vary from your shopping list, even if you see a spectacular buy. Prepare that list after, not before, a meal. The same applies to the shopping itself. Never go to the store on an empty stomach. Plan menus for a week and put on your shopping lists all the ingredients you need for the meals. Such planning will not only help you to stay on the diet, but will make life easier by making it organized.

If you are planning meals for others besides yourself, whenever possible, try to center the meal around the foods that you'll be eating as part of the diet. The others can simply have more of those foods than you will. And perhaps a side-dish or two can be prepared to fill out their calorie needs. Remember, too, that *everyone* will be better off cutting back on fat.

Don't shop from memory. If you've forgotten your list, go home and get it. Don't shop with others, unless they are also on the diet. Don't tempt yourself by buying snack foods or foods that were your favorites. And don't buy more food than you'll need for that week.

When you come home from shopping, immediately put all foods away out of sight. If you must keep snack foods in the house for other members of the family, keep them far away from areas you use frequently. If possible, have the children keep such foods in their rooms in tightly closed containers. Perhaps your spouse can take such foods off to the office or other workplace. Explain to your family that, at least for a while, just seeing those foods can sway you from your good intentions. Keeping them stored away will be an act of love on your family's part. It's a small thing to ask.

If there are foods in the house that you were particularly fond of and other members of the family don't eat, it's best to throw them out if you can't give them away. Don't worry about the waste.

Make it difficult for yourself to get to food quickly. Store foods in nontransparent containers so you can't see them. Remove the light bulb in the refrigerator to make it more difficult to find foods. Discard any leftovers lest you become tempted to eat them just to get them out of the house. Perhaps you can feed leftovers to your dog so you're not wasting food.

If you prepare food for your family, whenever possible do it when you yourself have already eaten. Cooking on an empty stomach can test the strongest resolve. Other family members can also eat the foods you'll be eating on this diet, along with carbohydrate items you'll avoid. Everyone can benefit by reducing fat intake. Again, ask them to go along with this out of love for you. But if it can't be done, don't let their foods tempt you.

While you're cooking, food aromas can be stimulating to the point of distraction. Minimize those aromas by turning on the kitchen exhaust fan and by covering pots of simmering foods.

Especially at the start of the program, stick entirely with the recipes provided in this book. And measure ingredients precisely and accurately to be sure that you're not consuming calories and carbohydrates you're not aware of.

This is the time to learn to measure food properly. To do so, you'll need some basic kitchen equipment. Buy a good food scale that weighs foods down to the fraction of an ounce. If you don't already have them, get measuring cups and spoons. Don't rely on your perceived notion of what an ingredient weighs or measures in volume. Take the time to make measuring a routine part of cooking. It'll help now and in the many years to come.

The recipes call for specific amounts of ingredients, all designed to stay within daily calorie limits and to maintain ketosis by restricting carbohydrates. Needless to say, it will defeat the purpose of such recipes if the ingredients are not measured precisely. During the period of stabilization and maintenance, when you are gradually adding portions of foods, you'll want those portions to be properly measured to ensure success.

When serving foods, put only the proper amounts on the table. Don't tempt yourself into taking second helpings. If your family eats with you, put your food on your own plate in the kitchen and don't eat from any other plates or serving utensils.

We start changing eating behavior by assessing when and where food will be eaten. Many overweight individuals eat on an almost continuous basis throughout the day. A careful and honest review of your habits will put your eating habits into perspective for you. As part of this program, we will ask you to restrict your eating to three meals and one snack per day. That's four eating times daily, and that should be enough to satisfy. If you've been eating more frequently than that, you'll have to break that habit to end the years of overweight.

Not only do we want you to limit yourself to three meals and a snack each day, we want you to eat those three meals and a snack every day. Don't try to improve on the diet or to speed up your progress by skipping meals. We want you not only to lose weight, but also to learn proper eating habits for the rest of your life. That means scheduling regular meals. We emphasize the word regular because it's best to have those meals at just about the same times each day. Many overweight individuals got that way by skipping a meal here and there and "making up for it" with huge meals later on in the day. Eating regular meals will help stabilize your blood sugar and your insulin level.

Remember, too, *why* you must eat. Although we all enjoy the tastes, appearances, and aromas of foods, the pleasures of physically chewing and swallowing, and the social rituals of eating, the basic reason we eat is to give our bodies nourishment. We should eat to live, rather than live to eat. All other reasons must be considered secondary, especially the many reasons we use to justify our unnecessary eating. We snack at parties to be social and celebrate. We gorge when feeling sorry for ourselves. We nibble to keep ourselves company when we're alone. We munch to have something to do with our hands while doing something entirely unrelated.

We've discussed why we eat and when; *where* we eat can be equally important. Especially if you've been eating virtually nonstop from morning till night, or if you've concentrated your eating into a period of the day, such as in the evening starting with dinner and ending with bedtime, you've been eating everywhere. Food has accompanied you into the living room, the bedroom, the laundry room, the bathroom, the office, the car, and beyond. Beginning now, there's only one proper place to eat your meals: at the dining room table.

For many overweight patients that's a stiff order, one that takes a lot of getting used to. But simply limiting your food consumption to the dinner table will automatically eliminate a large portion of calories typically consumed. But it also allows you to concentrate on eating, which will make you more satisfied.

At designated times of the day, prepare your food and serve it to yourself at the table, even if the table is outside the home, at the office or elsewhere. Make the plate of food attractive, perhaps by garnishing with parsley or a sprig of mint. Look forward to eating the food and enjoy every bite. Eat it without gulping. We want to slow down the process of eating.

Some well-known techniques of behavior modification for weight loss involve slowing down the speed of food consumption.

The researchers who first suggested this approach made the assumption that overweight men and women eat their food rapidly and that by slowing the process down they would eat less food and be more satisfied by it. While there is no evidence that overweight individuals eat any faster than slender people, by following some of these suggestions, one can decrease the amount of food consumed and enhance enjoyment of it. Even if you feel that you don't currently wolf down meals, you will benefit by employing some of the following suggestions.

Take small bites of food. Concentrate on tasting the food rather than swallowing it immediately. Focus on the effect of the food on your lips, teeth, and tongue. Chew it thoroughly. Decades ago, a researcher named Fletcher advocated the chewing of each mouthful of food exactly 28 times. The nation was filled with people "Fletcherizing" their food. While his rationale for the practice, that it aided proper digestion, has fallen under criticism and the practice is no longer followed, chewing food thoroughly has other benefits.

Swallow *before* you take the next bite. Put down your knife and fork while chewing, thus making a distinct separation between mouthfuls of food. You can practice becoming a food dallier by deliberately taking breaks in eating a meal. Even after food has been swallowed, wait a few seconds before cutting off the next bite. As time goes on, those delays between mouthfuls can increase from those few seconds up to half a minute and more.

Regardless of the type of food you're eating, do use utensils. Even if nibbling at finger foods, use a fork, if possible, to pick up the morsels. This helps to make you pay attention to what and how much you are eating, rather than absentmindedly putting food in your mouth. You might even try to eat some meals with chopsticks to slow the process down further.

When you're finished with your food at that meal, don't delay at the table. Get up and immediately clean off the plates, utensils, and cookware. If you're cleaning the plates of others, don't be tempted into taking even the smallest taste of any leftover uneaten food. Remind yourself that you will eat only what is on your plate while you are seated at the dinner table.

In all matters related to food for you and your family, try to enlist the cooperation of others. If they're not already doing so, your children and spouse can certainly share in the chores. In fact, the more you can separate yourself from the family's foods during the initial period of weight loss, the better off you'll be. And you'll also save yourself and your family from the anger and resentment that might arise in you when as a dieting person you must prepare, serve, and clean up after the meals that you're unable to enjoy yourself.

SUPPORT STRATEGIES

Love yourself enough to enlist the help of others. Expect them to love you enough to provide that help and to support, not sabotage, your weight loss efforts.

Most importantly, love yourself enough to follow through with your weight loss commitment even if you don't get the support of others. It can be difficult, but you can do it. The suggestions that follow are designed to help you in the coming days, weeks, and months of your weight loss and maintenance. Try reading only one section at a time, and integrate each suggestion into your life before going on to the next. In time, you'll be actively engaged in following several recommendations at once.

These support strategies are based on hundreds of cases of men and women who successfully lost weight with this program. Many ideas spring from the weekly support group meetings held in Dr. Ezrin's office during which patients exchange thoughts they've had during the week. They bring recipe ideas, newspaper items dealing with current events that relate to weight, and questions and concerns, and they receive information, answers, and comfort.

We regret that you're unable to come to these support group sessions since they are enormously helpful. You might consider forming a group of your own. We can at least tell you about thoughts and feelings that have come up repeatedly as new groups have formed over the years. We offer these with the sincere hope that as you read them, you'll feel that we're there with you in spirit and support.

Support Strategy 1: Tell the World

You've made a commitment to weight loss; this time you know you'll succeed. It's time to tell your friends, relatives, associates, and anyone who could possibly have an influence on your eating habits the good news. Tell them you've begun a program you have confidence in and that you will not sway from your resolve no matter what.

This is the time to be assertive. You don't have to be nasty in rejecting their offers of foods and drinks. To assert oneself, *Webster's New World Dictionary* states, is to insist on one's rights. Surely you have a right to be healthy and happy, and that's really what weight loss is all about.

If necessary, make a list of everyone who might be in a position to affect your diet. Make it a point to talk with each of them before a food situation comes up. Don't wait until you're visiting someone's home and they ask you to have "just one slice of this cake—I made it just for you." After all, you're a nice person, and you don't want to hurt anyone's feelings.

Explain to people that you're on "doctor's orders" not to eat certain foods. If further explanation is required, tell them that your body cannot tolerate simple carbohydrates, and for a while you're following a strict dietary regimen that's been medically documented to help those with conditions such as yours. It will be up to you if you want to go into the details of insulin resistance. But, regardless of circumstances, make it clear that you will not accept foods and drinks not permitted in the weight loss program. Perhaps you've never before been forceful about something terribly important to you. This is a good time to start.

One patient described what was, in perspective, an amusing story of how she had to "fight off" offers of a sweet potato pie during the Christmas holidays. Her hostess maintained that the pie was baked with absolutely no sugar. She didn't take into consideration that the pie consisted almost entirely of other carbohydrates. And to make matters even more amusing, she had substituted maple syrup for the sugar, since "that's natural." Moreover, the hostess said, "I baked it just for you." How can someone refuse an offer like that? But the patient did refuse, and she was proud of it.

Like so many things in life, the first time you refuse forbidden foods is the hardest. Sure, you'll be tempted. But if you've told your friends about your program, you won't want to fail in front of them. They'll be watching to see how you do. And as you say no to this and no to that, and tell more and more people that you're on this program, you start to feel real pride.

If you were a recovering alcoholic, it's not likely that your friends and loved ones would offer you a drink. If you had quit smoking cigarettes, they wouldn't constantly tempt you with "just one puff." Your program is just as important. You're doing it because you love yourself. If other people love you, they'll help, not hinder, your efforts.

Support Strategy 2: Keep the Cookie Jar Filled

Do you have a cookie jar that you keep filled with snacks for yourself and your family? Judith did, and she couldn't bring herself to put it away or to leave it empty on the kitchen counter. It was so cozy to have that cookie jar filled, but the temptation was horrid.

So Judith came up with a solution. Instead of cookies, she filled the jar with dog biscuits. That served a number of purposes. Obviously, she wasn't tempted to munch on them. Second, the cookie jar reminded her that she promised herself that she wouldn't give up the diet. And third, visitors to the house got an amusing, dramatic display of Judith's resolve.

If that approach is not quite up your alley, and you have a cookie jar that begs for filling, here's an idea that will help you today and for the rest of your life. Instead of sweet, caloric treats, fill your cookie jar with sweet, nonfood treats. Write ideas and suggestions for treats for yourself on pieces of paper and fill the jar with them. When you dip into the cookie jar, you'll pull out another way to give yourself a lift. Here are a few suggestions to put into the jar:

- Take a long, restful bubble bath.
- Give yourself a pedicure, complete with nail polish if you like.
- Make a phone call to someone you haven't spoken with in a long time. List some friends to call.
- Read a book you've been dying to read.

- Take a nap for just a few minutes to recharge your energies. Set a timer for 5 or 10 minutes.
- Make an appointment to get a massage.
- Write yourself a poem.
- Curl up for 15 minutes with a magazine.
- Work on a crossword puzzle.
- Do some knitting or crocheting.
- Ask your spouse if he or she wouldn't enjoy a "matinee." It's more fun to reach for a mate instead of a plate!
- Take care of a chore you've been putting off. (This one could probably fill a few slips of paper.) You'll be so glad to have finally done it!
- Pull out a tape and listen to a song you haven't heard for a long while.
- For women, fix your hair for the evening; do something fun with it. Perhaps braid in some colorful ribbon.
- Measure your lost inches.
- Take clothes to the tailor for alterations.

Think of things that really appeal to you. You can make those slips of paper more festive by rolling them into scrolls and tying them with ribbon. As you think of new ideas, keep adding them to the cookie jar. Be on the lookout for new ideas in magazines. Enjoy your sweet treats!

Support Strategy 3: Make a Deal

Lawyers use the phrase *quid pro quo,* literally, "this for that." Here's an example of how one patient used the concept of quid pro quo to lose weight.

Dorothy's husband had urged her to shed her extra pounds for quite a while. She, on the other hand, had hoped he would help with some household chores. So she offered a quid pro quo deal. George accepted, thinking that Dorothy wouldn't go through with her commitment. He began to help with the chores, and Dorothy began to follow the program.

To George's surprise, Dorothy stayed with it. When he neglected his share of the chores, she reminded him of the deal.

And, when Dorothy started to waiver in her resolve, George mentioned how he really didn't want to do those dishes that night. George and Dorothy resolved two difficulties in their marriage with one deal. Both were happy with the outcome.

Maybe this particular quid pro quo wouldn't work for you. Maybe you don't have a spouse to make a deal with. Perhaps you could make a deal with yourself. Is there something you'd really like to do or have? Something you've been denying yourself for quite some time? Perhaps it's a vacation or a trip to visit friends or family. Maybe it's a new piece of furniture or a subscription to a theater series. Most of us have something that we've denied ourselves for too long. So make a deal with yourself. Set a goal weight as the condition for realizing that dream.

Let's say it's the vacation that's part of your quid pro quo. Go to the travel agency and get some brochures and details of the trip. Find out when the flights depart. Mark your calendar for the date you'll leave. Go to the library or bookstore and find some reading material on your destination, and whenever you start to slip or be tempted, read about your paradise. Let the world know about it. Tell your friends that if you lose those pounds you're on your way.

Another way to arrange a deal with yourself is to promise that if you don't lose the weight, you'll deprive yourself of something you already have. That was the case for hundreds of policemen in Louisiana who were told that if they didn't conform to weight regulations, they would lose their jobs. That was enough negative motivation for all of them to comply and to lose the excess weight. Certainly you won't consider as drastic a deal as was forced upon those police officers. Your self-imposed deprivation must be more realistic in terms of your life, perhaps not going to a movie or concert as planned until you lose a specified amount of weight.

Whether you think you'd do better with positive or negative motivation, make your quid pro quo deal an act of love. Never forget: You're worth loving—you love yourself!

Support Strategy 4: Invest in Weight Loss

"Money talks." "You get what you pay for." "What's it worth to you?" These and other expressions in our language reveal the importance we all, to one degree or another, place on money. So let's see how you might relate weight loss to dollars.

If you were to go to a local weight loss center, you would pay a considerable sum of money for the program it offers. Some are more expensive than others, but even the least expensive programs will cost about $10 for each pound to be lost. Some commercial weight loss operations cost double or triple that amount. And they typically want their money, or at least most of it, right up front before you shed the first ounce.

What is your current financial status? Could you afford $10, $20, or $30 per pound? Do you have 20, 40, or 100 pounds to lose? You can make the calculation quite easily as to what weight loss in your case would cost. Would it be worth that amount of money? Of course it would. How can one set a price for health and happiness? So here's a strategy that has worked well.

Determine the amount of money you will "pay" to lose those pounds and inches. Take that money and put it into a bank, give it to a friend, or make some other arrangement to keep it stashed away. Then make a deal to get the money back. Instead of paying others to help you lose weight, pay yourself for getting the job done.

Set up a payment schedule. Draw out a given amount of money for each week you remain in ketosis. Or, predicate the payment on achieving a given amount of weight loss per week. Or, pay yourself for each inch lost or each pound lost or both.

Regardless of the terms of payment, however, you must make the promise that if you fail to deliver on your deal, you don't get paid. Not only that, but the money should be forfeited *forever*. Contribute the lost funds to a charity. Tell a close friend about your financial arrangement to make sure you can't get out of it. The most effective means of enforcing the arrangement is to have the friend be completely responsible for the money. Thus, each week he or she will either send you the amount you have earned or send it to the charity. Full compliance with the program means you lose nothing.

It's possible, of course, that you could lose the entire amount of money you set aside, but we don't think you will swell the treasuries of charities by much at all. This program is so effective that if you stick to it you're guaranteed success. Put your money where your mouth is!

Support Strategy 5: Shortcut to Feeling Good

What's the most intensely pleasurable memory you can think of that has nothing to do with food? Perhaps it was staring at the stars in a black sky aboard a cruise ship or out in the desert. Maybe it was holding your baby for the first time. Perhaps it was a sexual moment that remains the gold standard in your love life.

Really probe your memory. Come up with the ultimate in pleasant recall. Color in all the details. Think about every moment of the experience from the time it began to its completion. Surrender your consciousness completely to this recollection of pleasure.

Work on painting a mind picture of the pleasure for yourself at least once every day, and repeat it as often during the day as possible. You might notice that the pleasure becomes more intense every time you think about it.

Now, every time you conjure up that pleasant thought, give your right earlobe a gentle tug. You will begin to associate the tug with the pleasurable feeling. Soon the tug at the earlobe will be enough to remind you of the pleasant memory. The tug will make it easier to flood your thoughts with wonderful sensations. Finally the tug will be all it takes to make you feel great.

You can use this newly acquired, satisfying response to help with your weight loss efforts. Every time you start to think about forbidden foods, give a tug. When you're at a party with tables laden with treats, give a tug. Any time you're tempted to eat foods not permitted on the program, give a tug and start those pleasant associations flowing.

The time will surely come, and sooner than you might imagine possible, that you'll replace thoughts of food with thoughts of a completely different nature. As others indulge in their cakes and candies, you'll plunge into your pleasurable mental fantasy. No one need know what is going on in your mind. And all the while, you'll be further along the road to permanent weight control.

Support Strategy 6: You're in Good Company

It's part of human nature, when we are faced with a regrettable event, to ask "Why me?" Being on a diet evokes that kind of thought from time to time, and it can involve feelings that range from mild perplexity to bitterness and resentment. Why can't I eat those candies like my friends do? Why must I forego baked goods? Why can't I eat whatever I like without worrying about weight? Why me?

Well, it's time to put things into their proper perspective. Just about everyone has to control some aspect of diet. Take a look around you and you'll see that it's not only you who has to be careful. For openers, estimates state that up to one in nine Americans is an alcoholic. Alcoholics' very lives are threatened by their inability to consume alcoholic beverages safely. The only way to control the condition is to abstain completely from alcohol for life.

Then there are the many sufferers of food allergies and sensitivities. Some people cannot tolerate the lactose in milk. Drinking even a glass of it can lead to severe gastric symptoms. Others develop skin rashes from eating foods such as strawberries or tomatoes. The list of food sensitivities and their medical consequences have filled volumes.

But, you might interrupt, what about my friend who eats like a horse and never gains a pound? She eats anything and everything. While it's true that there are exceptions to every rule, closer examination usually reveals that the rule still applies. If a person consumes more calories than can be burned, weight will eventually and inevitably be gained. That friend may be doing extensive exercise you're not aware of or dieting except when with friends or limiting herself in ways you're not seeing. Perhaps she *is* blessed with a strong metabolism. For whatever reason, you are not!

You have plenty of company in terms of limiting the food in your diet. You are *not* the lone victim you sometimes feel yourself to be.

Support Strategy 7: Dealing with Special Occasions

Is there a special celebration coming up? Birthdays, anniversaries, graduations, religious holidays, Halloween, the holiday season from Thanksgiving to New Year's Eve are notorious food extravaganzas. The temptation is to say, "Oh well, it's just this once. One meal won't hurt."

On the face of it, that kind of thinking seems reasonable. The problem is that "just this once" tends to apply to so many food-related situations during the year. Take another look at the list above. You can probably add a few more special occasions that apply to your own life. If you treat them all as "just this once," before you know it you'll be lapsing from your diet on a regular basis.

Many people refuse to begin a diet between Thanksgiving and New Year's Day. Then they make a resolution to lose all the weight gained during that long period of eating huge quantities of highly caloric foods. Other people say they can't start dieting until after their birthday or until after their vacation or until after some other special occasion they've marked on the calendar. Pretty soon they've eliminated the entire year! For some people, there's *no* good time to begin to change the eating patterns that lead to and maintain overweight.

Any time is a good time to start dieting, especially on this program, because any time worth celebrating is worth highlighting with a commitment to future health and happiness. The forgone foods are a small sacrifice to make to achieve permanent weight loss.

Get out your calendar right now and mark all those times in the coming months and throughout the year when food temptations will be the strongest. The saying "Forewarned is forearmed" applies here. Start planning your strategies now so you won't be caught off guard when those special occasions come up.

What can you do to celebrate that has nothing to do with food? If you traditionally bake platters of cookies or gift boxes of fruitcake for Christmas presents, plan to make other kinds of gifts. How about homemade Christmas tree ornaments or floral arrangements? Scan through some magazines for specific suggestions and instructions.

Rather than going to a fancy restaurant to mark a birthday or an anniversary, why not get reservations for the theater or for a concert? Such outings would be far more special and out-of-the-ordinary than another meal, no matter how expensive.

If you are invited to a party at a friend's home, be sure the friend knows that you won't be eating the foods offered. Be assertive about this. And then to weaken the temptations, have your meal before you go to the party.

On Halloween this year, eliminate the temptation to sample goodies bought for trick-or-treaters by giving out nonfood items. Replace candies with coins, gift certificates, or trinkets. You'll also be doing a favor for the parents of the children, who would probably prefer such treats to tooth-decaying sweets.

Thanksgiving is a time of gorging. The U.S. Department of Agriculture once calculated that, given the standard fare of turkey and all the trimmings, the average American male will consume up to 7,500 calories at one seating. But even a lapse far less dramatic than that can knock you out of ketosis and off your weight loss program. Yet that same Thanksgiving dinner can provide the very foods you want while following this program. Select your 4 ounces of turkey breast, a lettuce salad, and some spinach or another permitted vegetable. Declare yourself thankful that, in the face of abundance, you've decided to love yourself enough to pass it by. You might even enjoy feeling just a little smug about your demonstration of self-control. You are in control, and the rewards are so worth it!

Support Strategy 8: Keep Busy

If you've ever wanted to get involved with a hobby, this is the time to start. For those intent on changing their dietary habits, the old Puritan saying, "The devil finds work for idle hands," holds true. If your mind and hands aren't otherwise occupied, they can too easily be persuaded to fill the void with food.

It's pretty difficult to eat a pint of ice cream while doing needlepoint. (And needlework is not only for women. Football player Rosie Grier made his love of needlepoint well known.) You might renew some pleasant childhood memories. When was the last time you built a model airplane or painted a picture? What was your special enjoyment?

Take a trip to the local toy or hobby store and see if any of the items there appeal to you. Don't hesitate to select something that appears to be a child's toy: a woodburning set or watercolors or modeling clay. Not only will these help you keep your mind and hands off food, but they might also prove to be wonderful ways to help you relax from the tensions of the day.

Consider also how you might be able to spend some of your spare time with others who need and would greatly appreciate your help. Think about doing some volunteer work at a children's hospital or a home for the elderly. Talk with your clergyman about how you can help in the community. You'll feel good about your contribution, you'll eliminate many moments of temptation, and, if you have a tendency to do so, you'll stop feeling sorry for yourself.

Support Strategy 9: When You Reach a Plateau

There comes a time in the life of all dieters, even those following this medically and scientifically superior approach, when they reach that dreaded stage known as a plateau, when even though they've done and are doing everything they're supposed to do, their weight stays the same. If it hasn't happened to you yet, it will. So it's best to be prepared to cope with this phenomenon.

The first thing to understand is that weight does not come off in a linear manner, with exactly the same number of pounds lost each day and each week. The first few days of any weight loss program will provide the greatest loss in pounds, largely because retained water weight is the first to go. From that point until goal weight is achieved, there will be peaks and valleys of loss.

Over the course of a week women typically lose 2 or 3 pounds and men 4 pounds, depending on the degree of overweight and physical activity. A given day might pass, however, when no weight loss occurs. That's why we suggest weighing yourself only weekly during weight loss and every other day after that. Weighing on a daily basis can be frustrating, because of those peaks and valleys.

Your body, not knowing why its supply of calories has suddenly been dramatically cut back, will start to switch gears, downshifting to a lower level of metabolism, in order to conserve the energy coming in. This mechanism can be a lifesaver when the body is confronted with impending starvation. But the body cannot know the difference between dieting and starvation. The result is a plateau in which weight loss abruptly comes to a standstill. One approach is to do absolutely nothing and wait for the plateau to pass. It will pass, but waiting can be frustrating, especially to those doing their best to succeed. However, there are some techniques that can end the plateau or make it less frustrating.

You can jolt your metabolism into increased action by stepping up your regimen of exercise. Add another 20- to 30-minute walk each day or another type of physical activity. Climb an extra two flights of stairs rather than taking an elevator, work some bicycle riding into your schedule, or perhaps you're ready to take on some tennis or racquetball. Any increase in physical activity will switch your body back into metabolic high gear.

Although it's true that your ultimate goal is to shed fat pounds, you still have some water weight at practically any stage of weight loss. During a plateau, therefore, you can eliminate another pound or two by practicing the technique of diuresis of recumbency, described on pages 61–62.

To make the plateau more tolerable, bear in mind that even though the pounds are not coming off, you will lose inches even during plateau periods. That's because you're still burning fat and replacing it with an equivalent weight in non-fat areas. This is a good reason to continue your body measurements throughout the period of weight loss; as long as you're losing inches and are in ketosis, you may not even mind a plateau in weight loss.

But no technique will be effective if the plateau is the result of not sticking with the program. The first thing to do is check to see that you are still in ketosis. If you are not, review your daily food intake in your diet diary. Perhaps a few extra carbohydrates have slipped into your diet and it's time to cut back again. Can you see times when you could have improved?

The plateau is a time to renew your commitment and resolve to make permanent weight loss a reality. It's *not* the time to give up. The plateau is a normal, natural part of weight loss, and it will pass. How fast it will pass depends largely on your attitude and approach.

Support Strategy 10: Coping with Stress

Stress is an inherent part of dieting. The better you are at defusing that stress, the more successful you will be in your weight loss efforts. If you feel somewhat irritable because you miss some of your old favorite foods, even though you're not hungry, you're no different from anyone else who has gone on the program before you. It's a natural reaction to miss the foods you love to eat. Those foods have been an integral part of your life, but remember that now you're trying to change your life-style for the better.

Think of people you've known who have quit smoking cigarettes. With dieting and quitting smoking, one feels as if one is giving up a "best friend." Certain foods or cigarettes were always there to help you celebrate when things were good or console you when things were bad. It's tough to say goodbye to these friends, even though we know they're not good for us.

Just as one can predict that the person who quits smoking will get through the state of withdrawal, we know that the dieter will learn to cope with the loss of certain foods. However, in the meantime you're still feeling stress, and knowing why or that it will eventually go away may not make you feel any better right now. There are two things you can do to lessen stressful moments.

Exercise has proved time and again to be effective in reducing diet-related stress. Not only is physical activity a substitute for eating, but it also has a relaxing, tranquilizing effect. Review the amount of activity you're getting each day, and see if you couldn't step up that level.

Sleep is always important for good physical and mental health, but it's even more important when you're under any kind of stress. A restful night's sleep can give you the energy and vitality to face the next day with renewed commitment to the weight loss program.

Relaxation techniques are essential components of a successful weight loss program. Are you taking the time each day to pursue a relaxed state? Remember, relaxing isn't a matter of collapsing in front of the television set at night. Whether it's yoga, meditation, hobbies, or other relaxing activities, relaxation techniques can greatly enhance the quality of your life. You owe yourself the 20 minutes or so a day that it takes to achieve a relaxed, stress-free state.

Support Strategy 11: Don't Be Afraid to Be Thin

Some people can become their own enemies, especially in the late stages of weight loss. After being insulated and protected by layers of fat for many years, they begin to have doubts about really wanting to shed that system of defense and give up their old familiar selves.

One patient had been severely overweight for all her teenage years and into early adulthood. She had never learned to deal with the attentions of men, since they seldom approached her. Suddenly, now that she was losing weight, all that was changing, and she was afraid. Her immediate response was to gain the weight back. But with the help of her brother, who accompanied her to dances and parties until she was able to cope on her own, she overcame her fear.

Others begin to fear that their obesity was an excuse for not getting ahead in their careers. What if the weight is lost and the promotion doesn't come along? Such fears may well undermine the weight loss effort.

Trying to hide under protective layers of fat is like covering your eyes so as not to see the negative aspects of life, and missing the positive aspects as well. Life is too rich to hide from it. Any time you begin to doubt yourself or your ability to live happily as a slender person, think again about all the reasons why you're a lovable person. It's not that you'll be more lovable when you lose the weight; you'll still be the same old you underneath, but with more confidence and self-esteem. And remember, you *weren't* happy being overweight.

You'll have to cope with receiving compliments. You'll have to deal with being treated equally with others, not adversely or patronizingly because of your overweight. You may have to learn a few new skills along the way. But it's a great new life waiting for you to enjoy. Love yourself enough to grab every moment of happiness.

Support Strategy 12: Traits That Predict Success

"Quitting cigarettes is easy—I've done it dozens of times." That old joke can be told about weight loss, too. The trick is not just losing weight, but keeping that weight off permanently.

There are certain personality traits that can predict failure in maintaining weight loss. Those most likely to regain lost weight, research has shown us, are men and women who demonstrate anxiety, avoidance of monotony, and a low degree of socialization. But those traits can be reversed, and, in doing so, you can greatly improve your chances for success.

To lessen anxiety, one must concentrate on those things that can promote relaxation, such as sufficient exercise, a good night's sleep, and specific relaxation activities.

Few people enjoy monotonous routines, but one can compensate for monotony in some things by substituting other activities at other times. For example, one might say that it's monotonous to be unable to break the meal plan routine by deciding at the moment to have ice cream or cheesecake for dessert. But if sufficient motivation and alternative activities are present, such feelings can be overcome. Your walks and new hobby can introduce much variety and spontaneity into your life.

Overweight men and women frequently have not learned social skills. It's difficult to say whether weight was the cause or the effect, the chicken or the egg. But one can make active efforts to become more social. For best results, such efforts should be gradual.

The best way to meet others with interests in common is to get involved in activities related to your own interests. Do you enjoy theater? Join a local drama group. Do you like modern art? Do some volunteer work at a museum. There are many people out there in the world who would enjoy your company. Volunteer work can help you feel involved and gradually more confident.

If none of these traits applies to you, we're confident that you'll lose weight and maintain that loss successfully for years and years to come. But if any of the traits is part of your personality, you can make some changes now. It will help in your efforts at weight loss, and it will enrich your entire life.

Support Strategy 13: When You're Angry

If you are the person primarily responsible for food preparation in your home, you might begin to feel some anger and resentment toward those who eat the foods you prepare when you yourself can't. These feelings can result in tense family relations and possible abandonment of the diet. Both consequences are undesirable, so steps have to be taken to offset hostile emotions.

After the Christmas/Hanukkah holidays, one patient was fit to be tied. She was angry at "having" to cook all the foods she couldn't eat. "Next year I'm going to Las Vegas," she said. It's not always possible to "run away from home," but it may be possible to abdicate at least some responsibility in the kitchen. If your family is willing to do so, why not encourage them to eat some meals out in restaurants? Or perhaps they could, at least while you're in the weight loss phase, order some of their meals from take-out establishments. This might also be a good opportunity to teach others in the family a bit of responsibility for themselves. Even the youngest child can take a role in food preparation, serving, and clean-up.

In any case, the first thing to do when feeling anger or resentment about having to prepare foods for your family is to have a frank discussion with them. Tell them that you understand the changes may be difficult for them, but also explain the importance of this diet to you. Success can mean enhanced health and happiness for the rest of your life. It may involve some changes in their routines and expectations, but aren't you worth such a small sacrifice?

Support Strategy 14:
Don't Let Your Loved Ones Sabotage You

There are people out there ready and willing to sabotage your efforts at weight loss. The closer you get to your goal weight, the more temptations they seem to come up with, along with what they believe to be good reasons for you to eat the foods you've been trying to avoid.

The best possible defense against these well-meaning individuals is to know their lines of persuasion in advance. Then you won't be surprised when you hear them, and you'll be able to come up with counterarguments.

Get ready to hear . . .

"But just this one little piece of cake won't hurt."

"But I don't think you're heavy. *You* don't have to lose weight. You're perfect the way you are. Eat!"

"Try this chocolate mousse. I made it with you in mind."

"What's wrong? Don't you like the food?"

"I read that this brand is OK for dieters."

"Maybe you should quit that diet. You're getting too thin. Do you want to be skinny?"

"Haven't you been on that diet long enough?"

"Some people are *born* to be skinny, some heavy. You can't change your genes. Don't bother trying."

"Lots of heavy people live to be 100."

"It's your birthday. Why not splurge a little?"

"Go ahead and have some. You can always go back to the diet tomorrow."

"I don't think you should give up *all* your favorites."

"When you really miss foods, you should have just a taste to get you through."

"You're not feeling well, and they say 'Feed a cold,' so enjoy this chicken soup I made just for you."

"Have some cake. It'll calm your nerves."

"It's not *natural* to eat so little."

"This candy is good for diabetics."

"We love you, Mom. We don't care if you're heavy. You won't be the same if you lose weight."

"I love you, dear. That's why I married you even though you were heavy. I just adore cuddling you. Won't you stop this dieting?"

These are the kinds of comments you can expect to hear from friends, relatives, and loved ones. Only *you* know how much you want to lose that weight. Don't let *anyone* stand in the way of your future health and happiness. Even if some people seem disappointed when you don't join them in eating certain foods, they will respect you for it.

Support Strategy 15: When You Fail

We'd like to think that everyone who begins this program will continue straight along until reaching goal weight and then maintain that loss for the rest of their lives, never once falling off the wagon. But we know that's just not to be. There's a good chance that you will slip. There's nothing wrong with falling down. But there's no reason in the world not to get right back up again.

Lest you think you're different from everyone else in the world, let us reassure you that many others have slipped and fallen before you. Those who respond by abandoning the program altogether tend to have in common a general lack of self-confidence and self-respect. Some, after giving in to temptation and gaining weight, look at themselves in the mirror with disgust. "I knew I couldn't do it," they say. "I don't deserve any better in life. There's no point in going on with this. I'm just a fat slob and no one cares about me anyway. Why should I care? I might as well eat."

That scenario has been played and replayed again and again. You very well may have some of the same feelings if you splurge and gain back some of the weight you lost. But you have to fight those feelings.

Everyone has little failures. No one is perfect. We do ourselves more damage by punishing ourselves for failing than by the failures themselves. So forgive yourself. Do so because you love yourself enough to get up and start again.

If you've brought some carbohydrates into the house, throw them out or give them away. Get right back onto the program and into ketosis. Be forewarned, however, that it may be more difficult to reenter the state of ketosis than it was to get into it initially. It might take a day or two more. But you can and will get back into ketosis.

There's a saying that every millionaire went broke once or twice before making his ultimate fortune. The same applies to those trying to lose weight. Failing once or twice may just be paving the way for success. Have faith in yourself. Love yourself. You can do it, and you will.

Chapter 13

INSULIN CONTROL FOODS AND RECIPES

One of the great advantages of the dietary aspects of this program is the wide variety of foods it allows you every day. In Chapter 8 we outlined a full two weeks of meal plans. You'll notice that you won't repeat any of the entrees, except for the occasional use of leftovers for lunchtime convenience. Using the recipes in this chapter, you'll be able to create week after week of delicious menu plans. Seek the widest variety of foods possible and don't let yourself slip into a rut of preparing foods the same way over and over. Give all the recipes a try. By the time you determine which are your favorites, you'll be well on your way to a slender new self.

Note: We have deliberately not included a breakdown of calories, fat, protein, and carbohydrates in the recipes for this program. The reason is simple: We want you to be able to follow the program without worrying about calories, and to learn to determine your own nutritional needs.

Spend some time with the lists of foods we've provided to acquaint yourself with their nutrition analyses. Then you'll know at a glance whether foods in question will be appropriate for you, whether you're in the weight loss, stabilization, or maintenance phases of the program.

Bon appetit!

EGG DISHES

There's no more traditional breakfast than the egg, which starts the day for people in countries all over the world. Because eggs contain a wealth of nutrients, are a marvelous source of protein, are low in fat and calories, and contain no carbohydrate at all, they are an excellent choice as a part of your weight loss program.

Of course, eggs do have a high cholesterol content, with more than 200 milligrams in one large egg. But many individuals can eat an egg a day without any elevation in cholesterol levels. If you don't know your cholesterol level, it's a good idea to have it checked; your physician can tell you how. If your cholesterol level is normal, you can continue to enjoy your daily egg. If it's slightly elevated, your physician may advise you to eat only two or three weekly. If your cholesterol level is quite elevated, you should eliminate whole eggs from your diet.

All the egg's cholesterol is found in the yolk; there is none in the white. If you are advised to eliminate whole eggs, you can use two whites instead of one egg. There are also a number of egg substitutes, which are made from egg whites and contain no cholesterol. These can be used to make scrambled eggs that can scarcely be distinguished from fresh eggs.

If you aren't already familiar with the many ways eggs can be prepared, here are a few of them.

Poached

In a small saucepan bring water to a gentle boil. Crack an egg into a small dish. Swirl the water in the pan into a little whirlpool and gently slide the egg into the center of the whirlpool. Let cook for 2 to 3 minutes. Remove with a slotted spoon.

Soft Cooked

Place an egg in a small saucepan of cold water, enough to completely cover the egg, and bring to a boil. Boil gently for 3½ minutes for the classic soft-cooked egg, a bit less for a runnier egg, and a bit more for a firmer one.

Hard Cooked

Place an egg in a small saucepan of cold water, enough to completely cover the egg, and bring to a boil. Cover the pan and turn off the heat. Let stand for 20 minutes. Remove the egg and hold it under cold running water for about 30 seconds. You might want to make several hard-cooked eggs at once, so you will have some to peel as needed.

Sunnyside Up

This classic egg dish is usually made with butter or oil, but this version eliminates most of those fat grams and calories. Spray some butter-flavored vegetable spray on a nonstick pan. Crack an egg into the pan over medium heat and fry until the white is no longer translucent and the yolk is done to your taste.

Scrambled

The trick to making perfect scrambled eggs is to beat them lightly in a bowl prior to cooking. Spray a nonstick pan with vegetable spray and start to heat. Pour the beaten egg into the pan. Cook over low heat, scrambling, until set. You may substitute one of the brands of cholesterol-free egg substitutes. For flavor variety, add a few drops of vanilla, almond, or orange extract while scrambling.

Basted

This delicious variation on the sunnyside-up egg is a cross between a fried and a poached egg. Proceed as for a sunnyside-up egg, but after putting the egg in the pan, pour 1 tablespoon of water over the egg and cover the pan. For those watching cholesterol, try using only the whites of two eggs instead of a whole egg.

Deviled

Slice hard-cooked eggs in half lengthwise, and place the yolks in a bowl. For each yolk add 1 teaspoon of nonfat milk and a dash each of paprika, onion powder, dry mustard, minced chives, and salt. Mash the yolks. Fill the egg whites with the yolk mixture, and sprinkle with paprika and chives.

BOUILLON

You'll come to rely on bouillon as you follow this weight control program. It's low in fat, carbohydrate, and calories, yet flavorful and satisfying. When you'd like a pick-me-up in the middle of the afternoon, reach for a steaming cup of chicken, beef, or vegetable bouillon. When sautéing or stir-frying various foods, use a tablespoon of bouillon instead of oil. You will also use bouillon in a number of recipes.

Several canned and instant bouillons (powders and cubes) are available. Choose the best ones by reading their nutrient labels. Most canned beef bouillons (or broths, the terms are interchangeable) contain just 1 gram of carbohydrate and only 16 calories per 8-ounce serving prepared according to label directions. There is more variation among the instant bouillon mixes. Weight Watchers packets, when mixed with water to make 6 ounces of bouillon, contain 1 gram of carbohydrate and 8 calories. Romanoff MBT brand supplies 12 calories and 2 grams of carbohydrate. It is a slight difference, but it can add up.

VEGETABLE DISHES

We encourage you to have vegetables every day on this program. Vegetables are a low-fat, low-calorie, nutrient-packed component of a balanced diet for everyone. Start now to get into the good habit of selecting a variety of vegetables to enjoy regularly. Remember that a serving size of vegetables is ½ cup cooked or 1 cup raw.

While you can simply open a can of green beans or defrost some frozen broccoli, you'll find the program much more enjoyable and healthful if you use fresh vegetables. Try some you haven't had in a while or never tried.

Although some nutrients are lost in canned vegetables, they can come in handy when you're in a hurry. Frozen vegetables contain more nutrients than canned, and you can measure out a serving for yourself and return the rest to the freezer. Try perking up the flavor of frozen and canned vegetables by adding snippets of fresh herbs such as basil and dill.

Properly prepared steamed or boiled vegetables are delicious, but even the most health-conscious dieter can get tired of them in their plain state day after day. However, the alternative is not to add butter or cream or other highly caloric sauces. Rather, explore the possibilities of using fresh and dried herbs and spices. More than ever before, fresh herbs can be found in most supermarkets. Simply adding a fresh herb to a fresh vegetable can transform a simple dish into a taste experience. Whether using fresh or dried herbs, start with small amounts and increase until you reach your own taste preference. Don't overdo it. You can use only one flavoring or mix them, according to your taste. Garlic and ginger, for example, go particularly well together, providing an oriental flavor when used with a dash of soy sauce. Here is a list of vegetables and some herbs and spices that go particularly well with them.

Asparagus: basil, garlic, sesame seed
Beans: savory, basil, chili powder, nutmeg, sage, dill
Broccoli: mace, oregano
Cabbage: dill, mace, oregano, caraway seeds
Carrots: cinnamon, dill, ginger, nutmeg, thyme
Cauliflower: chili powder, dill, nutmeg
Pea pods: marjoram, oregano, mint
Spinach: chervil, marjoram, nutmeg
Squash, winter: cloves, nutmeg
Turnips: dill, basil

Why limit yourself to the color and flavor of just one vegetable at a time? Mix two or three vegetables to make terrific combinations. Just make sure the total does not exceed the serving size of ½ cup cooked or 1 cup raw. By keeping several kinds in the freezer, you can mix to your heart's content. Here are a few combinations you might like to try. Use your imagination to come up with some of your own.

Brussels sprouts and carrot slices
Green cabbage and red cabbage
Carrots and celery with strips of red pimento
Carrot strips and french-cut green beans
Julienne strips of beets and carrots
Onions, mushrooms, and broccoli
Pea pods, mushrooms, and water chestnuts
Cauliflower and broccoli florets

Following are some simple recipes and basic preparation methods for a variety of vegetables.

Artichoke

Artichokes are a fun food. You'll enjoy picking the leaves off one at a time and scraping them between your teeth to get at the flesh. And when you've finished the succulent part of the leaves, you still have a couple of bites of the delicious artichoke bottom to savor. A serving of artichoke is ½ of one medium artichoke. Select artichokes that have tight rather than opened leaves.

To prepare, remove any discolored and small leaves at the base of the artichoke. Cut off the stem and the top of the globe. Snip off the tips of the leaves with scissors. Remove the small, pale, inner leaves at the top of the globe. Scrape out all of the fuzzy choke below the inner leaves. Rinse and drop into a bowl of water with some lemon juice added until ready to cook. In a saucepan just large enough to hold the number of artichokes you are cooking, bring to a boil enough water to cover the artichokes. Add 1 teaspoon of lemon juice, 1 clove of garlic, and 1 teaspoon of salt. Add the artichokes and return to boil. Reduce heat and simmer uncovered for 30 to 40 minutes or until the leaves pull off easily. Drain and serve either hot or cold.

Asparagus Chinese Style

Asparagus is a treat just steamed or boiled, but for some variety try this dish with a Chinese flavor. Trim off the hard ends of the spears. Cut the asparagus on a diagonal into 1½-inch pieces to make 1 cup (3 to 5 stalks). Add ½ teaspoon of salt to 1 cup of water in a shallow pan. Bring water to a boil and add asparagus. Cook 5 to 7 minutes or until just tender to a fork. While the asparagus is cooking, make a sauce by combining 2 tablespoons chicken bouillon, 1 teaspoon soy sauce, a dash of ground ginger, and a dash of Chinese five-spice seasoning. Drain the asparagus, return it to the pan with the sauce, heat quickly, and serve.

Beans with Basil

Snap off the tips of fresh beans and slice into 1-inch pieces. Place in a small saucepan with 1 cup of cold, salted water for each 1 cup of raw beans. Bring to a boil. Add two or three basil leaves. Cook for 5 to 10 minutes. Drain and serve.

Bean Sprouts

Chinese cooking isn't the only place for bean sprouts. Try them with a number of dishes to add a distinctive crunch. In a medium-sized skillet, bring 2 tablespoons of chicken bouillon to a boil. Add 1 cup of bean sprouts per person. Cover and cook for just 2 minutes. Don't overcook.

Beets

Many people have eaten only canned beets. Now's the time to enjoy the marvelous flavor of fresh beets. Select firm beets with a deep red color. Cut the greens off, leaving about an inch of stem, and cut the tails off, leaving about an inch. Wash the beets and leave whole. To enough water to cover the beets, add 1 teaspoon vinegar and ½ teaspoon salt per cup of water. Bring water to a boil, add the beets, lower the heat, and cook at a simmer for 35 to 45 minutes, until tender. Cool under running water and remove skins. Slice and serve. Or, wrap the whole beets in foil and bake in the oven at moderately high heat (375°) until tender (45 minutes to an hour depending on the size of the beet).

Broccoli

The bright green color of properly prepared broccoli adds excitement to any plate of food. The trick is not to overcook it. Trim off leaves and cut off as much stalk as you wish. Cut into florets and place in a large skillet with a cover. Add 1 inch of cold salted water, bring to a boil, and cover. Cook approximately 3 minutes, until broccolli is fork tender and emerald green.

Brussels Sprouts

These little cabbages are a nice change of pace. Shop for the smallest ones you can find, with tight leaves. Trim off any excess stalk, and, if you have the patience, pierce the stalk end with the tip of a knife. Bring 1 inch of salted water to a boil in a shallow pan. Add the sprouts, bring to a boil, cover, and cook for about 10 minutes or until tender.

Cabbage

Prepare red cabbage, green cabbage, or some of both by shredding enough to fill 1 cup per person. In a pot large enough to accommodate the cabbage, bring ½ inch of salted water with 2 tablespoons of vinegar to a boil. Put in the cabbage, cover, and cook 8 to 10 minutes.

Carrots

Cut carrots into rounds, strips, chunks, diagonals, or whatever shape you can think of. Each shape, it seems, affects the taste in the same way that pasta tastes different as spaghetti or shells. Look for bright, small carrots. Enjoy carrots both raw and cooked. Try shredding some into your dinner salad. Slice into julienne strips to nibble at during dinner. To cook, peel, slice, and boil in salted water for about 15 minutes. As with all vegetables, don't overcook.

Cauliflower

One medium head of cauliflower comes out to about four servings. Remove the heavy stalk and leaves and cut into small florets. Bring 1 inch of salted water to a boil in a medium skillet. Place the cauliflower in the skillet, cover, and cook for about 20 minutes. Perk it up by serving with colorful strips of red pimento.

Chinese Pea Pods (Snow Peas)

These flat, bright green pods shouldn't wait for a Chinese meal. They make a wonderful accompaniment to any dinner. Snap off the ends and remove any strings. Bring 1 inch of salted water to a boil, add the pea pods, and cook for just 2 minutes so they're still crisp.

Spinach

Rinse a bunch of spinach thoroughly before you remove the binding ties. With a large knife cut the stems off at the base of the leaves. Fill the kitchen sink with water and swirl the spinach leaves around in it to remove any residual sand. Shake the spinach dry and place in a large pot with only the water clinging to its leaves. Use a stainless steel, enameled, or coated pot. Do not cook spinach in aluminum. Cover and cook over a medium-high heat for about 3 minutes. Serve with a sprinkle of cider vinegar or just plain.

Zucchini

This versatile vegetable can be eaten raw or cooked. Cut it raw into julienne strips or shred it to add to a salad. Slice it or cut it into chunks and boil for about 7 minutes in salted water. Cut a small zucchini in half lengthwise, place it 6 inches under the broiler, and broil 10 to 12 minutes or until fork tender.

FISH AND SHELLFISH

For the health- and weight-conscious eater, the ultimate entree is fish and shellfish. High in protein and low in fat, these foods are rapidly replacing beef and pork on the dinner table. If you haven't already jumped on the fish bandwagon, this is the perfect time to do so.

The freshness of fish and seafood is the all important factor for taste. Fresh fish does not smell "fishy." The store itself should smell fresh and clean. Ask when the fish was received and what the freshest "catch of the day" is. On a whole fish, the eyes should be relatively clear and not sunken in. On fillets, be certain the skin hasn't begun to curl and that the flesh is moist. Ask the shopkeeper for advice on best quality, good buys, and cooking methods, and don't be afraid to try new varieties.

There's a simple rule when it comes to cooking fish. Regardless of the type or cut of fish, regardless of the method of cooking, cook for no more than 10 minutes per 1-inch thickness of fish. Whether it's a whole fish or a fillet, measure the thickest part of the fish. *Most* fillets and steaks will be no more than 1-inch thick. This rule applies to broiling, grilling, and sautéing. When fish is combined with other ingredients and baked, it may take longer. Fish is considered done as soon as it has lost its translucent color. You do not want to overcook any type of fish or shellfish. In the past one was advised to cook until the flesh began to "flake," but most chefs today would consider this overdone. You want the fish to be moist and juicy.

You can enjoy a wide variety of fish prepared in many ways. To get you started, we've provided some favorite recipes. Fish may not be "brain food," but it certainly is a smart choice.

Baked Fish Fillet

4 ounces fish fillet (sea bass or snapper is excellent)
1 tablespoon chopped tomato
1 pinch each tarragon, dill weed, finely chopped chives

Rinse the fish well under cold running water; pat dry with paper towel. Place the fish in a glass or ceramic casserole dish and cover with chopped tomato and seasonings. Cover. Bake in a preheated 350°F oven for 15 minutes.

Florentine Fish Fillet

4 ounces fish fillet
3 tablespoons chopped spinach
1 tablespoon chopped onion
1 pinch each thyme, salt, pepper

Rinse the fish well under cold running water; pat dry with paper towel. Place the fish in the middle of a 12-inch square of aluminum foil. Cover with the spinach, onion, and seasonings. Fold over the foil and seal tightly. Bake in a preheated 350°F oven for 10 to 12 minutes. Open immediately upon removal from oven to stop the cooking process.

Chinese Fish Steak

4 ounces fish steak (halibut, shark, tuna, swordfish)
3 tablespoons chopped mushrooms
½ cup chicken bouillon
1 teaspoon soy sauce
½ teaspoon each finely chopped garlic and fresh ginger
vegetable oil spray

In a small pan coated with vegetable oil spray, sauté garlic and ginger briefly. Do not let garlic brown. Add soy sauce and bouillon to pan, and heat to boiling. Transfer the bouillon mixture to a small casserole dish. Add the fish to the casserole and spread the mushrooms on top of it. Cover. Bake in a preheated 350°F oven for 15 to 20 minutes.

Salmon in Court Bouillon

4 ounces salmon fillet or steak
1 cup water
1 tablespoon lemon juice
2 bay leaves
6 peppercorns
1 garlic clove, quartered
3 slices onion
1 large sprig fresh dill

Mix all the ingredients except the salmon in a casserole dish. Place the salmon in the mixture and arrange the sliced onion over it. Cover the dish with a sheet of waxed paper. Bake in a preheated 350°F oven for 20 minutes.

Teriyaki Broiled Fish

4 ounces fish fillet or steak (a firm-fleshed variety, such as salmon or shark)
1 tablespoon soy sauce
1 teaspoon lemon juice
1 garlic clove, finely minced
½ teaspoon finely minced fresh ginger

Mix all the ingredients except the fish in a plastic food storage bag. Place the fish in the bag and marinate for 30 minutes or longer. Place the fish on a broiler tray or grill, and broil or grill for 10 minutes.

New Orleans Creole Fillet

4 ounces fish fillet (red snapper, grouper)
1 tablespoon each chopped tomato, onion, celery, green pepper
1 garlic clove, finely minced
1 tablespoon tomato juice
¼ teaspoon chili powder

Mix all the ingredients except the fish in a casserole dish. Place the fish in the dish and spoon the mixture over it. Cover. Bake in a preheated 350°F oven for 15 minutes.

Indian Fish Curry

4 ounces white fish fillet (cod, white fish, orange roughy)
1 tablespoon each chopped onion, mushrooms, tomato
1 teaspoon lemon juice
1 teaspoon curry powder

Mix all the ingredients except the fish in a casserole dish. Place the fish in the dish and spoon the mixture over it. Cover. Bake in a preheated 350°F oven for 15 minutes.

Blackened Fish

4 ounces fish fillet
1 tablespoon Cajun seasonings (purchase commercially)
2 tablespoons unprocessed bran
2 tablespoons beaten egg *or* egg substitute
vegetable oil spray

Mix the unprocessed bran with the Cajun seasonings. Dip the fish fillet first into the egg, and then into the bran mixture to coat it. Coat a pan with vegetable oil spray and heat on high heat. Sauté the fillet for about 3 to 4 minutes on each side.

Broiled Seafood Kebabs

4 ounces seafood (scallops, shrimp, fish chunks, or a mixture)
1 cup total raw vegetables (whole mushrooms, green pepper chunks, onions cut into quarters or eighths)
2 tablespoons lemon juice
1 garlic clove, finely minced
½ teaspoon salt
¼ teaspoon pepper

Mix lemon juice, garlic, salt, and pepper in a plastic food storage bag. Add the seafood and vegetables and marinate for 30 minutes or longer. Skewer seafood and vegetables alternately. Broil for 3 minutes on one side. Turn and broil for another 2 minutes.

Note: This dish includes both the protein food and the vegetable for a meal.

This 'n' That Seafood Soup

This type of dish was the origin of bouillabaisse and cioppino. As you purchase fish and shellfish and find an ounce of this and an ounce of that left over, save these morsels in the freezer. Then when you have enough for the recipe (or multiply it for the entire family), you'll have a treat!

> 4 ounces total seafood (shrimp, scallops, fish, crab, lobster)
> ½ cup water
> 1 teaspoon lemon juice
> 2 tablespoons chopped tomato
> 2 tablespoons chopped onion
> 1 pinch saffron
> 1 teaspoon salt
> ½ teaspoon pepper

Mix all the ingredients except the seafood in a pot and bring to a boil. Lower the heat, add the seafood, and cook 10 minutes at a slow simmer.

Oriental Seafood Stir Fry

> 4 ounces seafood, cut into even-sized pieces (scallops, shrimp, crab, lobster, or a mixture)
> 1 cup total vegetables, cut into even-sized pieces (bean sprouts, water chestnuts, mushrooms, broccoli, Chinese cabbage)
> 3 tablespoons chicken bouillon
> 1 tablespoon oyster sauce
> 1 teaspoon soy sauce
> 1 garlic clove, finely minced
> ½ teaspoon finely minced fresh ginger

Mix together 2 tablespoons of the chicken bouillon, oyster sauce, soy sauce, garlic, and ginger. Heat a large skillet or wok. Add the remaining tablespoon of chicken bouillon and quickly stir-cook the seafood and vegetables. Add the bouillon mixture and bring to a boil. Serve.

Note: This dish includes both the protein food and the vegetable for a meal.

Broiled Shrimp and Scallops

2 ounces shrimp
2 ounces scallops
1 garlic clove, finely minced
1 tablespoon lemon juice
1 tablespoon finely minced cilantro

Mix lemon juice, garlic, and cilantro in a plastic food storage bag. Add the seafood and marinate for 30 minutes or longer. Grill or broil for 3 minutes on one side. Turn and broil for an additional 2 minutes.

Salmon or Tuna Salad Sandwich

4 ounces canned salmon or tuna, packed in water
1 tablespoon each finely chopped onion, celery, green pepper
½ teaspoon dill weed
1 teaspoon lemon juice
½ teaspoon salt
1 teaspoon reduced-calorie mayonnaise
2 large lettuce leaves

Drain the tuna or salmon. Remove any skin and bones from the salmon. Mix all the ingredients except the lettuce leaves. Spread the mixture on one; cover with the second leaf to form a sandwich.

Salmon Patties

4 ounces canned salmon, packed in water
1 egg white
2 tablespoons unprocessed bran
1 tablespoon finely chopped onion
1 teaspoon minced parsley
1 teaspoon lemon juice
¼ teaspoon salt
¼ teaspoon pepper
vegetable oil spray

Drain the salmon and remove any skins and bones. Mix all the ingredients together and form two patties. Coat a pan with vegetable oil spray and heat on moderate heat. Sauté the patties until crispy on the outside.

Salmon Chowder

Here's a recipe to use all those scraps of salmon you have left over from other recipes. Freeze them until you have enough to make this delicious meal in a bowl.

4 ounces salmon chunks (skin removed)
1 cup chicken bouillon
1 tablespoon chopped onion
1 cup total vegetables, diced (carrots, parsnips, turnips)
¼ teaspoon salt
¼ teaspoon pepper
1 dash hot pepper sauce

Cook the vegetables in seasoned bouillon for 10 minutes. Add the salmon. Cook 10 additional minutes.

Note: This dish includes both the protein food and the vegetable for a meal.

Oven "Fried" Scallops

The main reason most of us like deep-fried foods is that wonderful crunch when we take a bite. This recipe duplicates the crunch and flavor without the fat and calories. You can do this same recipe with shrimp or fish fillets. For variety, change the seasonings in the bran mixture. You might try some of the commercial seasoning mixtures, such as lemon-herb.

    3 ounces bay *or* sea scallops
    1 beaten egg *or* egg substitute
    2 tablespoons unprocessed bran
    ¼ teaspoon each salt, paprika, ground pepper, garlic powder
    vegetable oil spray
    lemon wedges

Mix the bran with the seasonings in a plastic food storage bag. Dip the scallops into the beaten egg in a bowl. Drop a few scallops at a time into the bag and shake until coated. Place on a cookie sheet and spray with the vegetable oil spray. Bake in a preheated 400°F oven for 10 minutes. Serve with a squeeze of lemon.

Crispy Breaded Fish Fillets

    4 ounces fish fillet without skin
    2 tablespoons unprocessed bran
    ¼ teaspoon each paprika, salt, pepper, onion powder
    2 tablespoons beaten egg *or* egg substitute
    vegetable oil spray

Mix the seasonings with the bran. Dip the fish first into the egg and then into the seasoned bran to coat it. Sauté 8 to 10 minutes in a pan coated with vegetable oil spray.

Steaming Seafood

Have you ever wondered why fish tastes so fresh and moist when served in a Chinese or Japanese restaurant? It's because they *steam* their seafood. This technique is remarkably simple, yet most people don't attempt it in their own kitchens. And, if you're in a hurry, there's no faster way to prepare food. Just toss a 4-ounce serving into the steamer, set the timer, and in minutes it's ready to eat. All you need are a large pot or frying pan with a cover and a steaming rack. You can pick up a rack in any housewares department. Buy a large enough rack to fit into a large pot or pan.

Put 1 inch of water into the bottom of the pot. Place the rack in the pot; the water should not reach the surface of the rack on which the food will rest. Bring the water to a boil to produce steam in the pot. Place the food directly on the rack or put it in a plate on the rack. You can bring the plate of steamed food directly to the table.

Cover the pot. Steam for 10 minutes. Test for doneness. The fish should have lost its translucency and flake easily, but should be very moist.

You can use this same technique to steam shrimp, crab, clams, mussels, or other seafood. We've included a number of recipes for steamed fish to get you started. Once you try this technique and get the hang of it, you'll agree that it's one of the easiest ways to prepare delicious fish.

Oriental Ginger Fish

This recipe is meant to serve four. But you can use just ¼ pound of fish, make the whole recipe of sauce, and have the sauce ready to go for the next time you're in the mood for this taste treat.

1 pound fresh cod, whitefish, or rockfish fillets
2 tablespoons peanut oil
2 teaspoons grated fresh ginger
2 teaspoons dry sherry
1 tablespoon black bean sauce (optional)
¼ teaspoon hot pepper sauce (optional)
2 green onions, sliced into 3-inch slivers

Follow the general directions for steaming on page 237. Mix the ingredients except the fish and onion in a small bowl. Place the fish on a plate that can be used in the steamer, spread the sauce mixture over the fish, and top with slivers of green onions. Steam for 10 minutes.

Steamed Spinach and Salmon

If there was ever a dish that proved a diet can be delicious, this is the one. It's beautiful to serve and wonderful to eat. What a way to lose and maintain weight! The recipe serves four persons, but you can reduce the ingredients to serve yourself.

1 bunch fresh spinach, cleaned and stemmed (see page 229)
1 pound fresh salmon steak
½ cup chopped onion
2 tablespoons olive oil
½ teaspoon each fennel seeds, rosemary leaves, salt, pepper
lemon wedges

Follow the general directions for steaming on page 237. Combine the onion, oil, and seasonings in a small bowl. Place the spinach leaves on the steamer rack, put the salmon on top of the spinach, and cover with the seasonings mixture. Steam for 10 minutes. Serve with lemon wedges.

Steamed Salmon and Vegetables

This recipe serves four persons. During the weight loss phase, eliminate the potatoes in the recipe. Include them during the maintenance phase if you like.

1 pound fresh salmon steaks
2 cups broccoli florets
1 cup cauliflower florets
½ cup sliced onion
½ cup sliced mushrooms
2 cups red or new potatoes, cubed
1 large sprig fresh dill
2 tablespoons fresh thyme or 1 teaspoon dried
1 teaspoon salt
½ teaspoon ground white pepper
lemon wedges

Follow the general directions for steaming on page 237. Simply arrange all the fish and vegetables in the steamer and sprinkle on the seasonings. Steam for 10 minutes. Serve with lemon wedges.

Note: This dish includes both the protein food and vegetable for a meal.

Citrus Seasoned Steamed Fish

The aromas generated by this dish will have mouths watering throughout the house. You can vary the flavor by using different types of citrus: orange, lime, or lemon peel. Or you can combine the three. You'll find that this will become one of your favorite ways to remain faithful to the diet.

  1 pound fresh cod, whitefish, sea bass, or rockfish fillets
  ¼ cup fresh herbs, minced: basil, dill, or as available
  2 teaspoons fresh grated citrus peel (orange, lemon, or lime)
  1 tablespoon olive oil

Follow the general directions for steaming on page 237. Combine the herbs with the grated peel and olive oil. Spread the mixture evenly over both sides of the fish. Steam for 10 minutes.

POULTRY DISHES

Along with fish, poultry dishes should be among your principal choices of entrees. A 3½-ounce serving of roast chicken breast without the skin provides only 173 calories, 4.5 grams of fat, and no carbohydrate. A similar piece of turkey breast supplies 157 calories and a mere 3.2 grams of fat. Both supply generous amounts of protein. The calorie and fat contents soar, however, when you don't remove the skin. Chicken climbs to 222 calories and 10.9 grams of fat. Turkey goes up to 197 calories and 8.3 grams of fat.

Other types of poultry, while still devoid of carbohydrate as is all meat, have higher amounts of fat and calories. Roast duck with the skin has 337 calories and 28.4 grams of fat in the

3½-ounce serving. Goose contains 238 calories and 21.9 grams of fat in the same size serving.

Now we'll be the first to admit that having a piece of plain, roast chicken or turkey two or three times a week can become boring. We've all heard the jokes about the Thanksgiving turkey that stays around for weeks, far outliving its welcome on the dinner table. So you'll want to try as many ways as possible to prepare white-meat poultry. These recipes will please your tastebuds. Look for other recipes in magazines. The ground beef in most recipes can be replaced by ground poultry. Just be certain the carbohydrate count stays low so you can remain in ketosis.

Recipes that call for ground poultry meat are based on ground white meat of chicken or turkey. If your store does not carry the ground meat, ask your butcher to skin and bone a few breasts and grind them. Check packaged ground meat to be sure it is white meat and contains no unwanted and unexpected fat and carbohydrate.

Italian Poultry Burger

1 pound ground chicken *or* turkey breast
4 tablespoons unprocessed bran
1 teaspoon finely minced parsley
¼ teaspoon oregano
¼ teaspoon marjoram
1 garlic clove, finely minced
3 tablespoons chopped onions

Combine all the ingredients and form into four burgers. Grill or broil for about 3 minutes on a side.

Poultry Meatloaf

Here's a recipe the whole family will love. You can make it as one large loaf or four individual loaves. You may also wish to make an extra loaf to keep in the freezer for another time.

1 pound ground chicken *or* turkey breast
1 beaten egg *or* egg substitute
4 tablespoons unprocessed bran
1 tablespoon Worcestershire sauce
½ teaspoon Dijon mustard
1 large garlic clove, finely minced
3 tablespoons finely minced onion
¼ teaspoon each sage, black pepper, marjoram, celery salt
1 teaspoon salt

Combine all the ingredients and form into one large loaf or four small loaves. Bake in a preheated 350°F oven for 1¼ hours. Use a meat thermometer to check for doneness (175°F).

Chinese Stir-Fry

Have you ever wondered how a Chinese restaurant can offer so many different dishes? It's simply a matter of making different combinations of many ingredients, and you can do the same in your kitchen. You won't become bored with your diet program if you emphasize Chinese stir-fry cooking. You can have a different dish every day.

One day cook up some scallops with broccoli, another day have chicken with broccoli, and on another make chicken with bamboo shoots and baby carrots. The possibilities are endless, and they can be varied even more by changing seasonings. Oyster sauce and five-spice powder provide unusual tastes. You can change the flavor of a dish entirely by omitting those seasonings and adding two cloves of garlic. A teaspoon of Chinese hot chili sauce will turn any combination of a food into a fiery concoction. Chinese black bean sauce is particularly good with seafood.

Chinese cooking is both low in calories and healthful. You'll want to enjoy such dishes frequently, both when losing weight and when maintaining that loss. If you don't already have one, treat yourself to a good wok. Who deserves it more?

Italian Meatballs

1 pound ground chicken *or* turkey breast
2 tablespoons finely minced green pepper
2 tablespoons finely minced onion
1 tablespoon grated Parmesan cheese
1 large garlic clove, finely minced
4 tablespoons unprocessed bran
¼ teaspoon each oregano, black pepper, thyme, salt

Combine all the ingredients and form into 12 meatballs. Fry in nonstick pan sprayed with vegetable oil spray. Each serving is 3 meatballs.

Oriental Poultry Burgers

Here's a delicious twist on the standard burgers you've been eating. Try serving these Oriental burgers with bean sprouts or Chinese pea pods.

1 pound ground chicken *or* turkey breast
4 tablespoons unprocessed bran
1 tablespoon soy sauce
½ teaspoon freshly grated ginger
½ teaspoon powdered coriander

Combine all the ingredients and form into four burgers. Grill or broil the burgers for about 3 minutes on each side.

Florentine Chicken

4 ounces chicken breast (skinless and boneless)
1 cup fresh spinach *or* ½ cup thawed frozen spinach
1 tablespoon grated Parmesan cheese
1 tablespoon chicken bouillon
¼ teaspoon each thyme, salt, pepper

Combine the bouillon with the seasonings and mix with the spinach. Place the seasoned spinach on the bottom of a casserole dish and place the chicken breast on top of the bed of spinach. Sprinkle with cheese. Cover. Bake in a preheated 350°F oven for 30 minutes.

Poultry Burgers

Why not prepare several burgers and store them in the freezer? That way you can pop one out whenever you don't have the time for elaborate dinner preparations. When cooking, make an extra patty you can have later in the week as a sandwich for lunch.

> 4 ounces ground chicken *or* turkey breast
> 1 tablespoon finely minced onion
> 1 tablespoon unprocessed bran
> ¼ teaspoon paprika
> ¼ teaspoon salt
> lettuce leaves
> Dijon mustard
> thinly sliced onion rings

Combine the poultry, minced onion, bran, paprika, and salt and form into a burger. Grill or broil the burger but be sure not to overcook. Count on half the time needed for beef, about 3 minutes on each side. Serve on large leaves of lettuce with a dab of Dijon mustard and some raw onion rings.

Turkey Cutlets

Practically any veal recipe can be duplicated deliciously with turkey, at a real saving in fat and calories. Have your butcher skin and bone a large turkey breast and cut it into cutlets weighing 4 ounces each. You can package them separately and have them ready in the freezer for whenever you'd like to cook them. You may want to prepare two cutlets so you can enjoy one of them for lunch that week. Serve the cutlet as a sandwich on two large lettuce leaves with a dab of Dijon mustard.

4 ounces turkey cutlet
2 tablespoons unprocessed bran
1 beaten egg *or* egg substitute
vegetable oil spray

Dip turkey cutlet first into the egg or egg substitute and then into the bran to coat. Allow the coated cutlet to set for about 10 minutes; this helps to keep the coating firmer and less likely to crumble off when cooking. Spray pan with vegetable oil spray. Sauté the cutlet until crisp, about 3 minutes per side.

Chicken Cacciatore

4 ounces chicken breast (boneless and skinless)
¼ cup chicken bouillon
1 tablespoon each chopped onion, green pepper, tomato,
  mushrooms
1 garlic clove, finely minced
1 bay leaf
¼ teaspoon each oregano, thyme, salt

Cut chicken into strips. Sauté in a nonstick pan with the chicken bouillon until the chicken is no longer pink. Add vegetables and seasonings. Simmer until tender.

Note: If you increase the amount of vegetables to a total of 1 cup raw, this dish will then provide both your protein and vegetable allowance for a meal.

Turkey Soup

This is a great way to use up leftovers from a turkey roast. It takes little time to prepare. You can use it as a main meal for your family, perhaps with a sandwich on the side for those not on the diet. The easiest way to make the soup is to use canned turkey broth. If you feel energetic and have the time to do it, see the recipe on page 249 for homemade broth.

5 cups turkey broth
3 stalks celery, cut into ½-inch pieces
2 medium potatoes, cut into 1-inch cubes
2 carrots, cut into julienne strips
1 onion, quartered
1 teaspoon thyme
1 teaspoon salt
½ teaspoon pepper
¼ teaspoon sage
2 cups cooked turkey meat, cut into pieces

Add the vegetables and seasonings to your broth and bring to a boil. Reduce heat and simmer 45 minutes, until vegetables are tender. Add the turkey and simmer 5 more minutes to heat meat through.

Note: This dish includes both the protein food and the vegetable for a meal.

Chinese Chicken Stir-Fry

4 ounces chicken breast (skinless and boneless)
1 cup total raw vegetables: bean sprouts, water chestnuts, mushrooms, pea pods, broccoli, carrots, bamboo shoots
2 tablespoons chicken bouillon
1 tablespoon oyster sauce
1 teaspoon soy sauce
1 tablespoon unprocessed bran
¼ teaspoon Chinese five-spice powder

Cut chicken into small strips. Chop vegetables into bite-size pieces. Combine 1 tablespoon of the bouillon with the remaining ingredients to make a sauce. Heat the remaining tablespoon of bouillon to boiling in a large skillet or wok. Stir-fry the chicken until it loses its pink color. Remove it from the skillet. Stir-fry the vegetables until tender. Return the chicken to the skillet along with combined sauce. Heat to boiling, stirring. Serve.

Note: This dish includes both the protein food and the vegetable for a meal.

Yakitori

This delicious Japanese dish clearly illustrates why Oriental cuisine has kept people in the Far East healthy and slender for centuries. Yakitori is low in fat and carbohydrates. This recipe serves four people. Those not following the diet and those in maintenance will be able to have steamed rice along with the yakitori. Everyone can enjoy it with a salad.

    1 pound chicken *or* turkey breast (skinless and boneless)
    2 tablespoons chicken bouillon
    2 tablespoons soy sauce
    2 tablespoons dry sherry
    1 tablespoon fresh grated ginger
    2 garlic cloves, finely minced

Cut the chicken or turkey into cubes. Mix the remaining ingredients together to make a marinade. Marinate the poultry for 3 to 4 hours in a shallow dish in the refrigerator. Put the poultry cubes on skewers and grill or broil no more than 10 minutes.

Chicken Breast Mexicali

This dish is a great example of how a recipe can be adapted to suit your tastes and to provide variety as well. While the recipe calls for chicken breast, you can use the same ingredients and technique with fish fillets, turkey, or other kinds of meats. You'll be surprised at how easy it is to whip up such a festive dish even when time is short.

    4 ounces chicken breast (skinless and boneless)
    1 tablespoon chopped green pepper
    1 tablespoon chopped onion
    1 tablespoon chopped tomato
    1 garlic clove, finely minced
    hot pepper sauce to taste
    1 tablespoon chopped cilantro
    1 tablespoon chicken bouillon
    vegetable oil spray

Coat a nonstick pan with vegetable oil spray and heat. Sauté the chicken breast along with minced garlic clove until garlic begins to turn golden. Mix the remaining ingredients and pour over the chicken. Cover. Simmer gently for 20 minutes.

Chicken Curry

This dish is especially delicious if you add a part of your daily allotment of fruit to it. Try it with 2 tablespoons of chopped apple, pineapple, or pear. You might also add your meal's selection of vegetables when you cover and simmer the chicken. Just add an extra tablespoon of chicken bouillon.

4 ounces chicken breast (skinless and boneless)
2 tablespoons chopped onion
1 large garlic clove, finely minced
2 tablespoons chicken bouillon
¼ teaspoon curry powder (more if you like spicy food)
¼ teaspoon paprika

Cut the chicken into thin strips. Sauté in a nonstick pan with the chicken bouillon until white. Combine the remaining ingredients and pour over chicken. Cover. Simmer for 20 minutes or until fork tender.

Chicken à l'Orange

4 ounces chicken breast (skinless and boneless)
4 ounces diet orange soda
1 tablespoon each coarsely chopped onion and mushrooms
⅛ teaspoon each basil, rosemary, sage, salt, thyme

Mix the soda with the seasonings. Place the chicken in a small casserole dish and pour the soda mixture over it. Sprinkle onions and mushrooms over the chicken. Cover. Bake in a preheated 350°F oven for 30 minutes.

Sautéed Chicken Breast

You'll never believe this dish is low in calories. The buttery flavor is a real treat.

    4 ounces chicken breast (skinless and boneless)
    1 teaspoon lemon juice
    2 tablespoons chicken bouillon
    ¼ teaspoon imitation butter extract
    ¼ teaspoon dry mustard
    ⅛ teaspoon each powdered ginger and nutmeg

Cut the chicken into small strips. Sauté in 1 tablespoon of chicken bouillon until white. Combine the remaining bouillon with the other ingredients and pour over the chicken. Cover. Simmer for 20 minutes.

Homemade Turkey Broth

    turkey carcass and scraps
    3 quarts cold water (or water to cover)
    1 teaspoon salt

Place a turkey carcass and scraps in the water. Add the salt. Bring to a simmer and skim off any fat that rises to the surface. Simmer at least 3 hours. Do not allow to come to a fast boil, and skim several times. Allow to cool and skim again.

Chicken Cobb Salad

The original Cobb Salad was served at the Brown Derby restaurant in Hollywood many years ago. This version calls for ingredients to be coarsely chopped and mixed with dressing. The recipe serves four persons.

8 large lettuce leaves
6 cups head lettuce, chopped
2 carrots, chopped
2 green onions, chopped
1 cup red cabbage, chopped
2 cups cooked chicken breast, chopped
4 hard-cooked eggs, chopped
½ cup vinaigrette dressing (see page 255)

Arrange the lettuce leaves on the plates. Mix all the remaining ingredients and mound on the lettuce leaves.

Note: This dish includes both the protein food and the vegetable for a meal.

Turkey or Chicken Salad

This dish looks so festive you'll want to serve it to friends.

6 cups fresh spinach leaves
1 cup grapefruit segments
1 cup orange segments
2 cups cooked chicken *or* turkey breast, cubed
½ teaspoon dry mustard
½ teaspoon paprika
1 garlic clove, finely minced
½ teaspoon poppy seeds
¼ cup low-fat mayonnaise

On each plate, arrange spinach leaves to form a bed. Decorate the edges of the plate with alternating grapefruit and orange segments. Mix the remaining ingredients and place a scoop of the mixture in the center of each plate.

Note: This dish includes both the protein food and fruit for a meal.

Lemon-Mustard Chicken Wings

Though this recipe works best with wings, you can use other chicken parts. Also consider using turkey wings. This recipe serves four persons, so you can use it for the entire family or cut it down as necessary. You could make half the recipe so you could eat one portion now and save the other for tomorrow.

2 pounds chicken wings
1 tablespoon Dijon mustard
¼ cup lemon juice
¼ teaspoon lemon pepper
4 garlic cloves, minced
¼ cup corn oil

Combine all the ingredients except the chicken to make a basting mixture. Grill or broil the chicken, basting until done, about 20 minutes. Test for doneness by tugging at the wing joint; when the bones separate easily, the chicken is done.

Turkey Chili

The original chili was made without any beans at all. Translated literally, chili con carne means chili peppers with meat. So let's go back to the basics for this bean- and carbohydrate-free chili. The recipe feeds four.

1 pound ground turkey
1 cup chicken bouillon
½ cup green and red bell peppers, chopped
3 tablespoons chopped onion
2 garlic cloves, finely minced
1 teaspoon salt
1 tablespoon chili powder

In a nonstick pan, cook the turkey until crumbly. Add the remaining ingredients. Cover. Simmer for 30 minutes.

RED MEAT

We've all heard so much about fat and cholesterol in terms of heart disease that many people have cut back considerably on red meat or stopped eating it altogether. While it's true that red meat does contribute substantially to the total fat and cholesterol in the diet, it isn't necessary to eliminate it from the diet completely. Rather it's a matter of learning to use meats in the diet properly. In the past a serving of meat was often a huge slab of well-marbled steak or prime rib. That's just too much of the wrong kind of meat. A more proper serving is about 4 ounces of lean meat. Some cuts of beef are naturally leaner than others. Instead of prime rib, opt for the London broil.

Consider replacing beef with beefalo, a very low-fat cross between cattle and buffalo, with 4 grams of fat per 3.5 ounces. To order call Adams Processing at (615) 395-4819. Or how about buffalo meat by itself, or some exotic meats including elk and ostrich? Call the American Bison Meat Corporation at (619) 789-3044 to place an order or obtain a brochure. Venison is a low-fat delicacy found in many pricey restaurants. To learn where you can buy it for use at home, call Broadleaf Venison at (800) 336-3844.

The best advice is to eat a wide variety of foods and to enjoy them in moderation. With that in mind, here are some red meat recipes that are light and flavorful.

Beef en Brochette

With a meal like this one, you'll have a hard time believing you're on a diet. The recipe serves four persons.

Marinade:
½ cup red wine
¼ cup vegetable oil
1 teaspoon each Worcestershire sauce and catsup
1 garlic clove, finely minced
½ teaspoon each marjoram and rosemary

1 pound beef tenderloin
2 green peppers

2 onions
2 tomatoes
8 mushrooms

Cut the meat and vegetables into cubes and pieces to be threaded onto skewers later. Combine all the marinade ingredients and then mix with the meat and vegetables. Allow to stand 2 to 3 hours in the refrigerator. Arrange the pieces on skewers. Grill or broil to taste.

Note:: This dish includes both the protein food and the vegetable for a meal.

Beef Orientale

Even if you're in a hurry, and cooking just for one, you can make your meal a pleasant one. Here's an approach that works well.

4 ounces filet mignon
4 fresh mushrooms
½ green pepper
¼ onion
1 tablespoon soy sauce
1 teaspoon lemon juice

Cut the meat and vegetables into cubes. Mix the soy sauce and lemon juice and add the meat and vegetables. Allow to marinate for about 30 minutes. (That's just right to take a shower and get ready for the evening.) To cook, you have a choice: Skewer the meat and vegetables and broil or grill, or quick-fry the meal in a nonstick pan.

Veal and Blue Cheese

Here's just the ticket for jaded taste buds. This is a once-in-a-while treat because of the high fat content of cheese. But as part of a total, varied diet you can enjoy it without guilt. The best part is how easy it is to prepare.

3 ounces lean veal cutlet
1 ounce blue cheese
vegetable oil spray

Coat a nonstick pan with vegetable oil spray and heat. Pound veal thin. Over medium-high heat quickly cook the veal, 3 minutes on one side and 1 minute on the other. Crumble the blue cheese and sprinkle it over the meat. Cover. Cook for 1 minute.

Veal with Lime and Cilantro

4 ounces lean veal cutlet
juice of ½ lime
¼ cup chicken broth
1 tablespoon minced cilantro
¼ teaspoon salt

In a nonstick pan, bring the broth, cilantro, and salt to a gentle boil. Pound veal cutlets thin. Sauté the veal 2 to 3 minutes on each side. Add lime juice. Cover. Simmer for 5 more minutes.

Old-Fashioned Lamb Stew

This recipe can be made with either beef or pork. But if you haven't had lamb for a while, it's a nice change of pace with a flavor all its own. The recipe serves four persons.

1 pound lean lamb
1 cup each coarsely chopped carrots, celery, rutabaga or
   parsnips, onion
1 cup beef bouillon
3 bay leaves
6 juniper berries
2 garlic cloves, minced
1 teaspoon salt
1 teaspoon ground pepper
1 teaspoon marjoram
vegetable oil spray

Cut the lamb into ½-inch by 1-inch strips. Coat the bottom of a large, heavy pot with vegetable oil spray. Sauté the lamb until browned. Add ½ cup of the beef bouillon. Bring to a boil. Reduce heat, and simmer 30 minutes. Add the remaining bouillon along with vegetables. Cover. Cook for 30 minutes or until vegetables are fork tender.

Note: This dish includes both the protein food and the vegetable for a meal.

SALAD DRESSINGS

Even the freshest, crispest salad tastes better with a delicious dressing. But dressings can come packed with fat, calories, and even carbohydrate, ruining your otherwise good intentions. This is another example of how important it is to read the labels of food products. One oil and vinegar dressing may contain 0.6 grams of carbohydrate per tablespoon. But in another the carbohydrate content may rise to 6.6 grams. That can be just enough to get you out of ketosis and into trouble.

You'll want to watch the calorie and fat content as well as the level of carbohydrate in bottled dressings and packaged mixes. Ranch dressing prepared with regular mayonnaise has only 0.6 grams of carbohydrate per tablespoon, but 100 calories and 11 grams of fat.

There are some excellent dressings on the market that are low in calories, carbohydrates, and fat. Look for El Molino Herbal Secrets, Mrs. Pickford's Herb Magic, Pritikin, and Skinny Haven dressings in your supermarket and health food stores. Skinny Haven is a particular convenience because the dressings come in individual packets. You can easily carry one with you when you go out to dinner and enjoy your salad without guilt.

Homemade salad dressings are best of all. They're easy to prepare and they store well, so you can keep two or three kinds in your refrigerator.

Low-Cal Vinaigrette

Yield: 1 cup
Serving: 1 tablespoon
½ cup water
2 tablespoons oil
2 tablespoons fresh lemon juice
4 tablespoons cider vinegar
2 garlic cloves, minced
1 teaspoon Dijon mustard
1 teaspoon minced fresh basil
1 teaspoon minced fresh chives
1 teaspoon salt
1 teaspoon pepper (freshly ground if possible)

Blend all the ingredients together and store in the refrigerator.

Vinaigrette Variations

Exclude the garlic and herbs and add other ingredients as follows.

Dill Vinaigrette: 1 tablespoon minced fresh dill

Parsley Vinaigrette: 2 tablespoons minced fresh parsley

Curry Vinaigrette: 1 teaspoon curry powder
                    1 teaspoon ground coriander

Mexican Vinaigrette: 2 tablespoons fresh cilantro

GELATIN DESSERTS AND SNACKS

Many patients find sugar-free gelatin (sweetened with Nu-traSweet) to be an absolute lifesaver in dieting and in maintaining their weight loss whenever they crave a sweet for dessert or a snack. Experiment with different flavors and serve it different ways. Be sure to keep a supply in the refrigerator at all times. Here are just a few suggestions.

Checkerboard Gelatin

Prepare two colors of sugar-free gelatin, lemon and lime, for example, according to the directions on the package. Pour into flat pans and allow to set. Cut into 1-inch cubes. You can mix the cubes together in wine goblets to make a colorful attractive treat. Or stick toothpicks into the cubes to enjoy as finger foods.

Gelatin Salad

Stir in a variety of shredded greens before allowing the gelatin to set. Make individual salads in small bowls and glasses or a large salad in a serving bowl. You can form shapes using molds for a festive touch at the table. Dream up all kinds of combinations.

Lemon gelatin with radicchio
Orange gelatin with shredded lettuce
Lime gelatin with strips of spinach
Lemon gelatin with shredded celery, carrots, and radishes

Any combination such as these will use only a small portion of your daily allotment of greens. Remember that you're permitted the equivalent of one head of lettuce daily.

Gelatin on a Stick

Many of the low-calorie frozen confections available today have a large amount of carbohydrates in each serving. Sugar-free gelatin pops are a wonderful easy-to-make substitute.

Spray the inside of small tubular glasses with a bit of vegetable oil spray. Champagne flutes and cordial glasses work well. Prepare the gelatin according to package directions. Pour the gelatin into the glasses and allow to set. Insert popsicle sticks when you remove the gelatin from the glasses. The light spray of oil will let the gelatin slide out easily. Kids will love this idea.

Gelatin "Cookies"

If you've ever cut out cookies during the holidays, you know how much fun it can be. Why not bring out your cookie cutters and use them with gelatin? Just make the gelatin in shallow pans, filled to about the height of cutters. You can have green Christmas trees and red Santas even in July.

Gelatin and Fruit

Sugar-free gelatin is terrific for stretching your daily servings of fruit. While a few grapes may be gone in a moment, they last a lot longer when floating in a shimmering mold of gelatin. Use your imagination to create different combinations. Here are a few suggestions to get you started.

Red gelatin with thinly sliced apples
Green gelatin with a few seedless grapes
Orange gelatin with segments of Mandarin orange
Yellow gelatin with cubes of pears

• • •

To be absolutely certain you stay within your daily limits on fruit, which is high in carbohydrates, measure carefully. It's best to prepare the gelatin and fruit combinations in individual bowls or glasses so you don't accidentally eat more than a serving at one time.

Chapter 14

DOCTOR TO DOCTOR
Hyperinsulinism:
The Metabolic Trap in
Resistant Obesity

Calvin Ezrin, M.D.*

As with any weight loss program, we believe this one is best when followed under medical supervision. That is not to say that the program has any inherent danger. Quite the contrary, we believe it is safe and effective. But no one understands an individual's medical history and state of health as well as that individual's physician. And since this program is so directly concerned with health, the physician should observe its effects, particularly in obese diabetics.

We hope this book will act as a bridge between doctor and patient, offering to both a practical solution to a difficult problem. Weight loss has been frustrating to the medical profession and the public for years. By reading the book and following the program, patients will be able to take an active role in promoting their own health and well-being. Physicians will be pleased to observe positive improvements in their patients as they lose weight.

Most doctors simply don't have the time or the resources to educate and supervise every patient who could benefit from an

*Calvin Ezrin, M.D., is Attending Physician at Cedars-Sinai Medical Center and Tarzana Regional Medical Center in Los Angeles, Clinical Professor of Medicine at the University of California at Los Angeles, and author of numerous articles and medical textbooks. His specific area of expertise is endocrinology, and he is considered a world authority on the pituitary gland. He participated in historic research on glucagon with Dr. Charles Best, co-discoverer of insulin, at the University of Toronto, where he received his medical degree.

intensive program of diet and exercise. In addition, with developments in medicine occurring as rapidly as they do, no medical practitioner can expect to be on top of every advancement in health care.

We've written this book to be followed by individuals who have a significant amount of weight to lose. We've explained not only the day-to-day requirements of the program, but also the scientific rationale for why it works so well. We understand that many people who want to follow the program also want their physician to understand and approve of it. Diabetics will need the help of their doctors to adjust or withdraw their medication.

We suggest that patients either bring the book to their physicians or photocopy this chapter for them. It would be wonderful, of course, if every physician had the time to read the entire book, but this chapter will answer questions about the medical and scientific scope of the program and its underlying physiology. It has been written expressly for the physician. On a doctor-to-doctor basis, Dr. Ezrin has spelled out in detail his medical rationale.

• • •

There exists an unequivocal link between obesity and diabetes in the vast majority of cases. More than 90 percent of Type II diabetics are significantly overweight. And many obese individuals eventually develop diabetes. It has been said that if diabetic patients were simply to lose their excessive weight and engage in an exercise program, the manifestations of their disease would disappear. Yet that goal has been elusive.

Prevention and treatment of obesity are difficult. Most physicians are reticent to treat obese patients because the outcome is usually disappointing. Patients, in turn, are drawn to commercially available weight loss approaches that have little lasting effect.

Why are the long-term results of weight loss programs so dismal? For the individual who wants to lose just a few pounds and inches, typically for cosmetic purposes, caloric reduction and increased physical activity will suffice if such a program is adhered to for whatever period of time. But when weight gain reaches clinical signficance, that is to say in excess of 20 percent over ideal weight, obesity becomes increasingly resistant. Even when weight loss is accomplished, the well-publicized rebound effect and subsequent recycling become the rule rather than the exception. A major reason for such failure has been neglect of the importance of the role of insulin in the regulation of body weight.

Certainly insulin has its heroic side. But until recently the malevolent side of the hormone has been ignored. Ironically, the negative physiologic effects of insulin have been well documented. Insulin controls fat build-up and breakdown as well as salt and water retention. It is the fat-building hormones generating triglycerides from carbohydrate precursors in the liver and also in adipose tissue where they are stored as energy reserves. Insulin also blocks fat breakdown via inhibition of the lipolytic action of growth hormone, glucagon, and catecholamines on the hormone-sensitive lipase in adipocytes.

Insulin is the second most powerful salt-retaining hormone, next to aldosterone. Without excessive intake of calories, it can produce rapid weight gain from fluid retention alone. But why do obese individuals have an insulin problem? While I have concentrated on this problem for many years in my own clinical practice, significant attention has also been paid to the syndrome of insulin resistance in medical literature. The latter has been associated with elevations in triglycerides and blood pressure, increases in both total and LDL cholesterol, raised risk of heart disease, and, of course, obesity itself.

The insulin-resistant individual produces a significant amount of insulin by the pancreas, but that insulin is incapable of achieving normal glucose metabolism. Levels of glucose rise, and in an effort to compensate, the body produces yet more insulin. The resultant latter state is termed *hyperinsulinism*.

There are four major causes for the development of insulin resistance. First is obesity itself, developed over time, in which adipose tissue produces a substance that moves to muscle tissue to selectively block the blood sugar-lowering effect of insulin. The second cause is Type II diabetes in which insulin resistance may precede diabetes and may or may not be associated with obesity. Third, when blood sugar levels exceed 300, or perhaps even less, the hyperglycemia can trigger insulin resistance. The fourth cause is stress, whether physical, emotional, or traumatic, that increases insulin-neutralizing stress hormones including cortisol, adrenalin, and glucagon.

Adipose tissue produces a selective antagonist to the blood sugar-lowering effect of insulin. This has recently been identified as TNF-α (tumor necrosis factor-alpha) in mice. The more obese the patient, the more of this antagonist is produced. The normal pancreas readily responds to the antagonist by increased secretion of insulin which maintains normal blood sugar. Because the Type II diabetic pancreas secretes less insulin than normal, hyperglycemia results from a combination of obesity-related antagonism and inherent insulin resistance. However, sufficient extra insulin is often produced to favor weight and inhibit its loss. Because the other effects of insulin are not significantly impaired, the resultant hyperinsulinism produces a variety of metabolic changes favoring further weight gain. Measures designed to diminish insulin's weight-promoting influence are the basis of the Insulin Control Diet. This regimen restricts calories from fat and carbohydrates. The diet consists mainly of adequate protein with vitamin and mineral supplementation. Together with a stipulated program of physical activity, the program rapidly decreases insulin secretion, thus reversing its weight-enhancing effects.

Aerobic exercise is the only other modality besides insulin that can decrease blood glucose. It does so without involving insulin. Therefore, exercise further reduces the hyperinsulinism of obesity and also exerts an anabolic effect favoring muscle build-up. Thus, a low-carbohydrate diet and exercise are the favored prescription for treatment of obesity.

At first glance, a low-calorie diet seems inadequate to meet normal nutritional needs. In fact, once protein, vitamin, and mineral needs are provided, the remaining caloric requirements can readily be provided by mobilizing endogenous fat stores. Doing so establishes a state of mild, beneficial ketosis.

Ketones appear in the urine when insulin has been reduced sufficiently. This usually occurs within 48 hours on the Insulin Control Diet. Urine ketones are thus a reflection of satisfactory reduction of blood insulin levels. This degree of ketosis is never enough to upset acid/base balance. Indeed, this mild ketosis must not be confused with diabetic ketoacidosis with which it often is unjustly linked.

Ketonuria serves as an indicator of successful insulin reduction in this program and can be used to monitor the amount of carbohydrate in the diet. The diuretic effect of insulin reduction plus ketosis may deplete body sodium and water significantly with resultant postural hypotension. Therefore, at least one teaspoon of supplemental salt (5 grams) should be taken daily. If the patient is already on a diuretic it should be withdrawn gradually once ketosis is acheived and the salt supplement then added.

The physical and psychological benefits of ketosis are significant. As insulin levels are reduced, most patients experience relief from hunger and, in particular, from carbohydrate cravings. Hypertension often responds rapidly even before much weight is lost. Elevated triglycerides are very sensitive to insulin reduction responding rapidly to the ketotic state. An increased level of the neurotransmitter serotonin achieves a calming effect and allows for better quality sleep patterns.

Uric acid and ketones share a common renal excretory pathway. Uric acid levels may rise in the serum while following this regimen, sometimes to the point of frank gout, especially in susceptible male patients. Therefore, uric acid levels should be followed at monthly intervals. If needed, allopurinol should be prescribed to control hyperuricemia above 10 mg percent. Increasing fluid intake would also help to eliminate hyperuricemia. Routinely, at least 64 ounces of noncaloric fluid are prescribed, with more if required as indicated either by hyperuricemia or a strongly positive ketonuria.

Potassium supplementation is rarely needed, as there is no inordinate loss of the mineral on this program unless unrelated diarrhea or vomiting occur. The diuretic effect of the Insulin Control Diet is confined to sodium and water elimination, with no appreciable secondary hyperaldosteronism that might contribute to potassium depletion.

The major source of dietary calcium is limited on this program, owing to the carbohydrate (lactose) content of milk and other dairy products. Therefore, calcium intake should be supplemented by at least 1,000 mg of elemental calcium daily.

Initially, more weight is lost than can be accounted for by calorie deficiency. The diuretic effect of insulin reduction may produce a weight loss of 5 to 10 pounds in the first week. Therefore, a slower rate of loss, mainly from fat, is the rule. Women can expect a satisfying weight loss of from two to three pounds weekly, and men will lose three to four pounds a week, when diet and exercise recommendations are followed.

As weight loss progresses, metabolism decreases somewhat. This is an adaptive mechanism to prolong survival in times of starvation. The phenomenon involves a reduced conversion of thyroxine (T4) to triiodothyronine (T3) via decreased activity of five-prime deiodinase, an enzyme sensitive to carbohydrate stimulated insulin levels.

Increased exercise can compensate for the negative effects of hypometabolism including cold intolerance and a reduced rate of weight loss. In the stabilization phase of this program, hypometabolism can ultimately be advantageous because carbohydrates slowly added increase metabolism and thereby permit the addition of calories without a discouraging weight gain that frequently occurs at this time. (See Chapters 10 and 11 for details on stabilization and maintenance.)

For diabetic patients on oral hypoglycemic agents or insulin, expect a substantial decrease in drug requirements and reduced dosages as indicated by blood sugar levels. The beneficial ketonuria will not occur in the presence of exogenous insulin, and usually not with sulfonylureas. After withdrawal of these drugs, ketonuria can be used to monitor the level of insulin secretion.

Type II diabetes can be reversed with moderate weight loss, but the program should continue until the original goal weight is achieved to reduce insulin resistance as much as possible. The diet during weight loss has very little carbohydrate. Later, in the stabilization and particularly in the maintenance phases, much more carbohydrate will be consumed, requiring increased insulin action for its disposal.

Obese Type II diabetics are insulin resistant partly from obesity itself, but also from an inherent defect in glucose disposal that is independent of overweight. Compared to normal weight- and age-matched subjects, these patients are often hyperinsulinemic. But because they are unable to produce enough insulin to overcome this combined resistance, they are hyperglycemic. The Insulin Control Diet is the ideal treatment for the Type II diabetic because of the immediately decreased need to insulin. This is entirely owing to the program's very low carbohydrate content. Conversely, a high-carbohydrate intake, even within a reduced-calorie diet, would not confer this significant advantage.

The Diabetes Control and Complications Trial (DCCT) has shown that in Type I diabetics with insulin-dependent diabetes mellitus (IDDM), good control via intensive insulin therapy was extremely beneficial in delaying the onset and progression of retinopathy, nephropathy, and neuropathy. As 90 percent of diabetics have Type II, noninsulin-dependent diabetes mellitus (NIDDM), these benefits of good control could likely be conferred on a much larger number of patients. The mechanisms by which hyperglycemia cause the microvascular and neuropathic complications of diabetes are likely the same in both types of diabetes. Therefore, good control should be the goal in all patients, regardless of type.

A large body of evidence suggests that insulin itself is atherogenic. To achieve good control of Type II diabetes using the popular, relatively high-carbohydrate dietary regimens common in practice requires that exogenous insulin be added to overcome the insulin resistance characteristic of this disorder.

In a recent study, seventy-five NIDDM men were intensively treated with insulin and compared to a like number given standard insulin doses. After six months, glycosylated hemoglobin levels were less than 7.3 percent in the intensively treated group and a level 2 percent lower than the standard group was maintained for the duration of the study, which averaged 27 months. Between the two groups, there was no difference in weight, lipid levels, and blood pressure. Macrovascular events (myocardial infarction, congestive heart failure, cerebrovascular accident, amputation, and cardiovascular death) were significantly higher in the intensive insulin treated group.

Beyond the benefits of good blood sugar control, there are disadvantages to insulin therapy that should be acknowledged. Exogenous insulin slows weight loss in Type II diabetic patients on reducing diets. Weight gain is common when insulin therapy is instituted and is more than can be accounted for by storage of calories that were lost in the urine before better control was achieved. As well, the insulin-related weight gain is likely the result of appetite stimulation and salt and water retention.

To resolve the dilemma of the role of insulin in the management of Type II diabetes, we should strive to achieve excellent control with a minimum amount of insulin, whether exogenous or endogenous. This can often be achieved with the Insulin Control Diet program, including aerobic exercise, as detailed in this book.

The goal is a glycosylated hemoglobin level of less than 1.5 percent above the upper limit of normal for the assay used. If this cannot be achieved on diet alone after a satisfactory weight loss has removed a significant amount of insulin resistance, a sulfonylurea agent and/or Metformin should be added. If oral therapy fails, insulin treatment will be necessary.

In our experience, many obese diabetic patients can be so well controlled on the Insulin Control Diet that they no longer need exogenous insulin or oral hypoglycemic agents. However, advancing age with decreasing pancreatic reserve may lead to a gradual loss of blood sugar control even when ideal weight is maintained. For these patients, oral agents should be prescribed, followed by insulin if necessary.

Let me end on a very personal note. The concepts and the program I have just described may, indeed, seem radical to you at this time. They may even fly in the face of beliefs you have long held to be true. The natural reaction is to reject them out of hand. I ask you not to do that. Instead, allow yourself an open mind to test the Insulin Control Diet in your own management of patients. I believe that you and your patients will be rewarded with marvelous results similar to those I have experienced over the years.

The concepts of insulin resistance and their untoward physiologic effects have been well documented and will continue to receive increasing attention both in the medical literature and the lay media. It is one thing to describe and name a syndrome. It is another, very different and more important, thing to offer patients a practical treatment for that syndrome. Give the Insulin Control Diet a reasonable trial and I am certain you will agree that this is that treatment you and your patients have needed for years.

For inquiries write to:

The Ezrin Metabolic Center
18372 Clark Street. #226
Tarzana, CA 91356
(818) 996-3936 Fax: (818) 996-3655

COMPOSITION OF COMMONLY CONSUMED FOODS AND BEVERAGES

The following lists of foods show their caloric, carbohydrate, fat, and protein content. They should serve as a guide during your weight loss, stabilization, and maintenance programs—in other words, for the rest of your life. You don't have to memorize the exact composition of each food. The important thing is to be aware of the approximate amounts of calories, carbohydrates, and fats in what you eat.

Take a few minutes to glance through the lists now. As you plan your meals, review the food composition from time to time. We think you'll be surprised—even shocked—at how many calories and how much fat many of the foods contain. One glance at the listings for fast foods should be enough to make anyone vow not to eat them again. Whether you're trying to avoid calories, carbohydrates, or fat, most fast food restaurants serve up disasters.

These lists can cover only a few items. Don't forget to read the labels of the foods you purchase regularly.

Limits of space prohibit us from supplying data on each and every food you may eat or want to eat. We've tried to provide an overview. For a very extensive compilation of the carbohydrate, fat, and protein contents of a vast number of foods, we'd recommend the book *Food Values of Portions Commonly Used* by Jean Pennington. It's available in most bookstores.

Food	Serving Size	Calories	Carbohydrates (g)	Fat (g)	Protein (g)
Alcoholic Beverages					
Beer	12 oz	148	13.2	0.0	0.9
Beer, Light	12 oz	100	6.0	0.0	0.4
Liquers (54 proof)	1 oz	97	11.5	0.0	0.0
Daquiri	3½ oz	122	5.2	0.0	0.0
Manhattan	3½ oz	164	7.9	0.0	0.0
Martini	3½ oz	140	0.3	0.0	0.0
Gin, Rum, Vodka, Whiskey, Scotch					
80 proof	1 oz	65	0.0	0.0	0.0
86 proof	1 oz	70	0.0	0.0	0.0
90 proof	1 oz	74	0.0	0.0	0.0
94 proof	1 oz	77	0.0	0.0	0.0
100 proof	1 oz	83	0.0	0.0	0.0
Wine					
Champagne	4 oz	84	3.0	0.0	0.0
Red	3½ oz	76	2.4	0.0	0.0
White	3½ oz	80	3.4	0.0	0.0
Carbonated Beverages					
Coca-Cola	12 oz	144	37.5	0.0	0.0
Ginger ale	12 oz	113	29.0	0.0	0.0
Dr Pepper	12 oz	159	40.7	0.0	0.0
Root beer	12 oz	163	42.2	0.0	0.0
Seven-Up	12 oz	144	36.0	0.0	0.0
Tonic water	12 oz	126	31.2	0.0	0.0
Club soda, mineral water, water	12 oz	0	0.0	0.0	0.0
Diet soda	12 oz	0–2	0.0	0.0	0.0

Food	Serving Size	Calories	Carbohydrates (g)	Fat (g)	Protein (g)
Candy and Snacks					
Almond Joy	1 oz	151	18.5	7.8	1.7
Chunky	12 oz	143	17.9	7.1	1.9
Hershey's chocolate	1 oz	160	16.5	9.4	2.2
Nestle's Crunch	1 oz	160	19.0	8.0	2.0
Almonds	1 oz	176	5.5	16.2	5.2
Peanuts	1 oz	170	5.4	14.0	8.6
Jelly beans	10 pieces	66	16.7	0.0	0.0
Marshmallows	1 large	25	6.2	0.0	0.2
Corn chips	1 oz	153	16.6	8.8	1.7
Cracker Jacks	1 oz	114	25.5	1.0	0.8
Popcorn (air popped)	1 cup	54	10.7	0.7	1.8
Potato chips	1 oz	159	14.0	11.2	3.0
Pretzels	1 oz	111	22.4	1.0	2.6
Tortilla chips	1 oz	139	18.6	6.6	2.0
Dairy Foods					
American cheese	1 oz	106	0.5	8.9	6.3
Cheddar cheese	1 oz	114	0.4	9.4	7.1
Cottage cheese (1 percent fat)	1 cup	164	6.2	2.3	28.0
Cream cheese	1 oz	99	0.8	9.9	2.1
Gouda cheese	1 oz	101	0.6	7.8	7.1
Monterey Jack cheese	1 oz	106	0.2	8.6	6.9
Mozzarella cheese (part skim)	1 oz	72	0.8	4.5	6.9
Swiss cheese	1 oz	107	1.0	7.8	8.1
Buttermilk	1 cup	99	11.7	2.2	8.1
Whole milk	1 cup	150	11.0	8.0	8.0

Food	Serving Size	Calories	Carbohydrates (g)	Fat (g)	Protein (g)
Dairy Foods (continued)					
Lowfat milk (2 percent)	1 cup	121	11.7	4.7	8.1
Lowfat milk (1 percent)	1 cup	102	11.7	2.6	8.0
Nonfat milk (skim)	1 cup	86	11.9	0.4	8.4
Yogurt (lowfat)	1 cup	144	16.0	3.5	11.9
Yogurt (nonfat)	1 cup	127	17.4	0.4	13.0
Yogurt (fruit)	1 cup	225	42.3	2.6	9.0
Half & half	1 tbsp	20	0.6	1.7	0.4
Whipping cream	1 tbsp	52	0.4	5.6	0.3
Sour cream	1 tbsp	26	0.5	2.5	0.4
Desserts					
Angel food cake	2 oz	126	35.7	0.1	4.8
Boston cream pie	2 oz	332	54.9	10.3	5.5
Cheesecake (plain)	2 oz	150	37.8	14.3	6.0
Devil's food cake	2 oz	233	34.2	10.8	2.6
Chocolate chip cookies	2 oz	230	32.0	13.5	2.5
Oatmeal cookies	2 oz	260	34.0	12.0	2.0
Custard	½ cup	153	14.7	7.3	7.1
Danish pastry	1 oz	121	17.4	4.9	1.8
Doughnut	1 oz	151	21.7	8.4	4.5
Ice cream (10-percent fat)	1 cup	269	31.7	14.3	4.8
Ice cream (16-percent fat)	1 cup	349	32.0	23.7	4.1
Apple pie	4 oz	282	43.0	11.9	2.4
Lemon meringue pie	4 oz	250	42.0	10.0	2.0

Food	Serving Size	Calories	Carbohydrates (g)	Fat (g)	Protein (g)
Desserts (continued)					
Gelatin (sugar)	½ cup	81	18.7	0.0	1.6
Gelatin (w/Nutrasweet)	½ cup	8	0.0	0.0	1.6
Eggs					
Whole egg	1 large	79	0.6	5.6	6.1
Egg white	1 large	16	0.0	0.4	3.4
Egg substitute	¼ cup	30	1.0	0.0	6.0
Fast Foods					
Burger King Cheeseburger, regular	1 oz	350	30.0	17.0	18.0
Cheeseburger, Whopper	1 oz	740	52.0	45.0	32.0
French fries	1 order	210	25.0	11.0	3.0
Kentucky Fried Chicken Chicken sandwich	1	436	33.8	22.5	24.8
Fried chicken, drumstick	1	155	5.1	9.0	13.3
Fried chicken, extra crispy thigh	1	343	12.6	23.4	20.4
Long John Silver Fish sandwich	1	560	49.0	31.0	22.0
Fish, batter fried	3 pieces	549	32.0	32.0	32.0
McDonald's Egg McMuffin	1	327	31.0	14.8	18.5
Big Mac	1	563	40.6	33.0	25.7

Food	Serving Size	Calories	Carbohydrates (g)	Fat (g)	Protein (g)
		Meat			
Beef					
Composite,* cooked and trimmed	3 oz	192	0.0	9.4	25.0
Round steak, cooked and trimmed	3 oz	158	0.0	6.0	25.0
Sirloin steak, cooked and trimmed	3 oz	185	0.0	8.3	26.0
Rib steak, cooked and trimmed	3 oz	200	0.0	10.9	24.0
Pot roast, cooked and trimmed	3 oz	205	0.0	9.3	28.0
Tenderloin, cooked and trimmed	3 oz	183	0.0	8.9	24.0
Ground, (18% fat) cooked and trimmed	3 oz	192	0.0	14.4	24.0
Lamb					
Composite, cooked and trimmed	3 oz	176	0.0	8.1	24.0
Loin chop, cooked and trimmed	3 oz	188	0.0	8.9	25.0
Rib roast, cooked and trimmed	3 oz	211	0.0	12.9	22.0
Shank, cooked and trimmed	3 oz	168	0.0	5.5	28.0
Pork					
Composite, cooked and trimmed	3 oz	198	0.0	11.1	23.0
Loin chop, cooked and trimmed	3 oz	219	0.0	12.7	24.0

Food	Serving Size	Calories	Carbohydrates (g)	Fat (g)	Protein (g)
Meat (continued)					
Pork, *cont.*					
Loin roast, cooked and trimmed	3 oz	208	0.0	11.7	24.0
Spareribs, cooked and trimmed	3 oz	338	0.0	25.8	25.0
Tenderloin, cooked and trimmed	3 oz	141	0.0	4.1	24.0
Breakfast					
Bacon, crisp	3 slices	105	0.3	9.3	4.8
Canadian bacon	1, 1-oz slice	40	0.0	2.0	5.6
Pork sausage	1, 2-oz link	265	1.4	21.6	15.1
Luncheon					
Beef bologna	1, 1-oz slice	80	1.0	7.0	3.0
Hot dog, beef	1, 2-oz frank	150	2.0	15.0	6.0
Hot dog, chicken	1, 2-oz frank	120	4.0	9.0	6.0
Ham, (5% fat)	1, 1-oz slice	37	0.3	1.4	5.5
Salami, beef	1, 1-oz link	58	0.6	4.6	3.4
Turkey breast	1, 1-oz link	20	0.0	0.2	5.0
Poultry					
Chicken, white, roasted, w/o skin	3½ oz	173	0.0	4.5	30.9
Chicken, dark, roasted, w/o skin	3½ oz	205	0.0	9.7	27.4
Chicken, dark, roasted, w/skin	3½ oz	253	0.0	15.8	26.0
Duck, roasted, w/skin,	3½ oz	337	0.0	28.4	19.0
Turkey, white, roasted, w/o skin	3½ oz	157	0.0	3.2	29.9
Turkey, dark, roasted, w/o skin	3½ oz	187	0.0	7.2	28.6

Food	Serving Size	Calories	Carbohydrates (g)	Fat (g)	Protein (g)
		Poultry (continued)			
Turkey, all, roasted, w/ skin	3½ oz	208	0.0	9.7	28.1
		Fish and Seafood			
Bass, broiled	3½ oz	228	0.0	2.7	18.9
Clams, canned	3½ oz	98	0.0	2.5	15.8
Cod, broiled	3½ oz	162	0.0	0.3	17.6
Fillets, batter fried	2, 6-oz pieces	440	25.0	31.0	17.0
Fish sticks	4, 3½ oz pieces	176	6.5	8.9	16.6
Halibut, broiled	3½ oz	100	0.0	1.2	20.9
Lobster, broiled	3½ oz	91	0.0	1.9	16.9
Oysters, canned	3½ oz	76	0.0	2.2	8.5
Salmon, silver, canned	3½ oz	153	0.0	8.2	18.8
Salmon, broiled	3½ oz	182	0.0	7.4	27.0
Scallops, steamed	3½ oz	81	0.0	0.2	15.3
Tuna, canned in oil	3½ oz	190	0.0	10.0	25.0
Tuna, canned in water	3½ oz	118	0.0	1.7	26.0
		Grains, Breads, and Pasta			
Bagel, water	1	163	30.9	1.4	6.0
Blueberry muffin	1	126	19.5	4.3	2.4
Bread, corn	2 oz	160	26.0	4.0	4.0
Bread, wheat	1 slice	66	12.5	0.8	2.2
Bread, French	1 slice	70	12.6	1.0	2.4
Bread, rye	1 slice	66	12.0	0.9	2.1
Bread, sourdough	1 slice	68	13.4	0.5	2.5

Food	Serving Size	Calories	Carbohydrates (g)	Fat (g)	Protein (g)
Grains, Breads, and Pasta (continued)					
Bread, white	1 slice	66	11.7	0.9	2.0
Bread crumbs	1 cup	345	64.6	4.0	11.1
English muffin	1 muffin	135	26.2	1.1	4.5
Saltines	2 crackers	26	4.4	0.6	0.6
Triscuits	2 crackers	42	6.2	1.5	0.8
Wheat Thins	4 crackers	36	5.0	1.4	0.5
Noodles, cooked	¾ cup	107	20.1	1.2	3.9
Pasta, cooked	¾ cup	150	30.0	0.4	5.1
Rice, cooked	⅓ cup	80	15.0	0.0	3.0
Waffles	1 large	245	25.7	12.6	6.9
Cereals					
Composite bran cereals	⅓ cup	80	15.0	trace	3.0
Composite cooked cereals	½ cup	80	15.0	trace	3.0
Composite uncooked cereals	¾ cup	80	15.0	trace	3.0
Composite puffed cereals	1½ cups	80	15.0	trace	3.0
Cream of Rice, cooked	¾ cup	95	21.1	0.1	1.6
Cream of Wheat, cooked	¾ cup	100	20.8	0.4	2.9
Oatmeal, cooked	¾ cup	108	18.9	1.8	4.5
All Bran	1 oz	71	21.1	0.5	4.0
Cheerios	1 oz	111	19.6	1.8	4.3
Corn Flakes	1 oz	110	24.4	0.1	2.3
Frosted Flakes	1 oz	110	26.0	0.1	1.4

Food	Serving Size	Calories	Carbohydrates (g)	Fat (g)	Protein (g)
Cereals (continued)					
Grape Nuts	1 oz	101	23.2	0.1	3.3
Raisin Bran	1 oz	87	21.4	0.5	2.6
Shredded Wheat (1 biscuit)	1 oz	83	18.8	0.3	1.8
Wheaties	1 oz	99	22.6	0.5	2.7
Fruits					
Composite fresh fruit	½ cup	60	15.0	0.0	trace
Composite dried fruit	¼ cup	60	15.0	0.0	trace
Composite fruit juice	½ cup	60	15.0	0.0	trace
Apple, raw	1, 2-inch	60	15.0	0.0	trace
Applesauce (unsweetened)	½ cup	60	15.0	0.0	trace
Apricots, raw	1, 2-inch	60	15.0	0.0	trace
Apricots, canned	½ cup	60	15.0	0.0	trace
Avocado, California	1 medium	306	12.0	30.0	3.6
Banana	1, 9-inch	60	15.0	0.0	trace
Blackberries, raw	¾ cup	60	15.0	0.0	trace
Blueberries, raw	¾ cup	60	15.0	0.0	trace
Cantaloupe	⅓, 5-inch	60	15.0	0.0	trace
Cantaloupe, cubes	1 cup	60	15.0	0.0	trace
Cherries, raw	½ cup, large	60	15.0	0.0	trace
Cherries, canned	½ cup	60	15.0	0.0	trace
Figs, raw	2, 2-inch	60	15.0	0.0	trace
Fruit cocktail, canned	½ cup	60	15.0	0.0	trace

Food	Serving Size	Calories	Carbohydrates (g)	Fat (g)	Protein (g)
		Fruits (continued)			
Grapefruit	½ medium	60	15.0	0.0	trace
Grapefruit, segments	¾ cup	60	15.0	0.0	trace
Grapes	15 small	60	15.0	0.0	trace
Honeydew melon	⅛ medium	60	15.0	0.0	trace
Honeydew, cubes	1 cup	60	15.0	0.0	trace
Kiwi	1 large	60	15.0	0.0	trace
Mandarin orange segments	¾ cup	60	15.0	0.0	trace
Mango	½ small	60	15.0	0.0	trace
Nectarine	1, ½-inch	60	15.0	0.0	trace
Orange	1, 2½-inch	60	15.0	0.0	trace
Papaya	1 cup	60	15.0	0.0	trace
Peach	1, 2¾-inch	60	15.0	0.0	trace
Peaches, canned	½ cup, 2 halves	60	15.0	0.0	trace
Pear	½ cup, 1 small	60	15.0	0.0	trace
Pears, canned	½ cup, 2 halves	60	15.0	0.0	trace
Pineapple, cubes	¾ cup	60	15.0	0.0	trace
Pineapple, canned	⅓ cup	60	15.0	0.0	trace
Plum, raw	2, 2-inch	60	15.0	0.0	trace
Raspberries, raw	1 cup	60	15.0	0.0	trace
Strawberries, raw	1¼ cup	60	15.0	0.0	trace
Tangerine	2, 2½-inch	60	15.0	0.0	trace

Food	Serving Size	Calories	Carbohydrates (g)	Fat (g)	Protein (g)
Fruits (continued)					
Watermelon, cubes	1¼ cup	60	15.0	0.0	trace
Dried apples	4 rings	60	15.0	0.0	trace
Dried apricots	7 halves	60	15.0	0.0	trace
Dried dates	2½ medium	60	15.0	0.0	trace
Dried figs	1½	60	15.0	0.0	trace
Raisins	2 tbsp	60	15.0	0.0	trace
Dried prunes	3 medium	60	15.0	0.0	trace
Apple juice/cider	½ cup	60	15.0	0.0	trace
Cranberry juice	⅓ cup	60	15.0	0.0	trace
Grapefruit juice	½ cup	60	15.0	0.0	trace
Grape juice	⅓ cup	60	15.0	0.0	trace
Orange juice	½ cup	60	15.0	0.0	trace
Pineapple juice	½ cup	60	15.0	0.0	trace
Prune juice	⅓ cup	60	15.0	0.0	trace
Vegetables					
Composite cooked vegetable	½ cup	25	5.0	0.0	1.0–5.0
Composite vegetable juice	½ cup	25	5.0	0.0	1.0–2.0
Composite raw vegetable	1 cup	25	5.0	0.0	1.0–2.0
Composite starchy vegetables					
Beans, cooked	⅓ cup	80	15.0	0.0	3.0
Corn	½ cup	80	15.0	0.0	3.0
Corn on the cob	1, 6-in. cob	80	15.0	0.0	3.0
Lentils, cooked	⅓ cup	80	15.0	0.0	3.0
Lima beans	½ cup	80	15.0	0.0	3.0

Food	Serving Size	Calories	Carbohydrates (g)	Fat (g)	Protein (g)
Vegetables (continued)					
Peas, canned/frozen	½ cup	80	15.0	0.0	3.0
Plantain	½ cup	80	15.0	0.0	3.0
Potato, baked	1,3 oz	80	15.0	0.0	3.0
Potato, mashed	½ cup	80	15.0	0.0	3.0
Squash	¾ cup	80	15.0	0.0	3.0
Sweet potato	⅓ cup	80	15.0	0.0	3.0
Yam	⅓ cup	80	15.0	0.0	3.0
"Free" vegetables					
Cabbage, shredded	1 cup	24	5.4	0.0	1.3
Celery, raw	1 stalk	8	2.0	0.0	0.4
Chives raw, chopped	1 tbsp	3	0.6	0.0	0.2
Lettuce,					
butter	1 cup	14	2.5	0.0	1.2
iceberg	1 cup	13	2.9	0.0	0.9
romaine	1 cup	18	3.5	0.0	1.3
Parsley, chopped	1 tbsp	4	0.8	0.0	0.4
Spinach, raw	1 cup	26	4.3	0.0	3.2
Fats and Oils					
Butter	1 tbsp	108	0.0	12.2	0.0
Margarine	1 tbsp	102	0.0	11.4	0.0
Mayonnaise	1 tbsp	99	1.0	11.0	0.2
Mayonnaise, low-fat	1 tbsp	40	1.0	4.0	0.0
Oil (all types)	1 tbsp	120	0.0	13.6	0.0
Salad dressings					
Blue cheese	1 tbsp	77	1.1	8.0	0.7
Buttermilk	1 tbsp	58	1.2	5.8	0.5
Caesar	1 tbsp	70	1.0	7.0	0.0
French	1 tbsp	67	2.7	6.4	0.1
Green goddess	1 tbsp	68	1.2	7.0	0.1
Italian	1 tbsp	69	1.5	7.1	0.1
Italian creamy	1 tbsp	52	2.7	4.5	0.1
Oil and vinegar	1 tbsp	103	6.6	8.5	0.1
Thousand Island	1 tbsp	59	2.4	5.6	0.1

*Average composition for various cuts of meat, brands of processed food, or type of food.

BIBLIOGRAPHY

CHAPTER 2

Friedman, M. I., and I. Ramirez, "Insulin Counteracts the Satiating Effect of a Fat Meal in Rats," *Physiological Behavior* 40: 655–659, 1987.

Geiselman, P. J., and D. Novin, " The Role of Carbohydrates in Appetite, Hunger and Obesity," *Appetite* 3:203–223, 1982.

Harris, M. D., M. B. Davidson, and M. A. Bush, "Exogenous Insulin Therapy Slows Weight Loss in Type II Diabetic Patients," *International Journal of Obesity* 12:149–155, 1988.

Hirsch, J., and R. L. Leibel, "New Light on Obesity," *New England Journal of Medicine* 318:509–510, 1988.

CHAPTER 3

Avons, P., P. Ducimetiere, and R. Rakotovao, "Weight and Mortality," Lancet 1:1104, 1983.

Burton, B. T., W. R. Foster, J. Hirsch, and T. B. Van Itallie, "Health Implications of Obesity: A NIH Consensus Development Conference," *International Journal of Obesity* 9(3):155–170, 1985.

Dustan, H. P., "Obesity and Hypertension," *Annals of Internal Medicine* 103: 1047–1049, 1985.

Dyer, P., J. Stamler, D. W. Berkson, and H. A. Linberg, "Relationship of Relative Weight and Body Mass Index to 14–Year Mortality in the Chicago People's Gas Company Study," *Journal of Chronic Diseases* 27:109–123, 1975.

Gangemi, M., G. Meneghetti, O. Predebon, R. Scappatura, and A. Rocco, "Obesity as a Risk Factor in Endometrial Cancer," *Clinical Experiments in Obstetrics and Gynecology* 14(2):119–122, 1987.

Garfinkle, L., "Overweight and Mortality," *Cancer* 58(suppl. 8):18261829, 1986.

Rhoads, G. G., and A. Kagan, "The Relationship of Coronary Disease, Stroke and Mortality to Weight in Youth and Middle Age," *Lancet* 1:492–495, 1983.

Sorlie, P., T. Gordon, and W. B. Kannel, "Body Build and Mortality, the Framingham Study," *Journal of the American Medical Association* 243: 1828–1831, 1980.

Van Itallic, T.B, "The Perils of Obesity in Middle-Aged Women," *New England Journal of Medicine* 322:928, 1990.

Wadden, T. A., and A. J. Stunkard, "Social and Psychological Consequences of Obesity," *Annals of Internal Medicine* 103(6):1062–1067, 1985.

CHAPTER 5

Cincotta, A. H., and A. H. Meier, "Reduction of Body Fat Storage by Inhibition of Prolactin Secretion," *Experientia* 43(4):416–417, 1987.

Ezrin, C., J. O. Godden, and R. Volpe, *Systematic Endocrnology*, 2nd ed., Harper & Row, New York, 1979.

Ravussin, E., K. Acheson, O. Vemet, E. Danforth, and E. Jequier, "Evidence That Insulin Resistance Is Responsible for the Decreased Thermic Effect of Glucose in Human Obesity," *Journal of Clinical Investigation* 76:1268–1273, 1985.

Segal, K. R., B. Gutin, A. M. Nyman, and F. X. Pi-Sunyer, "Thermic Effect of Food at Rest, During Exercise, and After Exercise in Lean and Obese Men of Similar Body Weight," *Journal of Clinical Investigation* 76:11071112, 1985.

Yang, M. U., and T. B. Van Itallie, "Variability in Body Protein Loss During Protracted, Severe Caloric Restriction: Role of Triiodothyronine and Other Possible Determinants," *American Journal of Clinical Nutrition* 40:611–622, 1984.

CHAPTER 6

de Gastro, J. M., "Macronutrient Relationships with Meal Patterns and Mood in the Spontaneous Feeding Behavior of Humans," *Physiology & Behavior* 39:561–569, 1986.

Hartmann, E., "Effects of L-Tryptophan on Sleepiness and on Sleep," *Journal of Psychiatric Research* 17(2):107–113, 1982–83.

Wurtman, R. J., "Nutrients That Modify Brain Function," *Scientific American* 246:50–59, 1982.

CHAPTER 8

Blackburn, G. L., M. E. Lynch, and S. L. Wong, "The Very-Low Calorie Diet: Weight Reduction Technique," in *Handbook of Eating Disorders: Physiology. Psychology and the Treatment of Obesity, Anorexia and Bulimia*, ed. K. D. Brownell and J. P. Foreyt, Basic Books, New York, 1986.

CHAPTER 9

De Fronzo, R. A., R. S. Sherwin, and N. Kraemer, "Effects of Physical Training on Insulin Action in Obesity," *Diabetes* 36:1385–1479, 1987.

Gwinup, G., "Effect of Exercise Alone on the Weight of Obese Women," *Archive of Internal Medicine* 135:676–680, 1975.

Horton, E. S., "Metabolic Aspects of Exercise and Weight Reduction," *Medicine and Science in Sports and Exercise* 18:10–17, 1986.

Minuk, H. L., A. K. Hanna, E. B. Marliss, M. Vranic, and B. Zinman, "Metabolic Response to Moderate Exercise in Obese Men During Prolonged Fasting," *American Journal of Physiology* 238 (Endocrinology Metabolism 1):E322-E329, 1980.

Pacy, P. J., J. Webster, and J. S. Garrow, "Exercise and Obesity," *Sports Medicine* 3:89–113, 1986.

Pollock, M. L., H. S. Miller, R. Janeway, A. C. Linnerud, B. Robertson, et al., "Effects of Walking on Body Composition and Cardiovascular Function of Middle Aged Men," *Journal of Applied Physiology* 30:126–130, 1971.

Roberts, S. B., J. Savage, W. A. Coward, B. Chew, and A. Lucas, "Energy Expenditure and Intake in Infants Born to Lean and Overweight Mothers," *New England Journal of Medicine* 318:461–466, 1988.

Scheen, A. J., A. S. Luyckx, A. Fossion, and P. J. Lefebvre, "The Effect of Protein–Supplemented Fasting on the Fuel Hormone Response to Prolonged Exercise in Obese Subjects," *International Journal of Obesity* 7:327–337, 1983.

Terjung, R. L., and H. Kaciuba-Uscilkoh, "Lipid Metabolism During Exercise: Influence of Training," *Diabetes/Metabolism Review* 2(1,2):35–51, 1986.

Tremblay, A., J. P. Després, and C. Bouchard, "The Effects of Exercise Training on Energy Balance and Adipose Tissue, Morphology and Metabolism," *Sports Medicine* 2(3):223–233, 1985.

Woo, R., J. S. Garrow, and F. X. Pi-Sunyer, "Voluntary Food Intake During Prolonged Exercise in Obese Women," *American Journal of Clinical Nutrition* 36:478–484, 1982.

CHAPTER 12

Brownell, K. D., G. A. Marlatt, E. Lichtenstein, and G. T. Wilson, "Understanding and Preventing Relapse," *American Psychologist* 41:765–782, 1986.

CHAPTER 14

Abrara, G., Emanuele, N., Colwell, J., Henderson, W., Comstock, J., Levin, S., Nuttall, F. Sarvin, C., "Glycemic Control and Complications in Type 2 Diabetes: Design of a Feasibility Trial," *Diabetes Care* 15:1560–1570, 1992.

Bjorntorp, P., "Abdominal Obesity and the Development of Noninsulin-Dependent Diabetes Mellitus." *Diabetes Metabolism Reviews* 4:615–622, 1988.

Caro, J.F., "Insulin Resistance in Obese and Nonobese Man," *Journal of Clinical Endocrinology and Metabolism* 73:691–695, 1991.

DeFronzo, R. A., "The Effect of Insulin on Renal Sodium Metabolism: A Review with Clinical Implications." *Diabetologia* 21:165–171, 1981.

DeFronzo, R. A., Ferrannini, E., "Insulin Resistance: A Multifaceted Syndrome Responsible for NIDDM, Obesity, Hypertension, Dyslipidemia, and Atherosclerotic Cardiovascular Disease." *Diabetes Care* 14:173–194, 1991.

Ezrin, C., "Childhood Diabetes." *University of Toronto Medical Journal* 26:233–239, 1949.

Ezrin, C., Salter, J. M., Ogryzlo, M. A., Best, C. H., "The Clinical and Metabolic Effects of Glucagon." *Canadian Medical Association Journal* 78:96–98, 1958.

Ezrin C., Moloney, P. J., "Resistance to Insulin Due to Neutralizing Antibodies." *Journal of Clinical Endocrinology and Metabolism* 19:1055–1068, 1959.

Fontbonne, A., Eschwege, E., "Insulin-Resistance, Hypertriglyceridemia and Cardiovascular Risk: The Paris Prospective Study." *Diabete et Metabolisme* 17:93–95. 1991

Frayn, K. N., Koppack, S. W., "Insulin Resistance, Adipose Tissue and Coronary Heart Disease." *Clinical Science* 82:1–8, 1992.

Fujimoto, W. Y., Akanuma, Y., Kanazawa, Y., et al., "Plasma Insulin Levels in Japanese and Japanese-American Men with Type II Diabetes May be Related to the Occurrence of Cardiovascular Disease." *Diabetes Research and Clinical Practice* 6:121–127, 1989.

Haffner, S. M., Stern, M. P., Hazuda, H. P., et al, "Hyperinsulinemia in a Population at High Risk for Non-Insulin-Dependent Diabetes Mellitus." *New England Journal of Medicine* 315:220–224, 1986.

Janka, H. U., Ziegler, A. G., Standl, E., Mehnert, H., "Daily Insulin Dose as a Predictor of Macrovascular Disease in Insulin-Treated Non-Insulin-Dependent Diabetes." *Diabete et Metabolisme* 13:359–364, 1987.

Kanai, H., Matsuzawa, Y., Kotani, K., et al, "Close Correlation of Intra-abdominal Fat Accumulation to Hypertension in Obese Women." *Hypertension* 16:484–490, 1990.

Leibel, R. L., Rosenbaum M., Hirsch, J., "Changes in Energy Expenditure Resulting from Altered Body Weight." *New England Journal of Medicine* 332:621–620, 1995.

Letiexhe, M. R., Scheen, A. J., Gérard, P. L., et al., "Postgastroplasty Recovery of Ideal Body Weight Normalizes Glucose and Insulin Metabolism in Obese Women." *Journal of Clinical Endocrinology and Metabolism* 80:364–369, 1995.

Lippel, K., Tyroler, H., Gotto, A. M., Jr., Vahouny, G., "Relationship of Hypertriglyceridemia to Atherosclerosis." *Arteriosclerosis* 1:406–417, 1981.

Liu, Q. Z., Knowler, W. C., Nelson, R. G., et al., "Insulin Treatment, Endogenous Insulin Concentration and ECG Abnormalities in Diabetic Pima Indians." *Diabetes* 41:1141–1150, 1992.

Modan, M., Halkin, H., Lusky, A., et al., "Hyperinsulinemia as Characterized by Jointly Disturbed Plasma VLDL, LDL, and HDL Levels: A Population-Based Study." *Arteriosclerosis* 8:227–236, 1988.

Moller, D. E., Flier, J. S., "Insulin Resistance. Mechanisms, Syndromes, and Implications." *New England Journal of Medicine* 325:938–948, 1991.

Reaven, G. N. "Role of Insulin Resistance in Human Disease." *Diabetes* 37:1595–1607, 1988.

Ronnemaa, T., Laakso, M., Pyörälä, K., Kallio, V., Puukka, P., "High Fasting Plasma Insulin as an Indicator of Coronary Heart Disease in Non-Insulin Diabetic Patients and Non-Diabetic Subjects." *Arteriosclerosis and Thrombosis* 11:80–90, 1991.

Salter, J. M., Ezrin, C., Laidlaw, J. C., Gornall, A. G., "Metabolic Effects of Glucagon in Human Subjects." *Metabolism* 9:753–768, 1959.

Sato, Y., Shiraishi, S., Oshida, Y., Ishiguro, T., Sakamoto, N., "Experimental Atherosclerosis-Like Lesions Induced by Hyperinsulinism in Wistar Rats." *Diabetes* 38:91–96, 1989.

Singh, B. M., Palma, M. A., Nattrass, M., "Multiple Aspects of Insulin Resistance. Comparison of Glucose and Intermediary Metabolite Response to Incremental Insulin Infusion in IDDM Subjects of Short and Long Duration." *Diabetes* 36:740–748, 1987.

Stout,R.W., "Insulin and Atheroma: 20 Year Perspective," *Diabetes Care* 13:631–654, 1990

Uusitupa, M., Niskanen, L., Siïtonen, O., Pyörälä, K., "Hyperinsulinemia and Hypertension in Patients with Newly Diagnosed Non-Insulin Dependent Diabetes." *Diabete et Metabolisme* 13:369–374, 1987.

INDEX